Legends, Half-Truths, and Cherished Myths of the
The Drane Family

Daniel A. Willis

Copyright © 2012, Daniel A. Willis

First Edition

This book contains material protected under International and Federal Copyright Laws and Treaties. Any unauthorized reprint or use of this material is prohibited. No part of this book may be reproduced or transmitted in any form or by any means, electronic or mechanical, including photocopying, recording, or by any information storage and retrieval system without express written permission from the author.

ISBN: 978-1477504154

Printed in the United States of America

ALL RIGHTS RESERVED

Contents

Introduction — v

Simplified Drane Family Tree — ix

Chapter 1: Myths, Legends, and the Facts — 1

Chapter 2: The Anne Arundel County, Maryland, Dranes — 7
Including migrations to NE Tennessee, NE Alabama, and NW Arkansas

Chapter 3: The Baltimore Dranes — 39

Chapter 4: The Delaware Draines — 49

Chapter 5: The Prince George's County Dranes — 65

Chapter 6: The Montgomery County, Maryland, Dranes — 79
Including migrations to western Kentucky/Tennessee and to Philadelphia

Chapter 7: The Central Kentucky Dranes — 105
Including a migration to Boone County, Missouri

Photo Gallery — 131

Chapter 8: The Garrett County, Maryland, Dranes — 141
Including migrations to Wisconsin, South Dakota, Montana, Arizona, Texas, Missouri, and North Carolina

Chapter 9: The Pittsylvania County, Virginia, Drains — 161
Including migrations to Forsyth County, North Carolina, and Daviess County, Missouri

Chapter 10: The Rockbridge County, Virginia, Drains — 169
Including migrations to the Ohio River Valley and to Colorado

Chapter 11: The Central West Virginia Drains — 187

Chapter 12: The Western Pennsylvania Dranes — 195

Chapter 13: The Louisville, Kentucky, Dranes 201
Including migrations to Florida and Texas

Chapter 14: The Georgia Dranes 215
Including migrations to Alabama and Mississippi

Chapter 15: The Last Odds and Ends 235

Bibliography 237

Index 239

Introduction

I was a very fortunate child. I had three great-grandparents still living during most of my childhood. There was also a great-great-grandmother still alive at my birth, but she died before I ever got meet her. This source of historical knowledge of my family was invaluable.

My great-grandfather Ward lived just down the street from us, so I would see him often. He loved to tell stories from his youth about his parents and grandparents. I attribute my lifelong fascination with genealogy to him.

As many other people do, I endeavored to trace each of the lines of my ancestry to the extent possible. I have been highly successful, now having a recorded ancestry to at least the first ancestor to be on this continent for nearly all of my lines of descent. Many of my ancestors knew localized fame for one thing or another, but the line that has always held the highest interest for me is that of my maternal grandmother, the Dranes.

While still my early 20s, I began to seriously research my family history. This was still in days before the Internet, and research meant many hours in a library going through books that had been published indexing various documents and records from long ago. It also meant a lot of letter writing to county courthouses, churches, and cemetery offices.

Like many researchers, I got to a point where I was stuck. I often set aside the Drane research, and would spend time on the other lines of my ancestry. But I kept coming back to Drane, hoping a fresh look would give me inspiration for that elusive detail I needed to go back further.

My sticking point was David Drane of Rockbridge County, Virginia, who used the Drain spelling, because he was illiterate. I had no trouble finding the record of David's 1801 marriage to Jean Hayslet and details about several of their children. But I could not get past him to learn who his parents were.

Then the most wonderful happenstance took place. I was browsing the genealogy section at the Denver Public Library. Every time I went to get a book from the shelf, it was missing. Finally I decided someone else must be using the books I needed, so I started walking among the tables to see if I could find them. I did. They were all on the same table. I asked the middle-aged lady who was using them what family she was working on, because we seemed to be working in the same locations.

It turned out she was a second cousin to me. Being from the Appalachia region, we considered this quite a close kinship. It turned out that her grandfather was my great-granduncle who ran away from home as a teenager, and our family never knew what became of him. Now, I know he went to Kansas, and eventually to

Pueblo, Colorado. But finding this cousin and comparing our notes is what led to the breakthrough we both needed. It is stories like this that make genealogy so fascinating to me.

Once past David, I quickly found myself digging around in colonial Maryland for Dranes. I found several, not yet connected, families named Drane or Drain. Then the sorting out had to begin.

I had always been told, since childhood, that the Dranes in the United States were all related somehow and that we were all descended from a common ancestor who came from England in the colonial period. This has turned out to be very nearly true. There are now Dranes in every state that can be traced back to the same family that lived in colonial Maryland.

This book is an effort to compile the genealogy of all those branches into one grand, connected family.

The layout of the book is relatively simple. Each chapter will cover a geographic area where part of the family settled. It will begin in England, follow the immigrant ancestors to the American colonies, and then spread out as the family did.

Each chapter will begin with what biographical information I could find about each branch of the family, followed by a detailed genealogy of that branch. In order to protect the privacy of the living members of the family, this book will stop each line of descent at approximately the year 1900. Generations born after 1900 will not be included, but a comment "has issue" will be listed to indicate the family does indeed continue.

Only the male lines of descent are followed. If I was to try to trace out all of the female lines as well, this would quickly turn into something the size of an encyclopedia. It would also likely never get finished.

The genealogies are listed in an easy to follow outline. Each person is listed with their spouses, and under that are their children. Under each child is listed their children in turn. All of the American Dranes covered in this book can be traced to the common ancestor Thomas Drane of Sawbridgeworth, Hertfordshire, England. The outline numbering system begins with him.

The children of Thomas are listed with Roman numerals followed by a period (i.e., I. II. III. ...). Their children are lettered by capital letters and a period (i.e., A. B. C. ...). The third generation are numbered using Arabic numbers and a period (i.e., 1. 2. 3. ...). The fourth generation are lettered with lower-case letters and a period (i.e., a. b. c. ...).

Generations five through eight repeat the pattern, except, instead of a period after the letter or number, it will be a right parenthesis [e.g., II) A) 4) c)]. Generations nine through twelve recycle the pattern again, but the letters or numbers will be enclosed in parentheses [e.g., (II) (A) (4) (c)].

There are many places in this work where precise records are missing. To some degree, speculation had to be employed based on a variety of factors. The information provided is believed to be correct. Where there are conflicts between sources, footnotes are used for explanation. Furthermore, footnotes are used to cite sources, but not every detail is cited.

There are a few abbreviations used throughout the genealogical portions. Areas in England will be spelled out since most Americans may not be familiar with the shortened forms, but states in the U.S. will be presented using their standard two-letter post office abbreviations. Military ranks will also be abbreviated using their standard style.

A list of other abbreviations and symbols follows:
- *   born
- =   married
- +   died
- ...   unknown/missing information
- aft.   after
- ann.   annulled
- bap.   baptized/christened
- bef.   before
- btw.   between
- ca.   circa/approximately
- Co.   county
- CSA   Confederate States of America
- dv.   divorced
- Gov.   Governor
- Rep.   Representative (State or Congressional)
- Sen.   Senator (State or Congressional)
- dunm.   died unmarried
- W(VA)   a location in current day WV that was in VA at the time
- WWI   World War I
- WWII   World War II

A quick note must be made about the spelling of the name. Drane appears to be the usual spelling according to colonial and English records. It is also the most common spelling still in use. However, Drain, Draine, and occasionally Drayne are all used in reference to this same family. When it is clear that a branch of the family is using an alternate spelling, I will use that spelling as well. But I will assume the correct spelling is Drane until the research suggests otherwise.

After the publication of this book, a page will be added to my website www.dan-willis.com to record corrections that need to be made, or add information that is missing. I welcome all researchers of this family to inform me of any missing or incorrect data at my email: daniel@dan-willis.com

Daniel A. Willis
Denver
June 2012

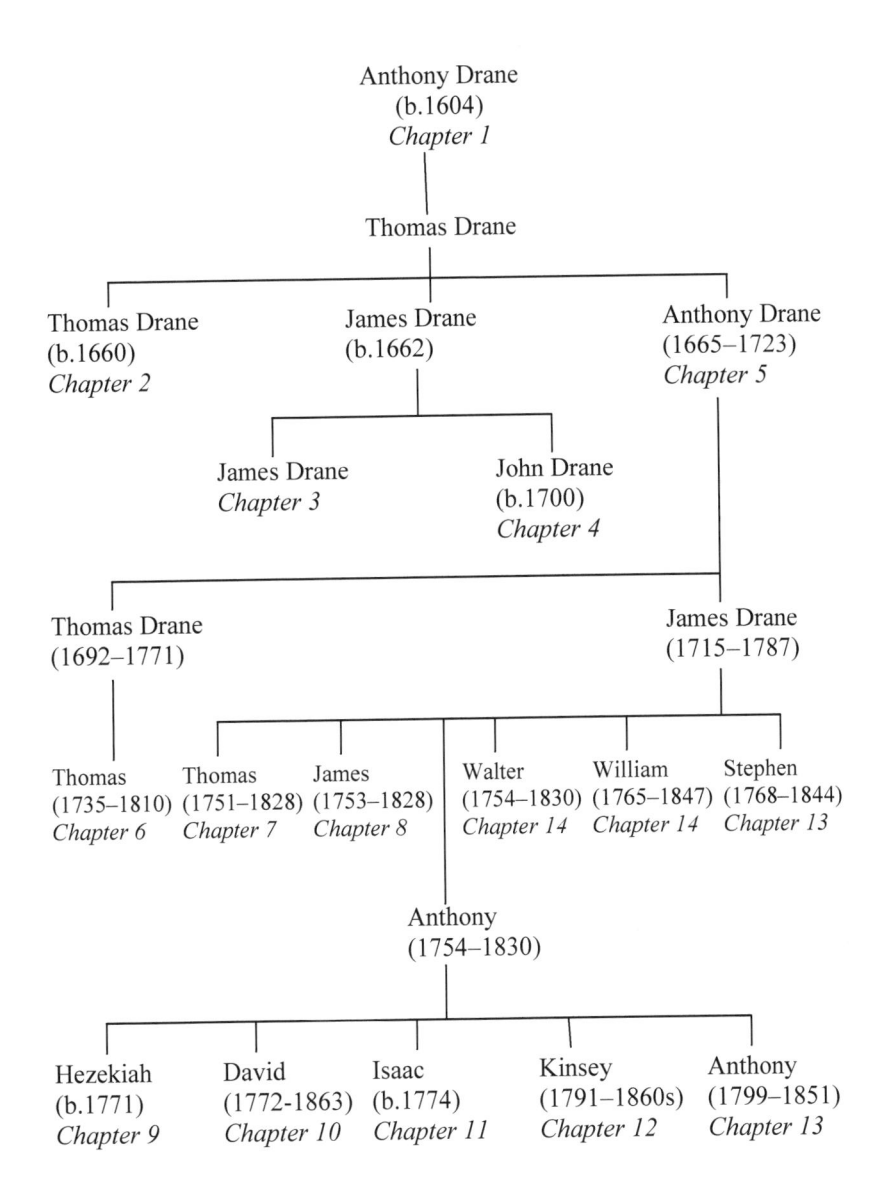

```
                    Anthony Drane
                       (b.1604)
                      Chapter 1
                         │
                    Thomas Drane
   ┌─────────────────────┼─────────────────────┐
Thomas Drane         James Drane          Anthony Drane
 (b.1660)             (b.1662)            (1665–1723)
 Chapter 2                                 Chapter 5
              ┌──────────┴──────────┐
          James Drane            John Drane
          Chapter 3               (b.1700)
                                  Chapter 4
                                                        │
   ┌────────────────────────────────────────────────────┤
Thomas Drane                                       James Drane
(1692–1771)                                        (1715–1787)
     │
 ┌───┴───┬─────────┬─────────┬─────────┬─────────┬─────────┐
Thomas   Thomas    James     Walter    William   Stephen
(1735–1810)(1751–1828)(1753–1828)(1754–1830)(1765–1847)(1768–1844)
Chapter 6 Chapter 7 Chapter 8 Chapter 14 Chapter 14 Chapter 13
                              │
                          Anthony
                        (1754–1830)
                              │
   ┌──────────┬──────────┬──────────┬──────────┐
Hezekiah    David      Isaac      Kinsey     Anthony
(b.1771)   (1772-1863) (b.1774)  (1791–1860s)(1799–1851)
Chapter 9  Chapter 10  Chapter 11 Chapter 12  Chapter 13
```

xi

Chapter 1
Myths, Legends, and the Facts

All Drane family researchers are probably familiar with some version of the story that has been told over and over since the 19th century relating how the Dranes came to this continent.

According to the telling I was familiar with, an old knight, Sir James Anthony Drane, who was a cousin to Lord Baltimore, was given a land grant for a few thousand acres in the colony of Maryland by his noble cousin, who was the proprietor of the colony.

Being a bit advanced in years, he did not wish to pull up stakes, so he sent several of his sons to settle the land in his place. The number of sons ranged from four to seven, depending on who was telling the story. These sons were then the ancestors of all of the Drane lines in the United States. My branch, the Prince George's County, Maryland, branch, were supposedly descended from the eldest son, James.

James Drane, so the legend goes, sailed with Cecilius Calvert, the 2nd Baron Baltimore, when he came to begin settling his colony, in 1637. James supposedly married to one Nancy Brandt or Brent, who was also closely connected to the Calvert family, shortly after arriving.

Over the years, many researchers tried, in vain, to hammer down the details of this story. Some of the sloppier work even assigned approximate years of birth and death to James and Nancy and extrapolates similar information for Sir James Anthony.

It is quite the romantic story, hinting at noble beginnings and grand familial alliances. Alas, it is all a fairy tale.

Some of the facts are easy enough to check out. Let's begin with Sir James Anthony Drane, Knight. The College of Heralds in the United Kingdom has always been a very meticulous organization, even when it was separate bodies in England, Scotland, Ireland, and Wales. It is a simple matter to check with the College if anyone named Drane, in any variation of its spelling, has ever been knighted. Their answer is no.

Some may be tempted to chalk the lack of record of a knighthood up to shoddy bookkeeping or missing records. This is simply not the case. Knighthoods can only come from one source: the monarch. They are bestowed upon an individual, not a family, and expire upon the death of that individual. For there to be a knight in the Drane family in the time period required to fit the legend, that knighthood would have to have been bestowed by either Queen Elizabeth I, King James I, or King Charles I. That covers a period from 1558 to 1649. Every knighthood bestowed by these monarchs is known and recorded. There are no lapses in information. So there simply is no such person as "Sir James Anthony Drane."

There is also the suspect close kinship to Lord Baltimore. The English noble families have well documented genealogies. It is quite easy to look at those families for connections to others. The only thing to consider here is which Lord Baltimore is supposed to be the cousin. The time frame limits it to the first two members of the Calvert family to carry the title, George and his son, Cecilius. Looking at both the paternal and maternal sides of their families, and those of their wives, there is no connection to the Drane family.

The next piece of the story to look at is the timing of the arrival of the Dranes to Maryland. The legend is they sailed with Lord Baltimore in 1637. On its surface, this is a possibility. The first trip to Maryland by any Lord Baltimore was the 1637 sailing of the 2nd Baron, Cecilius Calvert. He took two ships, the *Ark* and the *Dove*. Before going to Maryland, they were to go to Barbados, an already established English trading post, to pick up supplies and exchange some passengers.

There is only a partial surviving record of the names of the passengers who arrived in Maryland. This list only includes approximately one third of the people aboard and does not clarify if they came from England or boarded in Barbados. This has led for much speculation that the Dranes may have gone to Barbados several years previously then hooked up with Lord Baltimore's party. There was a prominent Brent family living in Barbados at the time, which fueled the speculation.

Despite the incomplete ship records, if there had been any Dranes on those boats, their names would eventually turn up in land records as the land grants were being handed out, taxes on them collected, etc. There are no records of any Dranes receiving any of the original land grants. In fact, no Drane appears in any records until 1701, when one Anthony Drane purchased

322 acres of the unimaginatively named land grant "Something," in Prince George's County, from John Demall. This Anthony Drane is the common ancestor of all of the Dranes who trace their lineage to Prince George's County.

Recordkeeping in the early days of Maryland was spotty at best. However, the records related to land ownership are still remarkably intact. While it may be possible there were Dranes in Maryland prior to Anthony, lack of any mention of them in these records makes it highly unlikely.

To put the final nail in the coffin of the legend, the Anthony Drane who purchased "Something" is now known to have not been born in Maryland. His baptism is recorded in St. Mary the Great's church in Sawbridgeworth, Hertfordshire, England, in 1665. There are several other members of his family recorded being in Sawbridgeworth in the years and decades leading up to his birth, so it does not appear the family even went to the colonies earlier and returned.

Therefore, the legend of Sir James Anthony, the connection to the Barons Baltimore, the 1637 sailing, and the original land grant have all been proven to be false information. So now let's talk about what the records do show to be the true story.

English church records are extraordinarily well preserved. There are many 16th and 17th century records of the Dranes throughout the area of England that is just northeast of London, namely, Hertfordshire, Essex, Suffolk, Cambridge, and Norfolk counties. Following the dates, it would seem Norfolk is where they originated, then migrated in a southwestwardly pattern with our branch landing on the Hertfordshire/Essex border by the mid-1600s in the village of Sawbridgeworth.

The Dranes who came to colonial America are all from the same immediate family. This family includes, among others, three sons, Thomas, James, and Anthony. These three names are repeated constantly through the generations of their descendants. The eldest and youngest brothers, Thomas and Anthony, respectively, appear to have come to the colonies together sometime in the late 1690s.

Anthony, as noted previously, purchased a large tract of land in 1701 in Prince George's County, on which he would build a plantation. His ability to do this suggests he came from money. The records of Sawbridgeworth did not indicate what the family did for a living, but having all of their family events recorded by the church is also an indication they were prominent members of the local society.

The Dranes of Prince George's County are the most prolific of the branches that came to the colonies. Most Dranes in the Unites States are descended from Anthony. The descendants of the other two brothers, Thomas and James, are senior, genealogically speaking, but are in much smaller numbers.

The eldest brother, Thomas, may have helped Anthony with the building of his plantation before moving on to Anne Arundel County to establish his own land and family. It is also possible he came to Maryland on a separate ship from Anthony, sailing directly to Anne Arundel. The middle brother, James, remained in England, but his son and namesake made the voyage to Maryland in early the 1700s, settling on the outskirts of the city of Baltimore.

James's younger son, John, also came to the colonies, but not by his own choice. He ran afoul of the authorities in Essex and was convicted of fraud. His punishment was to be exiled to the colony of Virginia. He did not remain there long, moving his way up to Delaware, where he founded his own branch of the family.

Anthony Drane (bap.17 Mar 1604 Shalford, Essex, England – ...)
son of Thomas Drane & Emily Jakes
1- **Anthony Drane** (...)
  = 1650 Stebbing, Essex; ...
  ancestor of the County Essex, England Dranes
2- **Thomas Drane** (...)
  = ...; **Elizabeth Dusten** (...)
  I. **Justinian Drane** (bap. 26 Nov 1659 Sawbridgeworth, Hertfordshire – ...)
    = ...
    A. **Justinian Drane** (...)
      =1 26 Apr 1733 Bishops Stortford, Herts.; **Mary Choat** (...)
      =2 12 Sep 1750 Chesterton, Cambridge; **Ann Prince** (...)
  II. **Thomas Drane** (1660 – ...)
    see Chapter 2
  III. **James Drane** (bap. 11 Apr 1662 Sawbridgeworth – ...)
    = 20 Oct 1684 Bishops Stortford, Herts; **Sarah Sell** (...)
    A. **James Drane** (...)
      see Chapter 3
    B. **John Drane** (1700 – ...)
      see Chapter 4
  IV. **Elizabeth Drane** (bap.22 Jul 1664 Sawbridgeworth – ...)
  V. **Anthony Drane** (1665-1723)
    see Chapter 5

Chapter 2
The Anne Arundel County Dranes
Including migrations to NE Tennessee, NE Alabama, and NW Arkansas

The senior most line of the Dranes to come to the colonies are the descendants of Thomas Drane, who was born in the winter of 1660–1661 in Sawbridgeworth, Hertfordshire. His baptism was performed on March 1st, indicating his birth was likely in the weeks prior to that. It is not known if Thomas married in England or waited until he got Maryland, but he is believed to have arrived in America approximately 1691, when he would have been about 30 years old.

It is possible that Thomas and his brother, Anthony, came together. They both first appear in Maryland right about the turning of the century from the 17th to the 18th. But Thomas settled in Anne Arundel County and Anthony in Prince George. The more likely scenario, from a nautical standpoint, would be for them to have travelled together into the Chesapeake Bay, landing at Anne Arundel County. To go to Prince George's first would have meant navigating up the Potomac which would have been fraught with difficulties in the 1690s.

However, it is also possible they came at different times. Anthony was definitely in Prince George's County in early 1701, but Thomas's arrival is a little less clear. It is derived from a few different facts as well as suppositions. The first is that there has not been found a marriage record for him in England. This lends substance to the theory that he married in Maryland, which, by extension, would mean he would have had to have been there long enough to meet and become engaged to a young lady.

Thomas's wife is not definitely recorded anywhere. But then, neither are most marriages prior to the 1720s in Maryland. There are references to a Deborah Drane, whose maiden name was Clark, who was of the right age bracket to be a wife to Thomas, but the only thing connecting them is being of the same age and in the same place. So that makes their marriage tenuous, at best.

Thomas's children began marrying in the 1720s, so their marriages are recorded, but these records typically do not include the names of the parents of the wedding's participants unless they are minors. The marriages of three people named Drane occur in Anne Arundel County in the period from 1719 to 1733. The tightness of the range of years indicates they are very likely siblings. Their names are Eleanor, Elizabeth, and James. While we have nothing to indicate their ages or dates of birth, from the years they got married we can infer they may have been born in this order. The two sisters, Eleanor and Elizabeth, married William Grimes and Charles Fazell, respectively. Both of these families continued on, but are outside the scope of this book.

This leaves the only surviving son, James. I say surviving son, because it was quite common in this period for several babies to be born to a couple, but only a few make it to adulthood. Given the time gaps between the marriages of the three surviving children, it seems likely there were others who did not make it. James's marriage and the christening of his first three children were all recorded in Westminster Parish in Anne Arundel County. He married Easter Hall, and together they had five surviving children: Thomas, John, James, Ann, and Elizabeth. One of the christened children was an earlier son named John, who lived only a couple of months.

The eldest of these children, Thomas, was a twin to the Baby John who died. The next baby born was also named John and that one lived to adulthood, becoming the ancestor to descendants covered in this chapter. James Jr. would become the father of the last Anne Arundel County Dranes. Anne would marry George Colbert, while Elizabeth became Mrs. Snowdon Taylor. One quick thing about Snowdon Taylor: Some researchers like to say the Dranes are related to President Zachary Taylor through this marriage. However, Pres. Taylor's ancestors have been well documented and Snowdon is not among them.

There is no documentation that the eldest son, Thomas, married or had children, but there is a Richard Drane in Arundel County who does not fit in with the children of Thomas's brothers, John or James, so it is rather easy to suppose he may be Thomas's son. However, after his 1806 marriage to Sarah Givins, he quickly falls off of the face of Earth, apparently without leaving any children, so his connection to the family, while not precisely documented, is also without much consequence.

The second surviving son, John, moved away from Anne Arundel County, and his descendants will make up the bulk of this chapter, so we will return to him shortly.

The youngest son, James Jr., married Sarah Todd somewhere around 1770 and had three known children: James III, Thomas, and Rachel. Rachel married John Sappington. While still children, James and Thomas were the subject of an inheritance dispute. Their mother died in 1786, already being a widow, leaving her children orphaned. They were assigned a guardian, one of their Grimes cousins. A few years later, her brother, Lancelot Todd, died childless and without a will. The probate court gave part of Lancelot's estate to the young James and Thomas. There is no further record of them after this, so it can be assumed they left no heirs of their own. There also does not seem to have been any inheritance for them from their paternal family. Any property this branch of the family had in Anne Arundel County appears to have been sold, or possibly destroyed in the Revolution.

Another possibility does exist for these branches that suddenly end. These lines of the Drane family are living during the period of the American Revolution. When the colonies formed a new nation and seceded from Great Britain, there were many colonists who still considered themselves subjects of His Majesty the King. Those who were unwilling to become Americans were obliged to return to England, or go to Canada. There is not a detailed accounting of who all left, so it is possible that some of these Drane lines did not die out, but that they simply packed up and left the United States.

Whatever became of the lines that disappeared from the American scene, one Drane from this branch remained. He was John Drane, the middle child of James and Easter. He is the first of this branch to have a recorded birth date, June 26th, 1736. What happens after that is a matter of some speculation.

There is a John Drane who would be born at about the same time, who was the husband of Rebecca Fancher. What little is known about John, and Rebecca for that matter, is learned after the fact when Rebecca, as a widowed Mrs. Drane, married a second time, to John Newman. It is her age at this marriage that places her date of birth at approximately 1737, only one year after the John Drane who was the son of James and Easter. When she married Newman, she brought several children into the bargain from her first marriage to a John Drane who died in Virginia in 1792.

Were Rebecca's husband and the son of Easter Drane the same person? The evidence is highly circumstantial and probably would not hold up in a courtroom, but it still falls in the "likely" category. Mostly it has been a process of elimination. Because Rebecca's husband was named John, it was tempting to try to stick him in with the Baltimore Dranes, which seem to have a John in every set of children born. However, those Johns are all documented and none were in the right age range or location to be Rebecca's husband. The Delaware branch was only just getting going, so did not have children old enough yet to be Rebecca's husband. The only other branch, the Prince George's County branch, is also well documented and was not missing anyone named John. This leaves the Anne Arundel County branch.

There is also an economic indicator. Both the Baltimore and Prince George's County branches were well off financially. The Anne Arundel branch has always seemed to struggle on this front. The John Drane who married Rebecca Fancher was not a man of money. The reason he took his family to the untamed frontier of the Smoky Mountains would have been to try to make his money off of the resources there, whether it be from trapping, mining, or lumber. Whether Easter Drane's son grew up to marry Rebecca Fancher or not, I am choosing to proceed with his descendants' story here, since I would otherwise have nowhere else to put it.

After the death of John Drane, his widow, Rebecca, married John Newman. By this time, she would have been a woman in her early 50s. It was also Newman's second marriage, and he also had his own children from the first marriage. They settled the northeastern tip of Tennessee, in Greene County, near the town of Greeneville. Greeneville had gained notoriety a few years earlier as the would-be capital of the proposed "State of Franklin," a failed statehood effort that was replaced by the formation of Tennessee in 1796.

Rebecca brought five teenaged children to her second marriage: Margaret, Kindness, James, John, and Rebecca. In the early 1800s, they each married in their turn. The girls became Mrs. John Reynolds, Mrs. John White, and Mrs. William Craddock, respectively. Rebecca Craddock would marry a second time, as an older widow, to Samuel Morelock. The boys, James and John, would continue the family, but would do so with the Drain spelling of the family. The reason for the spelling change is not clear, but could be tied to the fact they were quite young when their father died and had probably not had any contact with his family. Therefore, they simply may have never learned how to spell the name, so they spelled it the way it sounds, like a drain pipe.

James, the elder son, was born in 1780, according to his 1800 marriage certificate to Ruanna Sherill, which gives his age as 20 and hers as 18. Ruanna, although looking like a nickname, is the only name she was ever known by and was also a name handed down through several generations. She was from North Carolina, which only lies a few miles from Greeneville. James and Ruanna started a tradition that continues to this day: large families. They had twelve children, four of whom died young.

James served in the Tennessee militia during the War of 1812 and in the late 1820s started moving his family west to Arkansas. However, he did not make it that far. He passed away en route in Obion County, Tennessee which is just east of the Arkansas state line. His widow and six youngest children continued on the trek, settling in the northwestern edge of Arkansas. Rather than go with his family, James's eldest son and namesake migrated to northeastern Alabama. He was married twice and fathered a total of fourteen children between the two wives. The only surviving child to remain in Greene County was a daughter Mary who married Benjamin Hood in about 1830.

James's younger brother, John, continued the presence of Drains in Green County, and over the years they spread to neighboring Washington County, as well. John Drain was born in about 1782 and was married in Greene County, in 1810, to Margaret Lane. However, ten years later he left his wife and family to join his nephew in Alabama. Margaret received a divorce on the grounds of abandonment and was free to marry again to John Runnel.

When John left Margaret, he also left his five children, Thomas, John, Rebecca, Solomon, and Sarah. Thomas's and Rebecca's fates are not recorded, but it can be supposed they died without marrying. Sarah married Alfred McNab in 1845. Of the remaining sons, John and Solomon, John and his wife remained in Greene County, having five children. Their son, Wilton, went to Alabama during the Civil War, serving there in the Cavalry, but returned to Greene County, where he married Jennie Droak in 1867. There is no record of them having children. Wilton's brother, yet another John, also married in Greene County and had three surviving children, two daughters and a son, Edward, before moving to Maysville in Madison County, Alabama. He died there in 1909. Edward and his wife, Margaret, were living with them in 1910 in Maysville. Edward died in 1928. His descendants are believed to still be in northern Alabama.

Solomon Drain, the youngest son of John Drain and Margaret Lane, married twice, having four children with the first wife, Mary Holland. These four children are the ancestors of the present day Drains still in the Greeneville area. Their eldest child, a daughter named

Sarah, was born before Solomon and Mary's marriage. Solomon later gave a deposition after he married her mother claiming paternity and legitimizing her. His other children with Mary were John, Thomas, and James and were born between 1840 and 1850. The middle son, Thomas, died in 1864, unmarried, aged about 23.

John Wilson Drain, son of Solomon, remained in Greene County all of his life, dying there in 1915. He also married twice and fathered 10 children between the two. Most of his numerous descendants remain in northeastern Tennessee, but a few of his grandchildren went to the Great Lakes region to pursue the growing industries that swelled after World War II.

Solomon's youngest son, James, lived 1850 to 1911. He married Mary Malvina Falls in 1873. After their sixth and last child was born ten years later, they moved to Marion County, Iowa, settling near the town of Knoxville. Neither of the two sons, King Solomon, called "Bud," nor George, ever married. Any remaining descendants would be through the three daughters who did marry, Delilah, Nancy, and Ellie.

According to a great-great-granddaughter of Solomon, many of the members of this line of the family enjoyed a natural talent for music, learning to play several instruments. The most prevalent were the guitar or banjo. One grandson, William Reason Drain (1876-1959), even had a brief career as a musician on the radio. What kept this career short was the fact that he could not play without tapping his foot. The overly sensitive microphones of the day would pick up the sound of the tapping, leading to a musical legend being known only to his family and friends.

DeKalb County, Alabama Drains

James Drain, the son of James and Ruanna, married Nancy Sharp while still in Tennessee, but moved a few years later to DeKalb County, Alabama. Arriving in the mid-1830s, they were some of the first white settlers in what had recently been part of the Cherokee Nation. James and Nancy had ten children, all but two of whom lived to adulthood. After Nancy's death in 1871, James remarried, to Lydia Busby and had six more children, but only three of these made it out of infancy.

The eldest of James's and Nancy's children, John Green Drain, was known by his middle name. He married about 1850, but was dead by 1853, leaving no children. The second son was named Lorenzo, but is often called L.D. or Lon. His marriage to Catherine Mitchell produced eight children. Most of his descendants have remained in northern Alabama. One grandson, Sherman Drain, made the westward expansion and settled in Utah. His descendants still live in the West, but are spread throughout Utah, California, and Arizona.

James's and Nancy's third son, William, moved briefly to Mississippi, where his three daughters were born, but returned to northern Alabama, settling in Jackson County. The fourth surviving son had the unusual name Pearly. It is not clear where it came from, but a couple of his nephews would also be so named in his honor. Pearly served in the Civil War in the Alabama Infantry. After the war, he married Nancy Wynn. They had seven children; the descendants of his son Arthur, mostly remained in DeKalb County. His elder son, John, moved further south, most of his children living and dying in the Tuscaloosa area.

The youngest of James's children by his first wife, George Washington Drain, also remained in DeKalb County, becoming a pastor at the Piney Grove Baptist Church. Some of his descendants are still members there, along with the descendants of James's three children by his second wife, Lydia Busby.

Northwest Arkansas Drains

When the elder James Drain, husband of Ruanna Sherill, decided to move his family to Arkansas, he took his younger children with him. Although he did not make it, dying in Tennessee just shy of crossing into Arkansas, his widow and children continued the westward trek and settled in Franklin County, in the northwest corner of the state, in the early 1830s.

Ruanna lived to be very old. In 1870, she is listed on the census in Richland Township, Washington County, as an 89-year-old woman living with her son, G.W. When she went to Arkansas, she was joined by her sons, Washington and Wesley, as well as daughters, Sarah, Jennie, and Margaret. The family quickly spread out to inhabit not only Franklin County, but also Washington, Madison, and Benton Counties, too. To make matters a little confusing for this branch of the family, some of the descendants in the previous section lived in Huntsville, which is in Madison County, Alabama. Several of the descendants in this section lived in Huntsville, which is in Madison County, Arkansas. These are the type of things that drive genealogists to snatch their hair from their heads.

Ruanna Drain's son John joined his brother, James, when the latter went to Alabama, but only stayed there a short while. He joined the Army in the 1840s and went to fight in the Mexican-American War. He died during the conflict, not from the war itself, but from disease while in Mexico City. His widow, the former Susan Carr, took their six children and joined the majority of his siblings in Arkansas.

Washington Drain, whose full name was George Washington Drain, married Elizabeth Robbins once he reached Arkansas. In keeping with the times, they had twelve kids. All of the children and grandchildren lived, died, married, and produced more children in those same four counties in the northwestern corner of Arkansas. The children of the John Drain who died in Mexico City went on to marry and produce no less than 31 grandchildren. They all remained in Arkansas, as well. The youngest of the three brothers who went to Arkansas was Wesley. At least some of his 35-plus grandchildren branched out a little and moved across the Mississippi River into Missouri.

With the large number of Drains living in Washington, Franklin, Madison, and Benton Counties, Arkansas, one would think it very tempting to name the area "Drain's Corners" or something similar. But the locals there seem to have resisted this temptation.

Thomas Drane (bap. 1 Mar 1660/1 Sawbridgeworth, Herts., England –) immigrated approx.1690
= ...; **Deborah Clark**[1] (...)
A. **Eleanor Drane** (...)
    = 27 Oct 1719 Anne Arundel Co.; **William Grimes** (...)
B. **Elizabeth Drane** (...)
    = Dec 1725 Anne Arundel Co.; **Charles Frazell** (...)
C. **James Drane** (...)
    = 14 Aug 1733 Anne Arundel Co.; **Easter Hall** (ca. 1695 – ...) daughter of Henry Hall
    1. **Thomas Drane** (Apr 1734 Anne Arundel Co., – ...) (twin)
        = ...
        a. **Richard Drane** (...)
            = 4 Feb 1806 Anne Arundel Co.; **Sarah Gwinn** (...)
    2. **John Drane** (Apr – May 1734 Anne Arundel Co.) (twin)
    3. **John Drane** (26 Jun 1736 Anne Arundel Co[2]. – 1792 in VA)
        = **Rebecca Fancher** (ca.1737 – ...) =2nd John Newman
        a. **Margaret Drain**[3] (...)
            = 1803; **John Reynolds** (...)
        b. **Kindness Drain** (...)
            = 1805; **John White** (...)
        c. **James Drain** (ca.1780 – 5 Aug 1829 Obion Co., TN) served in War of 1812
            = Dec 1800; **Ruanna** Jane **Sherrill** (ca.1782 NC – aft.1870)
            I) **James Drain** (1804 TN – 1889 AL)
                =1 ...; **Nancy Sharp** (ca.1806 – 11 Feb 1871 AL)
                =2 1 Oct 1872 DeKalb Co., AL; **Lydia Busby**[4] (Jan 1854—...)
                issue of 1st:
                A) **Eliza** Jane **Drain** (22 Feb 1825 TN – ...)

---

[1] This is a huge supposition on the author's part. It is based on nothing other than Deborah appears to be too old to have been married to any of Thomas's children, and the only senior Drane known to be in the area at the time was Thomas.

[2] The baptismal record of John Drane shows him to be the son of James & Easter. Whether he is he same John Drane who married Rebecca Fancher is still not confirmed.

[3] It appears the children of John & Rebecca started using the Drain spelling, likely because they were not taught the Drane spelling, since they were separated from their paternal relatives and raised by John Newman, their stepfather.

[4] US Census: 1900 – Marshall Co. widowed w/sons Robert, Moses, and Chester.

 = 1850 DeKalb Co.; **Joel Sharp** (...)
B) John **Green Drain** (16 Apr 1828 TN – 9 Jan 1853)
 = 1849 DeKalb Co.; **Rebecca** Elizabeth **Coleman** (...)
no issue
C) **Lorenzo** Dow **Drain** (23 Dec 1829 TN – aft.1900[5])
served in the Cavalry in CSA
 = 1850 DeKalb Co; **Catherine Mitchell** (Jul 1833 – ...)
daughter of Humphrey Mitchell & Keziah Bynum
 1) **James** Humphrey Bates **Drain**[6] (Jun 1851 AL – ...)
  = 13 Sep 1873 Jackson Co., AL; **Mary Thomas**[7] (Dec 1857 AL – ...)
  a) **William P Drain** (12 Sep 1877 AL – 22 Oct 1965 Pottawatomie Co. OK[8])
   =ca.1900 Jackson Co. AL; **Pluma** Walter **Northcross** (21 Jul 1883 AL – 17 Sep 1980)
  has issue
  c) **Margaret** Pluma **Drain** (15 Mar 1883 AL – 29 Jun 1974 Gregg Co. TX)
   = ...; ... **Everett** (...)
  b) David **Lee Drain**[9] (May 1894 TX – ...)
   = ca.1917; **Lydia ...** (...)
  has issue
 2) **Mary A E Drain** (ca.1853 – ...)
  = 1877; **Alfred W Banks** (...)
 3) **Nancy** Keziah **Drain** (May 1856 – ...)
  = 1878; **John Reece** (Dec 1858 – ...)
 4) **John** Jesse **Drain** (ca.1860 – ...)
  = 1878; **Ellen** Nancy **Johnson** (17 Aug 1871 – 12 Sep 1947 Anniston, AL) daughter of Robert Johnson
  a) **Lorenzo Drain** (...)
   = 25 Dec 1913; **Lola Barnwell** (...)

---

[5] There is a marker for Lorenzo in the New Harmont Cementery in DeKalb Co., but it does not show a date of death. He was still alive in the 1900 Census, living in Thompson, Marshall Co. AL.
[6] 1900 Census: Baker, Howard Co. AR
[7] According to the 1900 census, she had 10 children, but only 3 were still living.
[8] William, Pluma and several of their descendants are burried in Tecumseh Cemetery, Pottawatomie Co. According to the obituary of one of his sons, the family moved to Oklahoma in the late 1920s.
[9] 1920 Census: Bryan Co. OK

    b) **Elizabeth Drain** (...)
      = 31 Aug 1919 Calhoun Co., AL; **James Hurley** (...)
    c) **Mary Drain** (19 Feb 1890 – 15 Oct 1961 DeKalb Co.)
      = ...; **Oscar Bearden** (1889 – 15 May 1971 Jackson Co., AL) son of John Bearden & Liza Harper
    d) **Jack O Drain** (11 Feb 1899 – 28 Oct 1937 Anniston)
      = ...; **Lexie** Virginia **Davis** (1 Jul 1900 – 5 Nov 1954 Anniston) daughter of Floyd Davis & Elizabeth Lathem
      has issue

5) **Rev. George** Washington **Drain** (7 May 1861 – 5 Apr 1924 Boaz, AL)
  = 1890; Sarah **Adeline Isbell** (13 Feb 1871 – 25 Dec 1940)
    a) **Rev. Charles W Drain** (4 May 1892 – 23 Apr 1950 Etowah Co. AL)
      = ...; **Mae D Fowler** (1 May 1896 – 13 Jul 1988)
      has issue
    b) John **Elmer Drain** (Jan 1894 – 15 Jul 1966 Huntsville, AL)
    c) **Rev. William A Drain** (5 Jan 1896 – 1 Feb 1952)
    d) **Sherman E Drain** (21 Nov 1897 DeKalb Co. – 9 Oct 1995 Salt Lake City, UT)
      = 26 Apr 1925 Salt Lake City; **Ruby** Ally **Williams** (19 Apr 1907 Salt Lake City – 2 Oct 1999 Salt Lake City) daughter of Thomas Williams & Lucy ...
      has issue
    e) **Gilbert L Drain** (ca.1905 AL – ...)

6) **Rev. Pearl H Drain** (ca.1864 – ...)
  =1 30 Nov 1882 Marshall Co.; Mary **Alabama Bearden** (27 Feb 1861 – 24 Oct 1910 Lawrence Co. AL)
  =2 ...; **Forrest Rogers** (19 Mar 1883 – 15 Jun 1985 Morgan Co. AL)
  issue of 1st:
    a) **Elisha H Drain** (Jan 1884 Marshall Co. – ...)
      = ca.1904 Lawrence Co.; **Novella Roaden** (ca.1885— ...)
      has issue
    b) **Idella Drain** (Aug 1887 Marshall Co. – ...)
    c) **Mose Drain** (5 Jul 1892 Marshall Co. – 18 May 1923 Danville, AL)
      = ...; **Shenobea Payne** (...) =2nd Earl Ogles
      has issue
    d) **Ellen Drain** (Nov 1893 Marshall Co. – ...)

  e) **Mary Drain** (Aug 1896 Lawrence Co. – ...)
  f) **John D Drain** (ca.1901 Lawrence Co. – ...)
  g) **Ernest Drain** (1 Sep 1903 Lawrence Co. – 24 Jun 1906 Lawrence Co.)
 issue of 2nd:
  h) a son (28 – 31 Jan1922 Danville)
 7) **Albert Drain** (22 Feb 1863 – 11 Jan 1944)
  = 20 Dec 1888; **Paralee Harper** (Jun 1867 – ...)
  a) **Alice Drain** (2 Oct 1889 – 2 Mar 1950)
   = ...; ... **King** (...)
  b) **Lorenzo D Drain** (Dec 1893 – ...) (twin)
  c) **Ida Drain** (Dec 1893 – ...) (twin)
   = ...; **Matt Rouzee** (...)
  d) **Leroy Drain** (Jun 1897 – 1 Feb 1919 Birmingham)
   = ...; **Gladys Fields** (...)
  e) **Joseph O Drain** (May 1898 – ...)
  f) **John Drain** (...)
   = ...; **Pauline** ... (...)
 8) **Kansada Drain** (29 Sep 1865 – 11 Feb 1944 Albertville, AL)
  = ...; ... **Samples** (...)
D) **William W Drain**[10] (15 Mar 1833 AL – ...)
 = ca.1853; **Elizabeth ...** (...)
 1) **Cornelia Drain** (ca.1854 MS – ...)
 2) **Nancy Drain** (ca.1856 MS – ...)
 3) **Josephine Drain** (ca.1858 MS – ...)
E) **Joel Drain** (27 Jul 1835 AL – 7 Mar 1838 AL)
H) **Pearley H Drain**[11] (1 Feb 1837 – 5 Dec 1903[12]) Army Sgt in CSA
 = 1866 Jackson Co.; **Nancy A Wynn** (21 Jan 1837 – 19 Dec 1903) daughter of John Wynn & Margaret Kennedy
 1) **Margaret Drain** (ca. 1868 – ...)
  = 19 Dec 1883 Marshall Co.; Hamilton "**Cub**" **Berry** (...)
 2) **John D Drain** (Oct 1869 – ...)
  = ...; **Mary Ann Richey** (Jan 1875 – ...) daughter of Jim Richey & Emma Liles
  a) **James** William **Drain** (Mar 1891 – 26 Jun 1957 Pickens Co. AL)

---

[10] US Census: 1850 – Jackson Co. AL; daughters born in MS though.
[11] US Census: 1880 – Marhsall Co. AL, 1900 – DeKalb Co.
[12] Buried in Piney Grove Cemetery, DeKalb Co. with many of descendants

= ...; **Esther** ... (...)
has issue
b) **Alta Drain** (27 Aug 1894 – 5 Nov 1896)
b) **Josie Drain** (25 May – 5 Aug 1895 DeKalb Co.)
c) **Magnolia F Drain** (1898 – 26 Aug 1970 Tuscaloosa Co., AL)
= ...; **William** Jesse **McPherson** (24 Oct 1896 – 5 Nov 1960) son of John McPherson & Sarah Milwee
d) **Wallace** Lee **Drain** (1902 – 21 Sep 1965 Pickens Co. AL)
= ...; **Alta** Estell ... (...)
e) **Edith** Myrtle **Drain** (5 Sep 1908 Dekalb Co. – 15 May 1970 Tuscaloosa Co.)
= ...; **Charles** Clayton **Fancher** (...)
3) Mary **Josephine Drain** (26 Dec 1871 – 5 Mar 1896 DeKalb Co.)
= ...; **John** Wesley **Tucker** (23 Feb 1868 – 18 Apr 1918 DeKalb Co.)
4) **Perlina Drain** (ca.1879 – ...)
5) **Arthur** Lee **Drain** (22 Dec 1881 – 23 Jan 1955 DeKalb Co.[13])
= ...; Phoebe C **"Lezby" Richey** (1882 – 1961 DeKalb Co.) daughter of Jim Richey & Emma Liles
has issue
6) **Dora Drain** (...)
= ...; **John Dickson** (...)
7) **June Drain** (...)
I) **Roan Drain** (...)
J) **Rev. George** Washington **Drain**[14] (3 Aug 1866 – 28 Jul 1937 Fort Payne, AL)
= 1899 DeKalb Co.; Sarah **Ada** Jane **Bailey** (6 May 1879 – 5 Apr 1962 DeKalb Co.)
has issue
issue of 2nd:
K) **Andy** Green **Drain** (1878 – 1925)
=1 ...; **Josie Heaton** (...)
=2 ...; **Bertha** ... (1884 – 1896)
has issue
L) **Robert** Murphy **Drain** (8 Jul 1880 – 22 Oct 1943

---

[13] Buried at Mount Flat Cemetery, DeKalb Co.
[14] George and Ada are buried at Piney Grove Baptist Church in DeKalb Co.

Marshall Co. AL)
= ...; **Jennie** Lou **Smith** (30 Jun 1882 – 23 Sep 1980 DeKalb Co.)
has issue
  M) **Mose** Allen **Drain** (17 Jun 1881 – 28 Mar 1957 Fort Payne, AL) (twin)
  = ...; **Temperance** Jane **Gilbreath** (26 Jun 1888 – 29 Jan 1965)
  has issue
  N) **Rose Drain** (* & + 17 Jun 1881) (twin)
  O) **Charley Drain** (1 Dec 1883 DeKalb Co. – 20 Dec 1889 DeKalb Co.)
  P) **Chester Drain** (Apr 1890 – ...)
II) **Elizabeth Drain** (...)
III) **Rebecca Drain** (+infancy)
IV) **Mary** Jane **Drain** (1811 Greene Co. – 30 Mar 1893 Granby, MO)
= ca.1830 Greene Co; **Benjamin Hood** (ca.1810 – 1875 Washburn, MO)
V) **Robert Drain** (1820 TN – ...)
VI) **David Drain** (ca.1818 TN – ...)
VII) George **Washington Drain** (ca.1823 Marion Co., TN – 7 Apr 1891 Franklin Co., AR) fought for CSA
= 8 Jul 1849 Washington Co. AR; **Elizabeth Robbins** (ca.1832 AR – bef.1910 Franklin Co.) daughter of Richard Robbins & Nancy Richards
  A) **Richard** David **Drain** (3 Apr 1850 Washington Co. – 4 Apr 1929 Washington Co.)
  = 11 Aug 1869; **Appie White** (Nov 1853 Washington Co. – Jun 1934 Washington Co.)
   1) **James** Washington **Drain** (Jun 1870 AR – ...)
   = ca.1890; **Elizabeth Evans** (Jan 1875 KY – ...)
    a) **Ida M Drain** (Oct 1894 – ...)
    = 27 Nov 1919 Madison Co.; **John** Lonzo **Lacy** (ca. 1874 – ...)
    b) Richard **Clarence Drain** (Apr 1896 – ...)
    = 26 Jun 1921 Washington Co.; **Ora** Esther **Allison** (19 Feb 1899 Madison Co. – 21 Jul 1971 Madison Co.) daughter of Sherman Allison & Martha Templeton
    has issue
    c) **Appie B Drain** (ca.1900 – ...)

= ...; **Jacob D ...** (...)
 2) **John** Wesley **Drain** (May 1875 Madison Co. – 1949)
   =1 ca.1893 AR; **Dolly** Ann **Malloy** (18 Nov 1876 AR – 24 Jun 1934)
   =2 10 Jun 1935 Washington Co; **Della Wadley** (ca. 1881 – ...)
   issue of 1st (none by 2nd):
   a) **Charley Drain** (Jun 1894 – ...)
   b) **Hoyt Drain** (Sep 1899 – ...) (twin)
     = ... Washington Co.; **Mary Beatty** (...)
   c) **Gracie Drain** (Sep 1899 – ...) (twin)
   d) **Paul Drain** (26 Jun 1905 Madison Co. – 10 Mar 1996 Franklin Co.)
     = ...; **Mary E Tye** (6 Jan 1908 MS – 2 Sep 1971 Franklin Co.)
     has issue
B) **James** Hiram **Drain** (22 Apr 1851 Washington Co. – 26 Oct 1932 Collin Co., TX)
 = 25 Dec 1877 Washington Co; **Nancy** Ann **Masters** (1 May 1852 – 17 Feb 1935 Collin Co.) daughter of John Masters & Ann Ball
 1) **Mary** Ann **Drain** (Nov 1879 – ...)
   = ...; **R Scott Phillips** (...)
 2) **Katy** Elizabeth **Drain** (ca.1880 – ...)
 3) George Washington "**Dud**" **Drain** (... – 26 May 1965 Dallas)
   = ...; **Estella Dunigan** (...)
 4) **John** Masters **Drain** (1886 Madison Co. – 1956)
   = ...; **Minnie C Russell** (...)
   has issue
 5) **Bertha Drain** (27 Feb 1887 – 20 Jul 1976)
   = 9 Apr 1902; **William** Tabble **Stibbens** (22 May 1883 – 24 Dec 1966)
 6) **Myrtle Drain** (ca.1888 – ...)
   = 10 Dec 1905 Franklin Co.; **Wallace Kirkendall** (ca. 1881 – ...)
 7) **Denver** Lee **Drain** (30 Apr 1894 – 8 Jan 1972 Dallas)
   = ...; **Mary ...** (...)
   has issue
 8) **James Drain** (ca.1896 – ...)
   = ...; **Mary Skelton** (...)

has issue
9) **Ernest** Jackson **Drane** (1897 – 14 Jun 1990 Collin Co.)
= ...; **Grace Titsworth** (...)
has issue
C) **Lottie** Louisetta **Drain** (ca.1853 Washington Co. – ...)
= ...; **George Monroe** (...)
D) **William** Alexander **Drain** (25 Nov 1854 Washington Co. – 30 Apr 1934 Madison Co., AR)
= ca.1882; **Mary** Isabelle **Olinger** (6 Jan 1855 AR – 5 Jan 1943 Madison Co.)
1) **John** David **Drain** (30 Sep 1885 – 8 Jun 1935 Madison Co.)
= 2 Aug 1908 Madison Co; **Mattie Murphy** (4 Nov 1885 Madison Co. – 10 Oct 1962 Washington Co.) daughter of Josh Murphy & Lizzie Parsley
has issue
2) **George** Washington **Drain** (19 Jul 1888 AR – 27 Feb 1979 Madison Co.)
= 5 Jan 1913 AR; **Ina** Alice **McConnell** (1 Sep 1896 – 3 Jul 1978)
has issue
3) Virginia **Lee Drain** (12 Feb 1890 – 13 Jun 1979 CA)
= 13 Oct 1912 Madison Co.; **Walter McConnell** (ca. 1893 – ...)
4) **Lillie T Drain** (Aug 1893 AR – 27 Feb 1942 Patrick, AR)
= 6 Dec 1910 Madison Co; **Monroe Hill** (Nov 1882 – Mar 1960 Crosses, AR)
5) **James** Sterman **Drain** (3 Jan 1891 Crawford Co., AR – 19 Feb 1978 Washington Co.)
= 2 Mar 1910 Madison Co; **Arizona Stacy** (16 Jun 1894 Washington Co. – Nov 1984 Madison Co.)
has issue
E) Nancy **Jane Drain** (ca.1858 Washington Co. – ...)
= 21 Dec 1879 Franklin Co.; **Silas Childers** (ca.1858 – ...)
F) **Wesley** Newton **Drain** (Apr 1859 Washington Co. – 1934 Pope Co., AR)
= 15 Apr 1883 Franklin Co., AR; **Nancy** Ann **Hill** (9 Jan 1859 – 1932 Pope Co.)
1) **Cora B Drain** (20 Jan 1881 Franklin Co. – 11 Oct 1945 Franklin Co.)

    = 18 Jan 1901 Franklin Co; **Miles** Fielder **Belt** (7 Nov 1875 Franklin Co. – 10 Jan 1944 Franklin Co.)
    2) **Nancy Drain** (ca.1888 – ...)
    3) **Dollie Drain** (ca.1895 – ...)
    4) **Mollie Drain** (...)
G) **Nora Drain** (+ young)
H) **Sarah Drain** (ca.1862 Washington Co. – ...)
    = 25 Jan 1880 Franklin Co.; **William Gardner** (ca.1852– ...)
I) **Salina Drain** (ca.1863 Washington Co. – ...)
    = ...; **Al Hendricks** (...)
J) **M Louisa Drain** (ca.1868 Washington Co. – ...)
    = ...; **Thomas Page** (...)
K) **Frances L Drain** (ca.1870 Washington Co. – ...)
    = 8 Oct 1897 Franklin Co., AR; **Aisom McCallister** (ca.1857 – ...)
L) **George** Washington **Drain** (15 Mar 1877 Franklin Co. – 10 Jan 1973 Edmund, OK)
    =1 14 Dec 1902 Franklin Co.; **Clara Staton** (4 Apr 1881 Franklin Co. –15 Nov 1909 Franklin Co.)
    =2 24 Mar 1912 Franklin Co.; **Polly** Ann **Belt** (3 Apr 1884 – 18 May 1956 Osage Co. OK) daughter of Newton Belt & Rachel Barnett
    has issue
VIII) **John Drain** (ca.1823 Marion Co. – 9 Nov 1847 Mexico City) died of disease during Mexican War
= 21 Jul 1840 DeKalb Co., AL; **Susan B Carr** (28 Feb 1818 TN – 2 Oct 1915 Madison Co., AR)
A) **Sarah** Emmaline **Drain** (Jun 1840 DeKalb Co. – ...)
B) **James E Drain** (ca.1841 DeKalb Co. – ...)
    = 3 Jun 1866 Washington Co; **Lucinda Watkins** (1845 AR – ...)
    1) Sarah **Emmaline Drain** (ca.1867 Madison Co. – ...)
    2) John **Enos Drain** (ca.1869 Madison Co. – ...)
    3) **John W Drain** (ca.1873 Madison Co. – ...)
    4) **Robert** Lee **Drain** (ca.1877 Madison Co. – ...)
C) **William** Burtis **Drain** (12 May 1843 Dade Co., MO – 7 Mar 1931 Washington Co.)
    =1 13 May 1866; **Susan L Dodd** (22 Oct 1844 TN – 17 Mar 1925 Washington Co.)
    =2 9 Oct 1927 Washington Co.; **Mary Samons** (ca.1869 – ...)

issue of 1st (none by 2nd):
1) **George Drain** (+young bef.1870)
2) **Mary** Elizabeth **Drain** (+ young bef.1870)
3) **Robert Drain** (ca.1868 – bef.1950)
   = ...; **Minnie Rowe** (...)
4) **Susan** Louise **Drain** (ca.1870 – bef.1950)
   = ...; **Thomas Hudson** (...)
5) **Mary Drain** (ca.1873 – bef.1950)
6) **William** Andrew **Drain** (8 Mar 1875 Madison Co. – 26 Aug 1950)
   = 28 Dec 1901 Washington Co; **Naurma Bookout** (10 Jul 1883 – 4 Jan 1930 Washington Co.)
   has issue
7) **John Drain** (ca.1879 – bef.1950)
   = 20 May 1901 Benton Co. AR; **Effie Robinson** (ca.1883 - ...)
8) **Emma Drain** (ca.1881 – ...)
   = 26 Feb 1899 Washington Co.[15]; **Lemuel Johnson** (ca.1878 – ...)
9) **Laura Drain** (ca.1888 – ...)
   = 22 May 1908 Washington Co; **William** Claud **Wilson** (ca.1884 – ...)
10) **Roy B Drain** (ca.1890 – bef.1950)
    =1 21 May 1914 Sebastian Co. AR; **Gona Bain** (ca.1892 – ...)
    =2 21 Aug 1920 Washngton Co; **Grace Hembree** (...)
D) **John** Wesley **Drain** (ca.1849 Madison Co., AR – ...)
E) **Thomas** Woodrow **Drain** (1 Sep 1855 AR – 14 Mar 1918 Madison Co.)
   = ...; **Laura Simpson** (Aug 1874 AR – ...)
   1) **Bertha Drain** (15 Jun 1885 Madison Co. – 3 Jan 1956 Galveston, TX)
      =1 24 Dec 1905; **Allen** Jackson **Holman** (ca.1880 – ...)
      =2 ...; **William** Henry **Spencer** (...)
   2) George Edward "**Burt**" **Drain** (28 Dec 1888 – 8 Mar 1950)
      = ca.1901 Wise Co., TX; **Mamie** Jane **Baldwin** (25 Aug 1891 – 16 Jan 1971)

---

[15] In her brother William's 1950 obituary, she is listed as Miss Emma Drain. Perhaps this marriage ended in divorce and she reverted to her maiden name.

has issue
3) **Jayson Drain** (Dec 1889 – ...)
4) **Albert** Stering **Drain** (Dec 1892 – ...)
= ...;
has issue
5) **Vera Drain** (Aug 1894 – ...)
6) **Ruby Drain** (23 Nov 1896 Madison Co. – 17 Jun 1971 Madison Co.)
= 4 Jan 1917 Madison Co.; **John** Lafayette **Thompson** (8 Nov 1894 Madison Co. – Oct 1970 Madison Co.) son of Henry Thompson & Ida Thornton
7) **Vernon Drain** (Nov 1899 – ...)
=1 15 Jun 1922 Madison Co.; **Arthea** Ruth **Kirk** (ca. 1904 – ...)
=2 22 Oct 1950 Madison Co.; **Ora Brown** (ca.1907 – ...)
has issue
8) **Dortha Drain** (ca.1902 – ...)
9) Thomas Toy "**Pete**" **Drain** (...)
= ...;
has issue

F) **George M Drain** (Dec 1861 AR – ...)
= ca.1888; **Jerome** [Jeramia?] **E Simpson** (Sept 1868 AR – ...)
1) **Jessie M Drain** (Jan 1889 AR – ...)
= 1909; **Grace** ... (ca.1889 AR – ...)
has issue
2) **Bonnie Drain** (Jul 1891 – ...)
= 22 Mar 1908 Madison Co; **J B Holman** (ca.1879 – ...)
3) **Hugh Drain** (Jul 1894 – ...)
4) **Ivie Drain** (Oct 1900 – ...)
5) **Loy M Drain** (ca.1902 – ...)
6) **Bert D Drain** (ca.1905 – ...)
7) **Marshall B Drain** (ca.1906 – ...)
8) **Leu Drain** (ca.1908 – ...)

IX) **Rebecca Drain** (...)
X) **Sarah Drain** (...)
XI) **Wesley Drain** (1829 TN – Aug 1856 Madison Co. AR)
= ...; **Martha J Dunaway** (May 1832 Madison Co. – 1923)
A) **John** Franklin **Drain** (1 Jan 1848 Madison Co. – 25 Aug 1918 Madison Co.)
= ca.1869 Madison Co; Barbara Ann Matilda "**Emma**"

Gardner (Jan 1855 Butler Co., MO – 1930) daughter of Lewis Gardner & Martha Miskel

1) James Alexander "**Johnnie**" **Drain** (15 Jan 1870 Madison Co. – 9 May 1968 Benton Co. AR)
   = ...; **Ardella** Elizabeth **Miller** (4 Oct 1884 – 31 Dec 1951 Benton Co.) daughter of James Miller & Anne Campbell
   has issue
2) Ruanna A "**Nannie**" **Drain** (12 Dec 1872 Madison Co. – 11 Jan 1924 Madison Co.)
   =1 10 Jun 1890 Madison Co; **John** William **Rogers** (14 Oct 1852 – 10 Aug 1919)
   =2 ...; **Squire Gros** (...)
3) **Wesley** Newton **Drain** (12 Dec 1874 Madison Co. – 12 Sep 1957 Washington Co.)
   = ca.1898; **Louisa** ... (Jan 1868 TN – ...)
4) **Johnnie A Drain** (* & + Jan 1877 Madison Co.)
5) **Willis** Andrew **Drain** (22 Jan 1878 Madison Co. – 1958 Washington Co.)
   = 6 Oct 1904 Washington Co; **Beulah Seamore** (ca.1884 – ...)
6) Robert **Lee Drain** (Jan 1881 Madison Co. – 1929 Washington Co.)
   = 19 Feb 1907 Washington Co; **Pearl Hartley** (1878 – 1952 Washington Co.)
   has issue
7) **John M Drain** (* & + 1883 Madison Co.)
8) **Martha** Sarah **Drain** (Apr 1885 – ...) (twin)
   = 12 Nov 1910; **L Monroe Miller** (...)
9) **John** Ulysses **Drain** (Apr 1885 – ...) (twin)
   = 2 Dec 1906 Madison Co.; **Marchie O Neal** (ca.1891– ...)
10) **Frances E Drain** (Apr 1887 Madison Co. – ...)
    = 6 Jun 1907 Madison Co; **James Spillers** (ca.1887 – ...)
11) **Columbia** Luellen **Drain** (26 Dec 1889 Madison Co. – 22 Mar 1979)
    = 29 Jan 1907 Madison Co; **William** Martin **Eubanks** (27 Sep 1876 Madison Co. – 20 Feb 1967 Madison Co.) son of Francis Eubanks & Easter Johnson
12) Merritt **Wade Drain**[16] (4 Dec 1891 Madison Co. – 5 Mar 1961 Washington Co.)

---

[16] Findagrave.com lists him as Marit, but does not provide a photo of the headstone to verify the spelling.

= 25 Jul 1920 Madison Co; **Altha** Elizabeth **Combs** (31 Mar 1905 – ...)
has issue

13) Louisa Bethena "**Bessie**" **Drain** (16 Oct 1893 Madison Co. – 17 Feb 1986 Washington Co.)
= 9 Apr 1914 Madison Co; Will **Joe Murphy** (10 Nov 1877 – 29 Jul 1951 Washington Co.)

14) **Homer M Drain** (Apr 1894 Madison Co. – 9 May 1986)
=1 15 Oct 1919 Madison Co; **Elsie** Dell **Combs** (ca.1900 – 7 Apr 1948 Washington Co.)
=2 ...; **Florence Stewart** (10 May 1900 St.Louis, MO – 18 Oct 2001 Washington Co.) daughter of John Stewart & Edna ...

15) Adda **Temperance Drain** (Oct 1897 Madison Co. – 1970)
= 14 Sep 1919 Madison Co.; **James F Clark** (27 Dec 1901 Hilton, VA – 26 Dec 1973 Washington Co.)

B) **Ruanna Drain** (Feb 1852 Madison Co. – 22 Aug 1905 Washington Co.)
= 1877; **Harrison** Davis **Spillers** (8 Feb 1846 IL – ... Cushing, OK)

C) **Samuel** Jackson **Drain** (7 Dec 1854 Madison Co. – 3 Mar 1938 Madison Co.)
=1 ...; **Sarah J Scruggins** (...)
=2 17 Jan 1888 Madison Co; **Safrona** Alice **Gardner** (15 Jul 1871 Madison Co. – 28 May 1949 Madison Co.) daughter of Lewis Gardner & Martha Miskel
issue of 2nd:

1) **Martha J Drain** (Apr 1889 Madison Co. – ...)
2) **Rhoda** Alice **Drain** (30 Jan 1892 Madison Co. – 21 Jan 1957)
= 18 Nov 1910 Madison Co.; **Robert E Watkins** (1889 – ... Carthage, MO)
3) **Flora D Drain** (8 Feb 1894 Madison Co. – 5 Jul 1966 Madison Co.)
4) Sarah **Ida Drain** (17 Jan 1897 Madison Co. – 25 Oct 1975 Madison Co.)
= 25 May 1948 Washington Co.; **Eual** David **Dunaway** (23 Jun 1917 Washington Co. – 27 Nov 1984 Madison Co.)
5) **Ruanna Drain** (Jul 1898 Madison Co. – ...)

= 14 Sep 1916 Madison Co; **Dalton Hill** (...)
6) **Adam** Vernon **Drain** (9 Oct 1903 Madison Co. – 2 May 1961 Washington Co.)
= 1 Oct 1924 Washington Co. (dv.); **Maggie** Mae **Miller** (1 Feb 1907 Madison Co. – 11 Mar 1979 Lebanon, OR) daughter of Jesse Miller & Sarah Eubanks
has issue
7) **Daniel** Boone **Drain** (4 Jan 1905 Madison Co. – 18 Jan 1990 Madison Co.)
= 6 Sep 1928 Madison Co; **Elmira** May **Clark** (...)
8) **Dela** Audrey **Drain** (9 Jun 1907 Madison Co. – 3 Feb 1991 Madison Co.)
= 21 Oct 1940 Madison Co.; **Audie** Ray **Combs** (...)
9) **Nervia Drain** (1912 – ...)
= 28 May 1933 Madison Co; **Clarence Meadows** (ca. 1905 – ...)
D) **Wesley** Newton **Drain** (25 Jan 1857 Madison Co. – 17 Nov 1927 Madison Co.)
= 15 Feb 1878 Madison Co; **Charlotte** Belle **Dunlap** (11 Jul 1861 – 19 Jul 1930 Madison Co.)
1) **M Larue Drain** (31 Jan 1879 Madison Co. – 14 Jul 1925 Madison Co.)
= 16 Mar 1902 Madison Co; Jeanette **Myrtle Faulkner** (1 Jul 1878 – 1 Apr 1963 Muskogee Co., OK)
has issue
2) **Otis A Drain** (Jun 1899 Madison Co. – ...)
= 19 Nov 1929 Washington Co; **Bonnie Wilson** (1904 –...)
3) **Thomas** Leonard **Drain** (19 Jul 1881 – 28 Mar 1948 Madison Co.)
= 18 Dec 1904 Madison Co; **Alwilda** May **Gardner** (28 Mar 1887 – 24 Mar 1979 Madison Co.) daughter of James Gardner & Elvia Ferguson; =2nd W. J. Patrick
has issue
4) **Temperance** Gertrude **Drain** (15 Oct 1884 Madison Co. – 18 Feb 1953 Pryor, OK)
= 27 Sep 1903 Madison Co; **Henry** Walker **Couch** (30 May 1881 Scott Co., VA – 1980 Pryor)
5) **Alfred C Drain** (7 May 1887 Madison Co. – 22 Apr 1961 Madison Co.)
= 11 Nov 1909 Madison Co; **Jennie Lollar** (9 Apr 1890 – 11 Dec 1979)

has issue
6) **George** Washington **Drain** (15 Jun 1889 Madison Co. – 27 May 1907 Madison Co.)
7) **Mary** Jane **Drain** (Apr 1891 AR – ...)
= 21 Jun 1908 Madison Co; **David** Marcelle **Thomas** (18 Apr 1884 Madison Co. – 18 Jun 1948 Haskell, OK)
8) **Andrew** Johnson **Drain** (21 Apr 1893 Madison Co. – 12 Oct 1964 Haskell)
= 18 Mar 1915 Madison Co; **Ica** Mae **Eubanks** (10 Apr 1894 – 10 Dec 1992 Haskell) daughter of Richard Eubanks & Amanda Rogers
has issue
9) **Effie L Drain** (25 May 1897 Madison Co. – 17 Aug 1957)
= 8 Mar 1916 Madison Co; **Benjamin** Franklin **Glenn** (27 Mar 1894 Madison Co. – 7 Mar 1945 Madison Co.)
10) Otis **Leotis Drain** (1901 – ...)
= 4 May 1931 Washington Co; **Bessie A Creech** (...)
XII) **Margaret Drain** (1830 TN – 1918 Washington Co.)
= ...; **Aaron Robbins** (ca.1818 – 1860) son of Richard Robbins & Nancy Richards
d. **John Drain** (ca.1782 MD – ...)
= 1 Sep 1810 (dv.ca.1820) **Margaret Lane** (ca.1790 – ...) =2nd John Runnel
I) **Thomas Drain** (... – ...)
II) **John Drain** (ca.1814 Greene Co. – 1855 Decatur, AL)
= ...; **Catherine ...** (ca.1820 TN – ...)
  A) **Martha E Drain** (ca.1839 Greene Co. – ...)
  B) **Wilton A Drain** (ca.1844 Greene Co. – ...)
    = 28 Apr 1867 Washington Co., TN; **Jennie Droak** (...) issue ?
  C) **Mary Drain** (ca.1846 – ...)
  D) **John Drain**[17] (Dec 1844 – 27 Mar 1909 Madison Co. AL)
    = ca.1865; **Frances Austin** (Dec 1845 – ...)
    1) **Ida Drain** (ca.1873 – ...)
    2) **Myrtle Drain** (1875 – 15 Feb 1953 Huntsville)
      = ...; **William Jones** (1869 – 1950)
    3) **Edward W Drain** (Dec 1878 – 14 Dec 1928 Decatur)

---

[17] John & Frances are living in Maysville, Madison Co. AL in 1900. Frances is listed as being the mother of 7 children, 3 of whom are still alive. Only Edward and his wife are living with them.

= ca.1898; **Margaret** ... (ca.1882 TN – ...)
   has issue
   E) **Elizabeth A Drain** (ca.1849 Greene Co. – ...)
III) **Rebecca Drain** (...)
IV) **Sarah Drain** (ca.1820 – ...)
   = 30 Sep 1845 Green Co., TN; **Alfred McNab** (ca.1824 – ...)
V) **Solomon Drain**[18] (4 Dec 1824[19] Greene Co. – 11 Oct 1903 Greene Co.)
   =1 16 Jun 1840 Greene Co.; **Mary** Ann **Holland** (12 Feb 1816 Greene Co. – 19 Sep 1888 Greene Co.[20]) daughter of Robert Holland & Sarah Jones
   =2 5 May 1889 Greene Co.; **Martha** Jane **Gilstrap** (7 Apr 1840 – 31 Jan 1902 Greene Co.) =1st John Darnell; =2nd William Wright; =3rd "Doc" Nash
   issue of 1st (none by 2nd):
   A) **Sarah** Ann **Drain**[21] (14 Oct 1839 Greene Co. – 28 Apr 1894 Cushman, AR)
      = ...; **Madison Falls** (9 Apr 1836 – 10 Jul 1924)
   B) **John** Wilson **Drain** (21 Mar 1841 Greene Co. – 13 Jan 1915 Greene Co.)
      =1 23 Oct 1862 Greenville, TN; Mary **Emma Davis** (15 Jun 1840 Greene Co. – 3 Aug 1886 Greene Co.)
      =2 8 Apr 1894 Greene Co.; **Mary** Ella **Tolley** (...)
      issue of 1st:
      1) **Thomas** Franklin **Drain** (18 Dec 1863 Greene Co. – 15 Jan 1944 Johnson City, TN[22])
         =1 ...; **Marsilla** Louise **Dugger** (2 Jan 1869 Greene Co. – 12 Jan 1912 Washington Co.)
         =2 ...; **Mary Evans** (...)
         issue of 1st (none by 2nd):
         a) **William** Robert **Drain** (28 Nov 1888 Greene Co. – 27 Jun 1927 Pontiac, MI)
            = 12 Jul 1914 Greene Co.; **Fannie** Pearl **Strickland** (11

---

[18] US Census: 1850 – Washington Co.; 1860 – Greene Co.
[19] Solomon gave a deposition in 1890, where he states he did not know what year he was born, but made up 1815 when he joined the service to make himself older. He estimated it was more likely 1824.
[20] Buried in Union Temple Cemetery, Greene Co. TN.
[21] In Solomon's 1890 deposition, he gave the dates of birth for his children. He also pointed out that Sarah was born before the marriage.
[22] Buried in Dotys Chapel Cemetery, Afton, TN.

May 1891 Washsington Co. – 24 Jul 1979 Greene Co.) daughter of Moore Strickland
has issue
  b) **George** Franklin **Drain** (4 Nov 1890 TN – 31 Mar 1923 Washington Co.)
    = ...; **Emma Thomason** (...) daughter of George Thomason & Amanda Crabtree
    has issue
  c) **Henry** Ward **Drain** (20 Oct 1893 TN – 10 Sep 1966 Knoxville, TN)
    = ...; **Maxie** Mae **Self** (7 Aug 1896 Greene Co – 10 Mar 1961 Greene Co.) daughter of William Self & Sarah Peters
    has issue
  d) **Jessie** Bressie **Drain** (Aug 1898 – ...)
    = ...; **James Miles** (...)
  e) **Iris** Pearl **Drain** (1899 – ...)
    = ...; **Benjamin Green** (...)
  f) **Luney** Edward **Drain** (10 Aug 1902 Washington Co. – 19 Aug 1978 Washington Co.)
    = 2 Feb 1925; **Eva** Pearl **Bayless** (17 Oct 1906 Washington – Jul 1979) daughter of Eddie Bayless & Fannie Carr
    has issue
  g) **Bertie** Mae **Drain** (10 Sep 1906 Telford, TN – 15 Jan 1990 Tecumseh, MI)
    = ...; **Worley** Franklin **Thomason** (21 Aug 1904 Greene Co. – 12 Jan 1956 Washington Co.) son of George Thomason & Amanda Crabtree
  h) a daughter (+ in infancy)
2) **Mary Drain** (ca.1865 Greene Co. – 1901)
3) Nancy **Virginia Drain** (ca.1866 – 28 Feb 1888 Greene Co.) dunm.
4) **James** Harvey **Drain** (10 Oct 1868 Greene Co. – 9 Nov 1952 Greene Co.)
  = 25 Aug 1890 Greene Co.; **Ida** Belle **Davis** (27 Sep 1873 – 27 Jun 1942 Greene Co.)
  a) **Ernest** Franklin **Drayne** (10 Jun 1892 Greene Co. – 26 Apr 1979 Washington Co.)
    = 1910; **Lena M Yokley** (...)
    has issue

b) **William** Harvey **Drayne** (25 Aug 1893 – Feb 1969 Sullivan Co., TN)
=1 31 May 1918; **Trula** Mae **Crabtree** (29 Jul 1896 Greene Co. – 17 Feb 1934 Greene Co.)
=2 ...; **Ada Oliver** (...)
has issue

c) **Risie** Katherine **Drain** (26 Apr 1895 Washington Co. – 3 Dec 1998 Greene Co.)
= 13 Dec 1920 Greene Co.; **George** Raymond **Charlton** (1901 Lovelace, TN – ...) son of Harvey Charlton & Sally Dykes

d) **Dewey Drain** (18 Sep 1898 – 17 Mar 1915 Greene Co.) dunm.

e) **Ott** Hubert **Drain** (1 Jun 1900 Union Temple, TN – 1957 Johnson City, TN)
= 16 Oct 1920 Greene Co.; **Leona** Bessie **Thornberg** (14 Jun 1901 Greene Co. – Jul 1981 Johnson City) daughter of Joel Thornberg & Alice ...
has issue

f) **Anna** Maude **Drain** (5 Mar 1904 Union Temple – 6 Mar 1992 Greene Co.)
= 1923; **Willard** Earl **Mathis** (...)

g) **Samuel** Edward **Drain** (23 Sep 1906 Union Temple – 14 Dec 1997 Knoxville)
= ...; **Fannie Pickering** (29 Jun 1901 Greene Co. – 18 Mar 1992 Knoxville) daughter of Isaac Pickering
has issue

h) **Motie** Mary **Drain** (13 Jan 1907 Union Temple – 30 Jun 2000 Greene Co.)
= 27 Feb 1932; **Herman** Reco **Charlton** (...) son of Harvey Charlton & Sally Dykes

i) John **Ivan Drain** (7 Apr 1913 Greene Co. – 28 Dec 1997 Greene Co.)
= 4 Sep 1937 Greene Co.; **Loos Thacker** (22 May 1915 Sedalia, MO – ...) daughter of Jim Thacker & Martha Lane
has issue

j) **Winnie** Juanita **Drain** (28 Jan 1917 Union Temple – Aug 1994 Akron, OH)
=1 ...; **William** Jefferson **Jones** (9 Nov 1916 TN – 20 Apr 1964 Akron)

  =2 11 May 1968 Carter Co.; Oscar **Leland Lyon** (9 Jan 1916 VA – 7 Sep 1996 Johnson City)
5) **Martha** Elizabeth "**Mattie**" **Drain** (23 Apr 1873 Greene Co. – 15 Aug 1946 Greene Co.)
6) **Sarah Drain** (9 May 1875 – 6 May 1946 Greene Co.)
  =1 8 Jan 1889 Greene Co.; **Lee Holt** (...)
  =2 26 Jan 1936 Greene Co.; **Eugene Jobe** (...)
7) **William** Reason **Drain** (15 Aug 1876 Greene Co. – 26 Jan 1959)
  =1 9 Jun 1901 Greene Co., TN; Nancy Jane "**Dolly**" **Walker** (27 May 1880 – 9 Oct 1915 Greene Co.) daughter of John Walker & Mary Reynolds
  =2 30 Oct 1918; **Eva** Gertrude **Holder** (5 Jul 1877 Greene Co. – 26 Nov 1960 Afton, TN) daughter of Manson Holder & Mary Ann Blakeley =1ˢᵗ Tilman Crabtree
has issue[23]
8) **John** Wilson **Drayne**[24] (10 Jul 1878 – 20 May 1959 Greene Co.)
issue of 2ⁿᵈ:
9) **Fannie** Pauline **Drain** (11 Apr 1893 Greene Co. – 22 Jun 1973 Washington Co.)
  = 3 Oct 1913; **William** Kelley **Jones** (13 May 1886 – 21 Feb 1964)
10) **Naomi** Mae **Drain** (8 Jun 1896 Greene Co. – 11 Feb 1979 Greene Co.)
  = ...; **Walter VanHooser** (24 May 1894 – 3 Mar 1977 Greene Co.)
C) **Thomas Drain** (6 Jul 1843 Greene Co. – 5 Feb 1864 Greene Co.) dunm.
D) **James M Drain** (9 Sep 1850 Greene Co. – 23 Dec 1911)
= 23 Jan 1873 Greene Co.; Mary **Melvina Falls** (18 Oct 1843 Greene Co. – 11 Jun 1918 Marion Co., IA)
1) **Delilah Drain** (3 Feb 1874 Greene Co. – 29 Jun 1931)
  = 26 Jul 1896; **George** Franklin **Ellison** (22 May 1876 Warrenburg, TN – 19 Oct 1961)
2) King Solomon "**Bud**" **Drain** (2 Nov 1875 – 28 Jun 1947) dunm.
3) Sarah **Orlena Drain** (2 Jan 1877 – 25 Aug 1966[25]) dunm.

---

[23] Some of William's descendants have adopted the Draine spelling.
[24] John changed the spelling as a young adult.

      4) **George Drain** (Jul 1882 – ...)
      5) **Nancy** Dessie Celinda Jane **Drain** (17 Jul 1883 – 25 Jul 1956)
      = 11 Jan 1917 Marion Co., IA; **Jacob** Mytes **Armstrong** (7 Jun 1878 – 2 Sep 1948)
      6) **Ella F Drain** (22 May 1886 – 12 Jun 1959)
      =1 ...; **Robert Bass** (1885 – 1957)
      =2 ca.1958; **Eugene** Oliver **Hegwood** (1873 – 1960) =1st Elmira Koder
  e. **Rebecca Drain** (... – aft.1867)
    =1 12 Oct 1812 Greene Co; **William Craddock** (... – 1849)
    =2 1852 Hawkins Co., TN; **Samuel Morelock** (...)
4. **James Drane** (+bef.1786)
  = ...; **Sarah Todd** (10 Jul 1747 – ca.1786) daughter of Lancelot Todd & Eleanor Ford
  a. **Rachel Drane**
    = 18 Dec 1790 Anne Arundel Co.; **John Sappington** (...)
  b. **James Drane** (...)
  c. **Thomas Drane** (...)
    = 17 Jul 1791 Anne Arundel Co.; **Elizabeth Todd**
5. **Ann Drane**
  = 16 Sep 1779 Anne Arundel Co.; **George Colbert** (...)
6. **Elizabeth Drane**
  = 7 Sep 1782 Anne Arundel Co.; **Snowden Taylor** (...)

---

[25] Orlena is buried in Greenwood Cemetery and shares a tombstone with her sister Ella.

Chapter 3
The Baltimore Dranes

The Dranes of Baltimore fall into two distinct family groups. The first are the descendants of James Drane of Sawbridgeworth, Hertsfordshire, who was a nephew of Thomas Drane who went to Arundel County. The second branch is from a wave of immigration which came from Ireland in 1849. It was headed up by brothers James and Richard. The question which remains is whether these two branches are related, and if so, how?

One noticeable difference between the two families is religion. The Sawbridgeworth Dranes were all Anglican. Once the United States was formed, they mostly became Methodists. The 1849 immigrants were Catholic. There are two likely explanations for these differences in the same family. The first, the families are from distantly related lines, one of which never converted to Protestantism. They would have likely gone to Ireland where they could practice the Roman Catholic faith with less fear of persecution.

The second possibility is based on the foundation upon which the colony of Maryland was first established. Because of religious strife in England, Roman Catholics there sought a place where they could practice in peace. Lord Baltimore, who had many Catholic relatives, chose to allow religious freedom in his new American colony. It is quite possible that some Dranes of the 1690s immigration converted back to Catholicism once they were someplace safe to do so. When Baltimore's colony became the State of Maryland, Catholics were suddenly not as welcome as they had once been. These Dranes may have chosen to go to Ireland, a Catholic nation at that time, only to be forced to flee 70 years later from the famines that plagued Ireland in the late 1840s.

Whatever scenario brought these two Drane families to Baltimore, they lived there together and both families will be included in this work.

The Dranes from Sawbridgeworth

The third of the Drane brothers born in Sawbridgeworth in the 1660s was James. He opted not to go to the New World, but remained in England with his wife, the former Sarah Sell. However, his eldest son, also named James, did take up the colonial challenge and also went to Maryland. Before migrating across the Atlantic, he married Susanna Down, in her hometown of Tolleshunt Knight, Essex, just across the county line from Sawbridgeworth, in 1724. Neither birth nor baptism records have been found for his children, but it seems likely they were all born in England. There is only evidence of one child, yet another James, going to Baltmore with his father, and the younger James would have been an adult at the time.

In keeping with the norms of higher society, the children of the younger immigrant James all married a little later than most of their contemporaries. While it was quite common for the children of the working class to marry in their late teens and early twenties, the merchant and noble classes tended to wait until their late twenties or even early thirties. A prevailing belief at that time was later marriages would produce fewer, but healthier, children, making it easier to keep estates mostly intact.

Thanks to some over-zealous soldiers in the War of 1812, most of the colonial civil records of Baltimore are now ash. However, the Westminster Parish of the Anglican Church was spared, preserving the marriage records of four of the five children of James and Susanna. Son Thomas seems to have married elsewhere, causing his marriage date and wife's identity to remain a mystery.

However, we do know that Thomas and his unnamed wife had three children, John, William, and Jane. Jane left Maryland to marry a New Englander by the name of John Gilman. They lived out the rest of their years in New Hampshire. William married in 1829, but no children were recorded for him. Elder brother John's line remains until the present day in the Baltimore suburbs.

John Drane married Margaret Kohlhaus, a daughter of German immigrants, in 1815. Later generations of Margaret's family would anglicize the name to Coalhouse. John and Margaret had four surviving children: William, Margaret, John, and Andrew. William became a police officer in Washington, D.C. He married Julia Kernan and fathered two daughters. Margaret married Patrick McKinley. John married twice, having a son by each of the wives. Andrew, named for President Jackson, moved northeast of Baltimore to Harford County. Some of his descendants still live there.

The younger son of Thomas and Susanna was also named John, likely the source of the name for his previously mentioned nephew. He married in 1784 to

Barbara Sollers, but was dead before the first census was taken in 1790. His widow, listed on that census as a head of household named Barbary, gave rise to a rumor that our family had connections to the island of Barbados, which figured into the Drane family myths.

The only known children of John and Barbara were John Jr. and Elizabeth. Elizabeth became Mrs. Thomas Evans in 1816. John Jr. would marry three times, but only appears to have surviving children by his second wife, Keziah Willem. His son, John III, himself being a product of a lack of imagination when it came to naming children, chose an elaborate, and patriotic, name for his own son: George Washington Lafayette Drane. Perhaps John was inspired by the recent celebrations marking the 100th anniversary of the birth of President Washington.

George W. L. Drane was an only child and so was his son, Charles. If any Dranes remain from this young branch of the descendants of Thomas and Susanna, it is through Charles's children, who were all born in the 20th century.

The Baltimore Dranes from Ireland

The Great Potato Famine hit Ireland beginning in 1845, reaching its depths in the winter of 1848-1849. During the period from 1845 to 1852, approximately one million people in Ireland perished from starvation and related diseases while another million emigrated elsewhere.

It was during 1849 that the Irish Catholic Dranes arrived in Baltimore. The family was made up of brothers James and Richard, with their wives and elder children. They were accompanied by a lady named Kate Drane who was similar in age to the brothers. It is unclear if Kate was an unmarried sister or perhaps the widow of a third brother. Richard's descendants are now believed to be extinct in the male line, although several descendants do continue through his daughters and granddaughters.

The surviving line is that of James Drane who was born in Ireland in 1823. While the descendants of the Sawbridgeworth Dranes mostly stayed to Baltimore's suburbs, this Irish branch lived in the city proper. Most of the family is buried in the New Cathedral Cemetery, but James and both of his wives are buried in a private family graveyard.

John was already married to Margaret Rice, or perhaps Reece, when they immigrated in 1849. They brought with them two small children, Ellen and John, and had seven more once in Baltimore. After Margaret's death, John married a lady named Mary, who gave him three more children.

The first of John's children to be born in the United States, David Drane, also served his country in the Civil War in the Navy. The only sons of John known to have married are Robert and Daniel, each fathering large families. Robert's and Daniel's grandchildren were all born after 1900, so are not included in this work, but they are quite numerous.

James Drane (ca.1695 Sawbridgeworth, Hertforshire – ...) son of James Drane & Sarah Sell
= 16 Jan 1724 Tolleshunt Knights, Essex; **Susanna Down** (...)
1. **James Drane** (ca.1726 in England – ...)
= ...
  a. **Rebecca Drane** (...)
    = 30 Apr 1789 Baltimore; **Joshua Gray** (...)
  b. **Rachel Drane** (...)
    = 31 Dec 1790 Baltimore; **James Richardson** (...)
  c. **Avis Drane** (...)
    = 21 Sep 1801 Baltimore; **Jacob Farney** (...)
  d. **Thomas Drane** (... – bef.1790)
    = ...;
  I) **John Drane**[26] (ca.1775 – aft.1850 Baltimore)
    = 29 Jul 1815 Baltimore; **Margaret Kohlhouse** (ca.1795 MD – ...)
    A) **William Drane** (1819 Baltimore – 24 Sep 1878 Washington, DC)
      = 12 Feb 1841 Baltimore; **Julia Kernan** (ca.1820 PA – ...)
      1) **Catherine Drane** (ca.1844 DC – ...)
      2) **Mary Drane** (ca.1846 DC – ...)
    B) **Margaret Drane** (ca.1821 Baltimore – ...)
      = 1840s; **Patrick McKinley** (ca. 1818 – ...)
    C) **John Drane** (ca.1823 – bef.1900)
      =1 ca. 1850; **Anna ...** (ca.1822 England – ...)
      =2 ca. 1872; **Priscilla ...** (May 1840 MD – ...)
      issue of 1st:
      1) **Willie Drane** (ca.1856 Harford Co. MD – ...)
      issue of 2nd:
      2) **Emma Drane** (ca.1873 Baltimore – bef.1900)
      3) **John J Drane** (Jul 1876 Baltimore – ...)
        = 1910s; **Ida ...** (ca.1885 MD – ...)
        has issue
    D) **Andrew** Jackson **Drane**[27] (17 Jul 1834 MD – 19 Feb 1908 MD)
      = 19 Nov 1869 Harford Co.; **Sarah Locher** (23 Feb 1843 MD – 10 Dec 1917)
      1) **Theresa E Drane** (Oct 1870 Harford Co. – ...)

---

[26] 1850 Census: Living in Baltimore (Ward 3) with McKinley family.
[27] Buried Fallston UMC Cemetery, Harford Co. MD, with a few family members.

  2) **Charles F Drane** (Nov 1872 Harford Co. – ...)
   = ...; **Mary** ... (ca.1884 MD – ...)
   has issue
  3) **Alice P Drane** (Apr 1878 Harford Co. – ...)
 II) **William Drane** (...)
  = 22 Dec 1829 Baltimore; **Margaret Norris** (...)
e. **John Drane** (ca.1750 – bef.1790)
 = 8 Dec 1784 Baltimore; **Barbara Sollers** (... – bet.1800/1810)
 I) **John Drane** (ca.1786 – ...)
  =1 8 Nov 1806 Baltimore; **Nelly Exter** (...)
  =2 28 Jul 1813 Baltimore; **Keziah Willen** (...)
  =3 14 Feb 1830 Baltimore; **Mary Gooding** (...)
  issue of 2nd:
  A) **John Drane** (1810's – ...)
   = 5 Apr 1831 Baltimore; **Catherine Lewis** (...)
   1) **George** Washington Lafayette **Drane** (13 Oct 1833 Baltimore – ...)
    = ...;
    a) **Charles Drane** (Jan 1871 Baltimore – ...)
     = ca.1899; **Ella Miller** (July 1872 MD – ...) daughter of Julius Miller & Missouri ...
     has issue
  B) **Mary Drane** (1810's – ...)
   = 27 Sep 1832 Baltimore; **Henry Long** (...)
  C) a daughter (1810's – ...)
 II) **Elizabeth Drane** (...)
  = 12 Dec 1816 Baltimore; **Thomas Evans** (...)

The Drains who came to Baltimore from Ireland in 1849:

I. **James Drane** (1823 Ireland – 27 Jun 1894 Baltimore[28])
=1 in Ireland; **Margaret Rice** (ca.1826 – ...)
=2 ...; **Mary** ... (1839 Ireland – 24 May 1890 Baltimore)
issue of 1st:
  A. **Ellen Drane** (ca.1845 Ireland – ...)
  B. **John Drane** (1846 Ireland – 16 Aug 1911 Baltimore)
    = ca.1875; **Mary Helen** ... (ca.1845 MD – ...)
    1. **John J Drane** (Jul 1877 – ...)
  C. **David J Drane** (25 Dec 1847 Baltimore – 9 Apr 1925 Baltimore) served in US Navy during Civil War
  D. **James Drane**[29] (ca.1852 Baltimore – ...)
    =...; **Charlotte** ... (ca.1853 DE – ...)
    1. **Charles Drane** (ca.1876 Wilmington, DE – ...)
  E. **Robert F Drane** (Jul 1854 Baltimore – 30 Sep 1907 Baltimore)
    = 1873; **Catherine Barry** (27 Mar 1855 Wales – 23 Nov 1940 Baltimore)
    1. **James Drane** (Mar 1873 Baltimore – 25 Nov 1884 Baltimore)
    2. **Robert J Drane** (Nov 1875 Baltimore – 1 Jun 1900 Baltimore)
    3. **David F Drane** (1878 Baltimore – 26 Oct 1898 Baltimore)
    4. **Mary Drane** (Jul 1879 Baltimore – 28 Oct 1943 Baltimore)
      =1 ca.1897; **Harry Talbert** (Sep 1873 MD – 12 Dec 1909 Baltimore)
      =2 ...; **Benjamin Harris** (6 Dec 1892 Baltimore – 19 Nov 1963 Baltimore)
    5. **John A Drane** (16 Aug 1881 Baltimore– Mar 1975 Baltimore)
      = ca.1912; **Kunigunde Selz** (1879 – 9 Mar 1950 Baltimore)
      she =1st August Reece (né Ries)
      has issue
    6. **Joseph P Drane** (9 Mar 1886 Baltimore – 30 Jan 1964 Baltimore)
      = ca.1908; **Margaret Trott** (May 1885 MD – 15 Nov 1967 Baltimore)
      has issue
    7. **Agnes Drane** (Jan 1888 Baltimore – 24 Feb 1889 Baltimore)
    8. **Charles J Drane** (Nov 1889 Baltimore – 20 Dec 1928 Baltimore)

---

[28] James and his wife are buried in a family plot. But most of his descendants are buried at New Cathedral Cemetery in Baltimore.
[29] 1880 Census: Wilmington, DE.

dunm.
   9. **Gertrude Drane** (6 Sep 1893 Baltimore – 27 Jun 1940 Baltimore)
   = 28 Nov 1912 Baltimore; **Joseph Frisino** (27 Mar 1893 Duluth, MN – 21 Mar 1971 Seattle, WA) son of Biaggio Frisino & Antoinette Genovese
   10. **Albert Drane** (15 Apr 1895 Baltimore – 13 Feb 1911 Baltimore)
F. **Margaret Drane** (ca.1856 Baltimore – ...)
G. **Mary Drane** (ca.1858 Baltimore – ...)
H. **Anne** Jane **Drane** (Jul 1862 Baltimore – 6 Feb 1865 Baltimore)
I. **Daniel A Drane** (12 Sep 1867 Baltimore – 29 Sep 1932 Baltimore)
   = ...; **Mary J ...** (ca.1866 MD – btw.1910/1920)
   1. **Bernard J Drane** (ca.1893 Baltimore – ...)
   = ca.1915; **Mary ...** (ca.1897 MD – ...)
   has issue
   2. **Albert A Drane** (8 Dec 1894 Baltimore – 15 Apr 1895 Baltimore)
   3. **Elmer A Drane** (28 Aug 1896 Baltimore – 28 Aug 1964 Baltimore)
   = ca.1920; **Catherine ...** (17 Mar 1899 MD – 16 Feb 1985 Baltimore)
   has issue
   4. **Lawrence Drane** (ca.1903 Baltimore – ...)
   5. **Margaret Drane** (ca.1906 Baltimore – ...)
issue of 2nd:
J. **Mary Drane** (...)
K. **Joseph Drane** (ca.1875 Baltimore – ...)
L. **Rose Drane** (ca.1879 Baltimore – ...)
II. **Richard Drane** (ca.1830 Ireland – ...)
= ...; **Alice ...** (ca.1834 Ireland – ...)
A. **James Drane** (ca.1860 Baltimore – ...)
B. **Mary Drane** (ca.1862 Baltimore – ...)
C. **Joseph Drane** (9 Nov 1864 Baltimore – ...)
   = ca.1892; **Mary Josephine ...** (21 Jun 1862 MD – ...)
   1. **Gertrude Drane** (7 Feb 1893 Baltimore – ...)
   2. **Marie Drane** (14 Jun 1896 Baltimore – ...)
   3. **Viola Drane** (10 Sep 1899 Baltimore – btw.1900/1910)
D. **Anne Drane** (ca.1866 Baltimore – ...)

Chapter 4
The Delaware Drains

James Drane of Sawbridgeworth who founded the Baltimore Dranes had a younger brother, John. John turned out to be a bit of an embarrassment for the family in Hertfordshire. In 1737, he was shipped off to the colonies as a felon. His precise crime has been lost to history, but it was one worthy of banishment, yet not severe enough to warrant a hanging.

John was taken to Virginia as a captive on the *Forward*, captained by John Magier. This penal transport was filled with nearly 50 other criminals which England felt a need to be rid of. The ship deposited her human cargo in Westmorland County, near the mouth of the Potomac. From that point, it fell to each passenger to find their own way and develop a life.

It is not clear how long John remained in Westmorland County, but it is easy to imagine he may have headed in the direction of Maryland pretty quickly, since he had family already established there. There are no records of him remaining in Maryland for any length of time, so it is quite possible his brother and cousins may have told him to keep moving when he showed up on their doorsteps.

Whatever adventures he went through to get there, he ended up in Sussex County, Delaware, with an unnamed wife and at least four children. The spelling of Drane changed often in this branch of the family. John, the felon, and his son, John, seemed to have both used Drane. John Jr.'s children all seem to have used Drain, but at least one branch of descendants then reverted to Drane. Another branch blended the two into Draine towards the end of the 19th century. For the remainder of this chapter, I will attempt to refer to each person using the spelling they appear to have used themself.

The Drains lived in or near the town of Lewes. Many of their descendants live in the vicinity to this day. Early Delaware records are rather scarce, so there is difficulty in pinpointing when most events happened until the early 1800s. Our first real records of the family are in the 1790 and 1800 censuses. By 1800, John's children were grown and starting their own families.

Besides the census, a few more important documents did survive. One is the 1779 marriage record of John Drain Jr. to Elizabeth Kollock. The Kollocks were among the original settlers of Delaware and were a very wealthy family. Their status is likely the reason we still have records of their lives. The second important early record to survive is the death certificate of John Drain Jr. dated 1784. John Jr.'s younger brothers were named Russell, Reuben, and Joshua, but little else is known about them. In fact, had Russell's name not appeared on a few documents as a witness, we would not even know of his existence. Reuben and Joshua both show up on the census from 1800 to 1830, but disappear without leaving any living sons. It is possible they may have had surviving daughters who married into other families.

In the 1790 census, John Jr.'s widow, Elizabeth, appears as a head of household with five children, four of whom are boys. All of the children are in the age range to be John Drain's children, so the assumption is he and Elizabeth had a child each year they were married before he died. There is no record of the name or what became of the daughter of this family. It is likely she married, which would cause her to turn up under a different, and unknown, surname in later records.

The four boys were Shepherd, Solomon, Reuben, and Daniel. Shepherd got his name from Elizabeth's father, who was also named Shepherd. The other sons seem to have been named from the Bible. Reuben and Daniel seem to have either died childless, or at least without sons.

Shepherd Drain and his wife, Sarah Moore, were the parents of at least ten children between 1800 and the mid-1810s. Their three daughters' married names were Margaret Frisch, Susanna Eskridge, and Sarah Callaway. Of the seven boys, Vernon and William died young. The youngest son, Albert, married and had children, but his male line goes extinct before the end of the 19th century.

The eldest son of Shepherd and Sarah was named for his paternal grandfather, John Drane. All of the records which include his name use the Drane spelling and his descendants use that spelling today as well. He married Rhoda Fletcher in 1827. According to the information from a family Bible, John and Rhoda moved to Portsmouth, Ohio, in 1835, and then on to Jo Daviess County, Illinois, in 1854. They had four children, three daughters and a son, James.

James Drane moved around a lot. He was born in Delaware before the family moved west, then married Susanna Phillips while they were in Ohio. James and Susanna went with his parents to Illinois, and their five children were born there. Later, James and Susanna moved on to Missouri and spent the rest of their lives moving around the Kansas City area, sometimes living on the Missouri side, sometimes on the Kansas side. Four of their children do not appear to have survived to adulthood. The one remaining child, John Leonard Drane, married twice and left seven children between the two wives. His descendants still call Kansas City home.

Shepherd and Sarah Drain's second son, Stephen Shepherd Drain, was known by his middle name and became a Methodist minister. Upon joining the ministry, he moved to Dorchester County, Maryland, where he served in several churches, mostly in the Cambridge area. He married Mary Creighton in Dorchester County in 1836. They had two sons, Vernon Creighton, who was named for Mary's father, and William Fisk, apparently named for the painter. William would leave an only daughter, Louisa, who was born 1878.

Vernon Creighton Drain lived from 1836 to 1900. He married Caroline Hurley in 1861, and they had five children. Like so many others in this branch of the family, only one of children left further issue to carry on the Drain name. That was his son, Dr. Shepherd Drain Sr. As his name may imply, there was also a Dr. Shepherd Drain Jr. Both were physicians specializing in homeopathic medicine.

The third son of the 18th century Shepherd Drain and his wife Sarah was Lorenzo Dow Drain. As we have seen in other parts of the family, it was quite common to name children after important figures of the day. We have already encountered at least one George Washington Drane and one Andrew Jackson Drane. Lorenzo is no different. Lorenzo Dow was a prominent

Methodist preacher who traveled the northeastern United States and was largely involved with the Second Great Awakening, a revival of Christian faith in the early 19th century.

Lorenzo Drain appears in most records as L.D. Drain. He and his wife, Eleanor, moved to Indiana, where they had two sons, William and George. Neither son married. The entire family is buried in Greendale Cemetery in Lawrenceburg, Indiana.

Lorenzo's next younger brother was Stanford Drain. Like his elder brothers, he also moved west. In 1836, Stanford, his wife, the former Sarah Parker, and their three young daughters moved to Shelbyville in northeastern Missouri. Sarah would have three more children before she died in 1850. The only son, Edwin, died young.

Stanford married a second time, in 1857, to Mary Lyell. Their only child, Vernon Lyell Drain, married Nellie Turner in 1892. Vernon and Nellie had three children: Benjamin, who died in the 1918 influenza pandemic, Katherine, and Vernon Jr., whose grandchildren still live in the Shelbyville area.

The descendants of Solomon Drain, the younger son of John Drane and Elizabeth Kollock, has caused quite a bit of confusion for genealogists over the years. Solomon died shortly before the 1850 census was taken. The 1850 census is very important to genealogical research because it is the first census that lists all of the members of a household by name, with pertinent information such as their ages, places of birth, and races. Although Solomon was dead, his children show up in this census with their race listed as "Mulatto."

I do not speak Italian, but I am reasonably convinced that mulatto is Italian for "muddle." It was a term used in the census to denote people who were of a mixed racial heritage. The most common usage was for the children, or later descendants, of unions between whites and blacks. But it could also mean Native American or Latino.

What made the issue so confusing in the case of the Draines in Sussex County, Delaware, was that in 1900, the census stopped listing this family as mulatto, but called them black. This would lead any reasonable person to assume they were the descendants of a white person (Solomon) and a black person (presumably his wife, but perhaps a slave). But, even the most reasonable of people would be wrong.

Extensive research has finally uncovered a reference to the marriage of Solomon Drain to Linea, a Nanticoke Indian. This marriage, while missing a marriage certificate, is recognized by the Nanticoke tribe, and several of Solomon's descendants are members of that tribe today. Why did the census call these people black in the early 20th century? I suspect the answer has more to do with the social attitudes of the day than with any ethnic reality.

Solomon and Linea had seven children: Abraham, Daniel, Robert, Jacob, James, Emmeline, and Elizabeth. All of the boys left descendants except Robert, who does not appear to have ever married. Abraham's wife was Harriet Parker, a sister to Sarah, who married Abraham's cousin, Stanford. They had twelve children, all of whom except the eldest remained in the Lewes area. That eldest son, John, moved to Philadelphia, where he married Elizabeth Elbert. They also had a large family with eleven children, all of whom remained in Philadelphia.

Solomon's second son, Daniel Draine, married twice but fathered all eleven of his children with his first wife, Levinia. The surviving male line descendants from Daniel are through his son, Gardner, and have also remained in the Lewes area. Also in the vicinity are the descendants of Daniel's brother Jacob.

The youngest of Solomon's sons was James. Like his nephew, he also moved to Philadelphia. However his descendants became extinct with the death of his son, Isaac, in 1910.

John Drane (bap.31 Mar 1699 Bishops Stratford, Essex, England – ...) convicted of a felony in Essex 1737, sent to Virginia
= ...:
1. **John Drane** (ca.1750 VA – 26 Sep 1784 Lewes, DE)
= 16 Mar 1779 Sussex Co., DE; **Elizabeth Kollock** (ca.1738 – aft.1810) daughter of Shepherd Kollock & Mary ...; =1st Gilbert Mariner
   a. **Shepherd Drain** (ca.1780 Sussex Co. – 24 Jun 1856 Sussex Co.)
   = ca.1799; **Sarah Moore** (1780s DE – aft.1850) dau of Matthias Moore & Easter Hearne
      I) **John Drane** (31 Oct 1800 DE – 6 Dec 1874 Jo Davies Co., IL)[30]
      = 5 Feb 1827 DE; **Rhoda Fletcher** (10 Jan 1801 Broad Creek, DE – 2 Dec 1894 Jo Davies Co., IL)
      A) **Harriet** Elizabeth **Drane** (14 Oct 1829 Sussex Co., DE – 3 Jun 1907 Hanover, IL)
      = 27 Jan 1852 Portsmouth, OH; **Abraham deGear** (18 Jun 1826 Clay Twp, Scioto Co. OH – 14 Jan 1911 Hanover, IL) son of Peter deGear & Catherine Hipsher
      B) **Sarah Drane** (ca.1831 DE – ...)
      = 10 Jan 1861 JoDavies Co. IL; **George H Soule** (...)
      C) **James Drane**[31] (Jan 1833 DE – ...)
      = 26 Jan 1854 Scioto Co.; Sarah **Susanna Phillips** (May 1837 OH – 10 Apr 1907 Clay Co. MO)
      1) **Saffronia Drane** (1857 IL – ...)
      2) John **Leonard Drane** (May 1860 IL – aft.1930)
      =1 ca.1883; **Nettie** ... (1864 – 6 Aug 1889 Clay Co. MO)
      =2 23 Nov 1893 Kansas City, KS; **Lillie Hinkle** (May 1870 MO – ...)
      issue of 1st:
      a) **Thomas Drane** (Oct 1883 MO – ...)
      = ...; **Merle** ... (ca.1896 KS – ...)
      has issue
      b) **Frank Drane** (Jun 1887 KS – ...)

---

[30] This Drane Family kept a Bible which was last heard of in the possession of one Betty Drane. In this Bible they relate they moved to Scioto Co., Ohio in 1835, and then on to Jo Davies Co., IL in 1854. John & Rhoda was buried in Thompson Cemetery, Thompson Twp, Jo Davies Co. IL

[31] 1900 Census: Clay Co. MO (Kansas City metro area). They are recorded as having had 5 children, 4 being alive in 1900; 1880: Jackson Co. MO; 1870: Macon Co. IL; 1860: Jo Davies Co. IL.

c) **James Drane** (Jan 1889 KS – ...)
issue of 2nd:
d) **Elsie Drane** (Oct 1894 MO – ...)
e) **Charles Drane** (Dec 1895 MO – ...)
f) **Carl Drane** (Nov 1898 MO – ...)
g) **Lee Drane** (ca.1901 KS – ...)
3) **May Drane** (ca.1863 IL – bef.1880)
4) **Francis Drane** (ca.1866 IL – ...)
5) **William Drane** (ca.1870 IL – ...)
D) **Susan Drane** (ca.1838 OH – ...)
E) **John Drane** (22 Nov 1840 Portsmouth, OH – 1 Jul 1927 Stockton, IL[32])
= 5 Feb 1863 JoDavies, Co. IL; **Sylvia A Bowker** (3 Feb 1844 IL – 11 Apr 1924 Stockton, IL)
  1) **Rhoda R. Drane** (ca.1864 IL – ...)
  = ...; Leonard **Lee Schultz** (...)
  2) **Leona A. Drane** (1866 IL – 1947)
  = ...; **Grant Typper** (1866 – 1919)
  3) **Joseph** Ira **Drane** (Aug 1871 IL – 1945)
  = 1 Sep 1900; **Mae Pulfrey** (3 Jun 1877 – 1964)
  has issue
  4) **Oran** John **Drane** (23 Jan 1880 Rush Twp, Jo Davies Co. – ...)
  = 6 Mar 1901; **Minnie Pulfrey** (20 Aug 1879 Rusp Twp – ...)
  has issue
II) **Rev.** Stephen **Shepherd Drain** (1806 Sussex Co., DE – 12 Nov 1844 Greensborough, MD)
= 24 Apr 1836 Dorchester Co. MD; Mary **Creighton** (20 Aug 1815 MD – 23 Dec 1878) daughter of Vernon Creighton
  A) **Vernon** Creighton **Drain** (1 Apr 1836 MD – 4 May 1900 Dorchester Co. MD)
  = 8 Mar 1861 Cambridge, MD; Mary **Caroline Hurley** (ca.1842 MD – ...) daughter of ... Hurley & Mary ...
    1) **Mary Drain** (ca.1865 MD – ...)
    2) **Lela** Gay **Drain** (ca.1867 MD – ...)
    3) **Sims Drain** [male] (ca.1869 MD – ...)
    4) **Charles Drain** (ca.1862 MD – ...)
    5) **Dr. Shepherd Drain** (Aug 1876 MD – 6 Aug 1945 MD)
    = ca.1896; **Maud Houck** (Jun 1877 MD – Dec 1967

---

[32] John & Sylvia are buried in the Ladies Union Cemetery, Stockton, IL

Baltimore) daughter of Harry Houck & Mary Hinton
   a) **Leila Drain** (Sep 1896 MD – ...)
   b) **Vernon** Creighton **Drain** (Nov 1899 MD – ...)
   d) **Theresa Drain** (ca.1903 MD – ...)
   c) **Shepherd Drain** (Aug 1905 Baltimore – 1957 Baltimore) = 1927; **Dorothy Conser** (1906 MD – ...)
   has issue
 B) **William** Fisk **Drain** (ca.1840 – ...)
 = 27 Oct 1875 Dochester Co.; Mary **Louisa Creighton** (ca.1851 – ...)
 1) **Louisa Drain** (ca.1878 – ...)
III) **Lorenzo** Dow **Drain** (ca.1810 Sussex Co., DE – Sep 1881 Lawrenceburg, IN)
= ...; **Eleanor** ... (10 Nov 1812 Bethel, DE – 4 Nov 1901 Lawrenceburg)
 A) **William B Drain**[33] (...)
 B) **George C Drain** (1840 IN – 17 Mar 1891 Greendale, IN)
IV) **Stanford Drain** (16 Nov 1811 Sussex Co., DE – 20 Nov 1892 Shelby Co., MO) went to MO in 1836
=1 18 Mar 1833 Laurel, DE; **Sarah** Weatherly **Parker** (19 May 1816 Parkersmill, MD – 8 Sep 1850) dau of Elisha Parker & Mary Weatherly
=2 5 Jan 1857 Shelby Co., MO; **Mary Lyell** (... – bef.1880) =1st ... Turner
 A) **Miranda** Jane **Drain** (1834 DE – ...)
 B) **Mary** Ann **Drain** (ca.1836 DE – aft.1911)
   = 15 Feb 1855 Shelby Co., MO; **John** Wright **Jacobs** (5 Aug 1824 Greene Co., TN – 7 Apr 1906 Clarence, MO) son of Lewis Jacobs& Anna Wright
 C) **Margaret Drain** (ca.1838 DE – ...)
 D) **Matilda Drain** (...)
 E) **Edwin Drain** (ca.1842 MO – ...)
 F) **Elizabeth Drain** (ca. 1847 MO – ...)
issue of 2nd:
 G) **Vernon** Lyell **Drain** (21 Jan 1864 Shelby Co., MO – 5 Jan 1941 Shelbyville) elected as Prosecuting Attorney of Shelby Co. 1892 & 1896
   = 17 Feb 1892 Shelbyville, MO; **Nellie Turner** (8 Oct 1864 Nodaway Co. MO – 5 Feb 1930 Shelbyville) daughter of

---

[33] Unreadable tombstone in Greendale Cemetery, buried with Lorenzo's family.

George Turner & Martha Moreman
1) **Benjamin** Stanford **Drain** (Sep 1896 Shelbyville, MO – ca.1918) died of influenza while fighting in World War I
2) **Katherine Drain** (Jul 1898 Shelbyville – ...)
3) **Vernon** Lyell **Drain, Jr.** (18 Apr 1903 Shelbyville – 25 Jun 1990 MO)
= 8 Jun 1942 Shelbyville; **Virginia** Mae **Zahn** (...)
has issue
V) **Vernon Drain** (... – bef.1856)
VI) **William Drain** (... – bef.1856)
VII) **Albert Drain** (1800's – ca.1841)
= ...; **Govy** ... (... – aft.1850)
  A) **Halsey Drain** (ca.1827 – ...)
  = ...; **Mary** ... (ca.1831 – ...)
    1) **George Drain** (ca.1856 – ...)
    2) **Annie Drain** (ca.1858 – ...)
  B) **George Drain**[34] (Sep 1828 – ...)
  = ...; **Mary** ... (ca.1842 GA – ca.1881)
    1) **Louisa** Ivy **Drain** (ca.1866 MS – ...)
  C) **Daniel Drain** (ca.1834 – ...)
  D) **Elizabeth Drain** (Jun 1841 – ...) unm. in 1900
VIII) **Margaret** Ann **Drain** (...)
= ...; ... **Frisch** (...)
IX) **Susanna Drain** (...)
= ...; **Eskridge** (...)
X) **Sarah Drain** (... – bef.1856)
= 13 Jun 1837 Sussex Co.; **Jonathan Callaway** (...)
b. a son (ca.1781 – ...)
c. **Solomon Drain** (ca.1782 – 12 May 1850)
= ...; **Linah**[35] (...)
I) **Abraham Drain** (ca.1808 Sussex Co. – ...)
= ca.1833; **Harriet Parker** (ca.1817 Sussex Co. – ...)
  A) **John Drain** (ca.1834 Sussex Co. – 16 Mar 1883 Philadelphia, PA)
  = 15 Mar 1863 Philadelphia, PA; **Elizabeth Elbert** (1839 Stanton, DE – 8 Feb 1903 Philadelphia)
    1) **Jane Drain** (ca.1863 – ...)
    = 1883; **Seldon** James Madison **Brock** (18 Jan 1861 VA – 9 Nov 1914 Philadelphia)

---

[34] 1880 Census: Jackson Co. MS; 1900: widowed in Philadelphia
[35] Linah was a Nanticoke Indian; her name was alternately spelled Linea.

2) Elizabeth **Amanda Drain** (1 Mar 1865 Philadelphia – 20 Nov 1931 South Media, PA)
= ca.1892 Philadelphia; **James** Henry **Wilson** (Jan 1872 Kent Co. DE – ...)
3) **Harriet Drain** (ca.1867 – ...)
4) **Mary** Matilda **Drain** (ca.1868 Philadelphia – Sep 1869 Philadelphia)
5) **Joseph** Albert **Drain** (15 Jan 1869 Philadelphia – 11 Dec 1959 Philadelphia)
= 29 May 1890 Philadelphia; **Agnes** Crofton **Clark** (26 Sep 1872 – 22 Dec 1933 Philadelphia) daughter of Whittington Clark & Sarah Wright
  a) **Jennie Drain** (Feb 1892 – 1928 Delaware Co. PA)
  = ...; **Egbert T Scott** (12 Mar 1884 – 4 Dec 1969 Delaware Co.)
  b) **Sadie Drain** (Jul 1894 – ...)
  c) **Harry** Joseph **Drain** (28 Apr 1896 Philadelphia – 14 Sep 1971 Darby, PA)
  = 3 May 1928 Philadelphia; **Anna Juhascik** (...) daughter of John Juhascik & Rosalia Michek
  has issue
  d) **Gladys Drain** (18 Sep 1903 Philadelphia – Nov 1984 Gloucester, NJ)
  = ...; ... **Finney** (...)
6) **John Drain** (ca.1874 – ...)
= ...; **Flora** ... (...)
  a) **Harriet Drain** (1894 Philadelphia – ...)
7) **Lucy Drain** (ca.1877 Philadelphia – ...)
= ca.1895; **Samuel** Horace **Durham** (Apr 1875 Kent Co. – ...) son of George Durham & Elizabeth Seeney
8) **Thomas Drain** (28 Dec 1879 Philadelphia – ...)
= ...; **Margaret Ray** (...)
has issue
9) **Flora Drain** (10 May 1881 – 4 Aug 1915)
= ...; **James H Byard** (...)
10) a child (* & + 26 Sep 1883 Philadelphia) (twin)
11) a child (* & + 26 Sep 1883 Philadelphia) (twin)
B) **Solomon Drain** (ca.1837 Sussex Co. – ...)
= ...; **Elizabeth** ... (Sep 1849 DE –
1) **Solomon Drain** (Sep 1869 DE – ...)
= ...; **Edna** ... (...)

has issue
   2) **Daniel Drain** (Sep 1874 DE – ...)
  C) **Elizabeth Drain** (ca.1838 Sussex Co. – ...)
  D) **Daniel Drain** (ca.1842 Sussex Co. – 10 Feb 1920 Lewes)
    = ...; **Adeline** ... (ca.1855 DE – ...)
   1) **Daniel Drain** (ca.1869 Sussex Co. – ...)
   2) **Solomon Drain** (ca.1874 Sussex Co. – ...)
   3) **John Drain** (ca.1876 Sussex Co. – 14 Jan 1941 Lewes)
    = ...; **Mary Miller** (ca.1871 Angola, DE – 11 Apr 1942 Lewes) daughter of Isaac Miller & Comfort Burton
    a) **Thomas Drain** (ca.1891 DE – ...)
    b) **Sallie** Ann **Drain** (ca.1892 DE – 6 Mar 1935 Millsboro, DE)
     = ...; **John W Clark** (ca.1891 DE – ...)
    c) **Howard Drain** (...)
  E) **Sarah Drain** (ca.1843 Sussex Co. – ...)
  F) **Hannah Drain** (ca.1845 Sussex Co. – ...)
  G) **Margaret Drain** (ca.1847 Sussex Co. – ...)
  H) **Ellen Drain** (ca.1852 Sussex Co. – ...)
  I) **Adeline Drain** (ca.1855 Sussex Co. – ...)
  J) **Harriet Drain** (16 Mar 1861 Sussex Co. – 17 Nov 1929 Milton, DE)
    = ...; **William J Dredden** (ca.1870 DE – ...)
  K) **William Drain** (1865 Sussex Co. – 1940 Kent Co.)
    = ...; **Cordelia Durham** (1869 – 1941 Kent Co.) daughter of George Durham & Elizabeth Seeney
  L) **Mary Drain** (ca.1868 Sessux Co. – ...)
II) **Daniel Drain** (1827 DE – 16 Sep 1900 Laurel, DE)
=1 ..; **Lavinia** ... (ca.1831 PA – bef.1880)
=2 ...; **Mary** Proctor **Johnson** (5 May 1833 Philadelphia – 14 Mar 1896 Philadelphia) daughter of Clark Johnson & Lydia Lecount
issue of 1st:
  A) **Armenia Drain** (ca.1848 Sussex Co. – ...)
    = ...; **James Kimmey** (ca.1845 DE – ...)
  B) **Elmira Drain** (ca.1851 DE – ...)
  C) **Daniel Drain** (ca.1852 DE – ...)
    =...; **Eliza** ... (ca.1859 DE – ...)
   1) **Solomon Drain** (ca.1874 – ...)
   2) **John Drain** (ca.1876 – ...)
  D) **Gardner Drain** (2 Mar 1853 Sussex Co. – 25 Feb 1951

Dover)
= ca.1878; **Roxana Wright** (2 Dec 1858 Sussex Co. – 27 Feb 1931 Sussex Co.) daughter of Frederick Wright & Selena Farmer
1) **Amanda Drain** (ca.1879 Sussex Co. – ...)
2) **Cora Drain** (8 Mar 1885 Sussex Co. – 20 May 1954 Delaware City, DE)
3) **Daniel Drain** (6 Mar 1887 Sussex Co. – 1980) served in World War I
   =1 ...; **Elsie** Ann **Shelton** (7 Jan 1899 DE – ...)
   =2 ...; **Margaret** ... (1895 – 1988)
   has issue
4) **Luther Drain** (25 Oct 1890 Sussex Co. – 28 Nov 1961 Lewes)
   = 18 Feb 1918 Sussex Co.; **Minnie Hall** (1901 – 1992 Sussex Co.) daughter of Irvin Hall & Clara Johnson
   has issue
5) **William** Edward **Draine** (24 Aug 1894 Lewes – 8 Jun 1970 New Castle Co. DE)
   =1 24 Oct 1920 Lewes (dv.); **Nora** Delema **Street** (15 Nov 1901 Warwick, DE – 21 Apr 1988) daughter of Robert Street & Matilda Jackson
   =2 18 Mar 1965 Milford; **Mary** Edna **Mosely** (25 Jul 1910 Milford Neck, DE – 21 Nov 1978) daughter of Andrew Mosely & Angela Coker
   has issue
6) **Habrick Drain** (1 Mar 1896 Sussex Co. – ...)
7) **Martha Drain** (20 Oct 1898 Sussex Co. – 8 Sep 1918 Sussex Co.)
8) **Frank Drain** (ca.1901 DE – ...)
   = ...; **Lydia** ... (...)
E) **Andrew Drain** (ca.1858 Sussex Co. – ...)
F) **Florence Drain** (1859 Millsboro, DE – 1939 Millsboro, DE)
   = 28 Jan 1880; (**Chief Wyniaco**)[36] **William** Russell **Clark** (30 Nov 1855 Millsboro – 8 Oct 1928) son of James Clark & Nancy Harmon
G) **Miranda Drain** (ca.1860 – ...)
H) **Laura Drain** (ca. 1861 DE – ...)
I) **Willard Drain** (1863 DE – 1945 Cumerland Co. NJ)
   = 1910s; **Florence** ... (1876 NJ – 1956 Cumberland Co.)

---

[36] Chief of the Nanticoke tribe.

no issue
J) **De Lange Drain** (ca.1867 DE – ...)
= 1908 Philadelphia; **Mary J Valentine** (...)
K) **Herschel Drain** (ca.1871 DE – ...)
III) **Robert Drain** (1827 DE – 27 Dec 1878 Philadelphia)
IV) **Jacob Drain** (ca.1830 DE – Aug 1901)
= ...; Mariah **Anne Wright** (ca.1837 DE – ...)
A) **Robert B Drain** (ca.1856 Sussex Co – ...)
= ...; **Margaret Wright** (ca.1862 Sussex Co – 12 Mar 1943 Sussex Co.) daughter of Philip Wright & Hannah Johnson
1) **William** Oliver **Drain** (21 Jun 1878 Sussex Co. – 21 Sep 1924 Sussex Co.)
2) **Jacob W Drain** (11 Feb 1880 Sussex Co. – 11 Jul 1965 Rehoboth, DE)
= ...; **Nellie G Daisey** (14 Mar 1884 DE – 7 Aug 1945 Rehoboth) daughter of Nancy Daisey
has issue
3) **Margaret J Drain** (1883 DE – 11 May 1960 Lewes)
=1 ...; **William Street** (...)
=2 ...; ... **Harmon** (...)
has issue[37]
4) **Annie Drain** (Feb 1885 Sussex Co. – ...)
5) **Clarence Drain** (Jul 1890 DE – ...)
= ...; **Anna** Louise **Maze** (ca.1893 PA – ...)
has issue
6) **Nelson Drain** (Nov 1892 DE – ...)
= ...; **Maggie Morris** (...) daughter of Edward Morris & Emma Dell
has issue
7) **Helena C Drain** (Dec 1898 – ...)
= 5 May 1917 Rebohoth Beach, DE; **Harvey** Hickman **Harmon** (14 Dec 1896 Lewes, DE – 25 Jul 1931 Millsboro) son of David Harmon & Ella ...
B) **Jacob W Drain** (26 Jun 1859 DE – 1 Dec 1927 Lewes)
= 29 Dec 1881 Nassau; **Adeline Wright** (Apr 1861 DE – ...) daughter of Philip Wright & Hannah Johnson
1) **Mary Drain** (Mar 1881 DE – ...)
2) **Sallie A Drain** (Nov 1882 DE – ...)
has issue:

---

[37] Margaret's children carried the Drain surname, but, since they were born after 1900, are not being included.

a) **Herschel Drain** (7 Apr 1900 – 20 Jun 1984)
   = ...; **Minnie V. Clark** (24 Jan 1898 – 23 Sep 1993 Milford) daughter of John Clark & Margaret Jack
   has issue
   3) **Emily Drain** (Jan 1900 DE – ...)
  C) **Mary Drain** (ca.1863 Sussex Co. – ...)
  D) **Anne Drain** (ca.1866 Sussex Co. – ...)
   = 18 Nov 1881 Nassau, DE; **George Coursey** (ca.1860 DE – ...)
  E) **Martha Drain** (ca.1872 Sussex Co. – ...)
  F) **Clara Drain** (ca.1878 Sussex Co. – ...)
 V) **James Drain** (15 May 1832 DE – 23 Dec 1906 Philadelphia)
   = 27 Jun 1859; **Sarah Harmon** (ca.1836 – ...) daughter of Woolsey Harmon & Julia ...
  A) **Isaac Drain** (May 1860 DE – 29 Dec 1910 Philadelphia)
   = ...; **Sarah** Elizabeth **...** (ca.1871 MD – ...)
   1) **Gertrude Drain** (ca.1882 Philadelphia – 1 Jan 1888 Philadelphia)
   2) **Helen Drain** (Mar 1889 Philadelphia – ...)
   3) **Robert Drain** (* & + 1890 Philadelphia)
   4) **Emma Drain** (Nov 1896 Philadelphia – ...)
   5) **Harold Drain** (15 Apr 1900 Philadelphia – 18 Jul 1907 Philadelphia)
  B) **Mary Euvenia Drain** (14 Aug – 4 Oct 1861 Lewes) (twin)
  C) **Electra Drain** (14 Aug 1861 Lewes – 9 Aug 1885 Lewes) (twin)
   = ...; ... **Stewart** (...)
  D) **Woolsey Drain** (ca.1864 DE – 28 Mar 1899 Philadelphia)
  E) **Sarah Drain** (ca.1869 DE – ...)
  F) **James Drain Jr.** (ca.1871 DE – ...)
 VI) **Emmeline Drain** (ca.1839 DE – ...)
 VII) **Elizabeth Drain** (...)
   = ...; ... **Hancock** (...)
  d. **Daniel Drain** (ca.1783 DE – aft.1850)
   = ...; **Mary ...** (ca.1800 DE – ...)
   issue ?
  e. a daughter (ca.1784 Sussex Co. – ...)
2. **Russell Drain** (...)
3. **Rueben Drain** (...)
4. **Joshua Drain** (...)

Chapter 5
The Prince George's County Dranes

The youngest of the Sawbridgeworth Dranes was Anthony, baptized in February 1665/6. Keep in mind the reason for the double dating was that England had not yet adopted the Gregorian calendar, so what the rest of Europe called February 1666, England was still calling 1665.

Anthony Drane came to the colonies in 1690, give or take a year or so. He may have travelled with his older brother, Thomas, or perhaps Thomas came a little later. In any event, Anthony married very shortly after arriving, suggesting perhaps arrangements had been made for the union prior to sailing. His wife was Elizabeth Mockbee Nichols, the only surviving child and heiress to the fabulously wealthy William Nichols and his wife, the former Mary Mockbee. The Nichols and Mockbee families owned thousands of acres of what was then Prince George's County. Some of their territory was ceded to the federal government for the construction of the District of Columbia. Both families were part of the original immigrants who travelled with Lord Baltimore in 1637. It is this connection that may have led later generations to be confused about whether the Dranes were also in Lord Baltimore's party.

Anthony probably lived with his in-laws when he first arrived in Maryland. After a few years of marriage, his family was starting to grow, so it would have been necesary to establish his own home. In the spring of 1700, Anthony purchased an 109-acre tract of land for 32 pounds, 14 shillings. Compared to the average wages of the day, this was a very large sum of money. However, in today's terms, it would be about $4300. So he got the land for a pretty good price.

He called the land and the plantation he built on it Greenfield which suggests that is all he had to start with, a green field. The larger tract of land that Greenfield was broken off of was curiously named "Something." One can only imagine how it got that name. Personally, I can see the new owners getting there with their land grant in hand and saying, "Isn't that something?" Or, perhaps, "We got to call it something." Anthony cultivated his land and turned it into a profitable tobacco plantation.

Greenfield was situated about three miles north of the present-day town of Upper Marlboro, with the Collington Branch of the Patuxent River forming its western border. One of Anthony's descendants, Nellie Kettering, made a big fuss in the 1890s about her family owning some of the property that formed Washington, D.C. It was assumed she meant her Drane ancestors, leading many to believe Greenfield was in present-day Washington. Descriptions and plat maps from the early 18th century make it clear that is not the case. However, the Nichols and Mockbees did own land that lay west of Anthony's plantation and some it did eventually get incorporated into the District of Columbia, but those landowners would not have been direct ancestors of Nellie. They would have been distant cousins.

Anthony and Elizabeth had at least seven children: Thomas, Anthony, Eliza, Ann, Mary, Rachel, and James. Eliza married George Hardie, Ann married George Becket. Mary married twice, first to a second cousin, William Nichols, and then to Arnold Livers. All three daughters left numerous descendants that continue to the present day. The youngest daughter, Rachel, was still unmarried in 1734, but may have married later.

Anthony died in 1723. In his will, he divided the land between his three sons and also left some personal effects to his daughter Mary. He called her "Mary, wife of William Nichols," so she was already married by then, and William was apparently still alive. William would be dead by 1729, when Mary married Arnold Livers. Anthony made his wife his executrix and provided for her to retain the plantation during her lifetime, before it was divided among the boys. As it turned out, Elizabeth outlived their son Anthony, so the plantation was divided between Thomas and James.

Elizabeth Nichols Drane died in 1742. Eight years prior to her death, she had already deeded the land to her children. In 1734, she gave it to sons Thomas and James and daughter Rachel. She also left a portion to her granddaughter, Rebecca Drane, but did not mention which son was Rebecca's father. Since Anthony Jr. was not mentioned, it can be safely assumed he was already dead at the time. Therefore, it would be a reasonable guess that Rebecca was his surviving child and heiress.

Thomas Drane, the eldest son, lived to be old man of 79, a rarity for the time period. He did not leave a will, so his wife, the former Susannah Magruder, was made the administratrix for the estate. She remained at Greenfield for the remainder of her life, but her only survivng child, also named Thomas, moved his young family to Kentucky shortly after her death.

James Drane, the youngest son, built a second house on Greenfield after he married Elizabeth Tyler Pottinger, a widow, in 1743. Elizabeth's mother, Susanna Duvall, was also from one of Maryland's original families. Elizabeth died ten years later, leaving two surviving sons, Thomas and James Jr. Both boys were still babies at the time, so James Sr. remarried very quickly to give them another mother, this time to Elizabeth Piles. The Piles family was very prominent in colonial Maryland, several members serving in government positions under the colonial governors. But it is Elizabeth's mother, Elizabeth Cooke, who has the most prominent ancestry. One only has to go back a few generations to start seeing noble titles among her ancestors. Ultimately they will lead back to the Percys, who were the Dukes of Northumberland, and through them, to King Edward III by way of his son, Lionel, Duke of Clarence. With this royal lineage, it may well have been tempting to call James Drane's second wife to be named Elizabeth his own personal Elizabeth the Second.

Elizabeth Piles Drane would give her husband ten more surviving children. There is no record of how many died in infancy, but it can be assumed a few did, going by the gaps in their survivors' birthdates.

James died in 1787, at the age of 68. His widow later married John Woodward. By 1787, the Dranes had expanded their property to over 200 acres, picking up a few parcels here and there as they went. Elizabeth had also inherited some land from her father. James divided the property among his twelve children. Ultimately the children sold the plantation, dividing up the proceeds. Of James's eight sons, only Anthony remained in Prince George's County, his brothers scattering to the four winds. Their stories will be told in subsequent chapters. Marriage records have been located for all of the daughters except Eliza. Some of their descendants remained in Prince George's, but many also moved away.

After the sale of Greenfield, Anthony moved to small parcel of land just southwest of Bladensburg, which he had inherited from his mother and had been part of the larger parcel owned by his maternal grandfather, Leonard Piles. Anthony would be the last Drane to be an owner of any significant amount of land in Prince George's County. Upon his death, the Bladenburg property was left to a daughter, which removed it from the Drane family.

Anthony Drane, whose full name according to his cemetery record is William Anthony Drane, married Ann Smith in 1801. However, he already had at least three sons by that time, so there must have been a first wife. Very thorough searches have not turned up a marriage certificate for this first wife, so her name remains lost to history. Ann Smith is often listed as the mother of the three older boys, even though it would be biologically impossible, as she was only eleven when the first was born. However, there can be no doubt she adopted these boys and raised them as her own when she married their father.

The total number of Anthony's children requires a little guesswork. There are also a few sons who other researchers have attributed to Anthony, but that cannot be where they go. My research gives Anthony eight children, the three by his first wife plus five more with Ann Smith. The first three were Hezekiah, David, and Issac. Each will be the founders of their own families who settled in Virginia. His sons by Ann were Haddock, Gustavus, George Washington, Kinzie, and Anthony. Issac and Kinzie are educated guesses, made mostly by process of elimination. There is enough detail known about each one to suggest Anthony is his father, but no documentation stating it explicitly. They will each discussed in further detail in their own chapters.

Haddock, who was named for his maternal great-grandfather, Haddock Smith, appears to be the only son to remain in Prince George's County, although he did also live at times in Washington, D.C. He married Mary White and had one child, James Anthony, who was born about 1808. James married Elizabeth Graham and moved to Athens County, Ohio. Their descendants, who use the Drain spelling, mostly remain there today. However, one son, Isaac, married a Drain cousin, Emily, from the Harrison County, West Virginia, Drain line, and moved there. Their descendants are listed here, but for Emily's family, see Chapter 11.

Gustavus Savage Drane was born in 1789. He went to West Point and continued a lifelong career in the Army, most famously being the commander of Fort Mifflin in Pennsylvania. He married Margaret Caldwell of Alabama, but they did not have any children. He died in 1846 and is buried in Laurel Hill, near Philadelphia.

Washington Drane moved to Fairfax County, Virginia where he founded the village of Dranesville. He established a general store there that also served as an inn, a tavern, and the town's post office.

He married Anna Maria Dade in 1816. They had five children before Washington died in 1832. Two of the boys died young, elder daughter, Maria, remained a spinster, and younger daughter, Anne, married John Farr, her step-brother. John's father, also named John, was married to Washington Drane's widow. It would be the Farrs that continued running the Dranesville Tavern, but after the Civil War, the establishment closed. Dranesville itself would have likely been a forgotten village if it had not been the site of a small Civil War battle on December 20, 1861.

Apparently Dranesville never really made it as a town. The Dranesville Tavern still stands, though, and has recently been refurbished to its original state. It serves as a historical site, tourist spot, and popular wedding reception venue.

Washington's only surviving son, Baldwin Dade Drane, named for his maternal grandfather, moved to the national capital and became one of the political movers and shakers of post-Civil War Washington. As a professional lobbyist, he was well known about town simply as B.D. Drane.

B.D. married Saphronia Ashford in 1857. Her father, Craven Ashford, had himself been a Washington powerbroker in his day. They had four sons and a daughter. The daughter appears to be the only one to have gotten married. All of his sons were alive in the 1900 census, but disappear after that. Two of the sons, Samuel Dade and Edward Washington, became actors, but only Samuel found any success. Mostly a stage actor, Samuel did make a couple of appearances in silent films, as Sam D. Drane, most famously playing Abraham Lincoln in *The Crisis* (1916) and Mutt in a *Mutt and Jeff* serial made in 1911.

Anthony's two youngest sons, Kinsey and Anthony, moved away and added their own branches to the family tree. They will be discussed in later chapters.

Anthony Drane (bap. 21 Feb 1665 Sawbridgeworth, Hertfordshire – 27 Mar 1723 Prince George's Co., MD[38])
= ca.1690 Prince George's Co.; **Elizabeth** Mockbee **Nichols** (ca.1669 – 1742 Prince George's Co.) daughter of William Nichols & Mary Mockbee

  A. **Thomas** Osborn **Drane** (ca.1692 Prince George's Co.[39] – 1771 Prince George Co.[40])
    = ...; **Susannah Magruder** (ca.1713 – aft.1773) daughter of Nathan Magruder & Rebecca Beall
    1. **Thomas** Offutt **Drane Sr.** (1735 – 1810)
      see Chapter 6
    2. **Cassandra Drane** (ca.1742 – ...)
  B. **Anthony Drane** (ca.1693 Prince George's Co. – bef.1734)
    = ...
    1. **Rebecca Drane** (bef. Nov 1734 – ...)[41]
  C. **Eliza Drane** (...)
    = 4 Oct 1720 Prince George's Co.; **George Hardie** (...)
  D. **Ann Drane** (...)
    = 17 Nov 1724 Prince George's Co.; **John Beckett** (...)
  E. **Mary** Ann **Drane** (ca.1702 Prince George's Co. – ca.1742 Frederick Co., MD)
    =1 bef.1723; **William Nichols** (... – bef.1729)
    =2 1729 Frederick Co., MD; **Arnold Livers** (ca.1702 – ...)
  F. **Rachel Drane** (...)[42]

---

[38] Maryland Calender of Wills. Anthony Drane's Will was probated Jun 1723. In his Will he leaves his land to his sons, Thomas, Anthony and James, and names his wife Elizabeth as Executrix. He also mentions daughter Mary, wife of William Nichols.

[39] Prince George's Co. Land Records. In 1760, Thomas gave his age as 68, making his dob ca.1692.

[40] Prince George's Co. Liber 6, folio 274. Thomas Drane died without a Will and his wife was made Administratrix of the estate. 1771 was the year she filed a final account of Thomas Drane, suggesting he had died shortly before. However, there was also an inventory of his estate in 1773, a year often given as his date of death.

[41] In 1734, Elizabeth Drane, as a widow, gifted land to her two surviving sons, Thomas and James, and her unmarried daughter, Rachel. She also named her granddaugther, "Rebekah Drane," but did not indicate which son was Rebecca's father. Since the original Will of Anthony Drane stipulated the land should go to his three sons, it would be a reasonable guess that Rebecca was Anthony's daughter and heiress.

G. **James Drane** (1715 Prince George's Co.[43] – 28 Apr 1787 Prince George's Co.[44])
=1 23 Jul 1743 Prince George's Co.; **Elizabeth Tyler** (11 Jul 1717 Prince Georges Co., – 1753 Prince George's Co.) daughter of Robert Tyler & Susannah Duvall; =1st Samuel Pottinger
=2 23 Dec 1753 Prince George's Co.; **Elizabeth Piles** (ca.1730 Prince Georges Co., – ca. 1803 Prince George's Co.) daughter of Leonard Piles & Elizabeth Cooke; =2nd John Woodward[45]
issue of 1st:
1. **Thomas Drane** (1751 – 1828)
   see Chapter 7
2. **James Drane** (1753 – 1828)
   see Chapter 8
issue of 2nd:
3. William **Anthony Drane**[46] (bap.Sep 1754 Prince George's Co.[47] – 27 Dec 1830 Prince George's Co.[48])
=1 ...
=2 23 Dec 1778 Upper Marlboro, MD[49]; **Ann Smith** (1761 – bef.1810) daughter of James Smith & Ann Burgess
issue of 1st:
a. **Hezekiah Drain** (bef.1772 – ...)
   see Chapter 9
b. **David Drain** (1772 – 1863)
   see Chapter 10
c. **Isaac Drain** (ca.1774 – btw.1810/1820)
   see Chapter 11
issue of 2nd:
d. **Haddock Drane** (1782 – ...)

---

[42] Rachel is mentioned as a recipient of land from her mother in 1734, at which time Rachel was apparently unmarried.
[43] Prince George's Co. Land Records. In 1780, James Drane is stated to be "about 65 years of age" which puts his birth ca.1715.
[44] Register of Wills, Prince George's Co. Divided his substantial property between children James, Thomas, Anthony, William, Walter, Benjamin, Stephan, Hiram, Eliza, Eleanor, Ann, and Charlotte.
[45] Elizabeth Drane married John Woodward 9 Nov 1796 in Prince George's Co.
[46] Name established as William Anthony by cemetery records. Burried with wife, Ann, at Rock Creek Cemetery, Washington DC.
[47] Baptized at St. Barnabas Episcopal Church, near Upper Marlboro, MD.
[48] Death notice in *The National Intelligencer* (Washington, DC) 3 Jan 1831.
[49] Prince George's Co. Marriage Records.

= ...; **Mary White** (...)
I) **James** Anthony **Drain** (ca.1807 VA – bef.1860)
   = ...; **Elizabeth** Jane **Graham** (ca.1808 MD – 10 Feb 1882 Athens Co. OH)
   A) **John Drain** (Feb 1829 Athens Co. – 18 Feb 1911 Athens Co.)
      = ...; **Nancy Brown** (+bef.1880)
      1) **Archie Drain** (28 Jan 1867 Athens Co. – 20 Aug 1933 Athens Co.)
         = aft.1900; **Agnes ...** (...)
      2) **John Drain** (Oct 1870 Athens Co. – ...)
      3) **Jacob Drain** (ca.1872 Athens Co. – 16 Sep 1899 Columbus)
         = ...; **Susan ...** (Oct 1876 OH – ...)
         a) **Ida Drain** (May 1896 Athens Co. – ...)
      4) **Charles Drain** (May 1874 Athens Co. – ...)
      5) **Amanda Drain** (Sep 1875 Athens Co. – ...)
   B) **Edward Drain** (ca.1831 Athens Co. – ...)
   C) **Isaac Drain**[50] (Mar 1838 Athens Co. OH – 22 Nov 1915 Shinnston, WV)
      =1 26 Jan 1862 Harrsion Co., (W)VA; **Nancy Carroll** (...)
      =2 14 Oct 1868 Harrison Co.; **Emily** Jane **Drain** (1856 – 17 Apr 1931 Shinnston, WV) daughter of Harrison Drain & Rose Collins *see Chapter11*
      issue of 1st:
      1) **Senora Drain** (...)
      2) **Robert Drain** (...)
      issue of 2nd:
      3) **Eliza** Louisa **Drain** (+young)
      4) **Francis Drain** (1872 Harrison Co. – 1882 Harrison Co.)
      5) **William** Goff **Drain** (7 Jul 1877 Harrison Co. – 15 Jan 1961 Shinnston)
         = ...; **Dessie** Dorothy **Drain** (Jan 1887 Harrison Co. – 7 Apr
         1945 Shinnston) daughter of Granville Drain & Minerva Ashcroft *see Chapter 11*
         has issue
      6) **Manual Drain** (1881 Harrison Co. – 1884 Harrison Co.) (twin)

---

[50] Isaac Drain was severely wounded at Ft. Gregg, VA, while serving in the Union Army and was medically discharged.

  7) **General Drain** (1881 Harrison Co. – 1884 Harrison Co.) (twin)
  8) **Viola Drain** (May 1883 Harrison Co. – ...)
  9) **Earl Drain** (Jun 1885 Harrison Co. – ...) unm.
  10) **Martha Drain** (Jul 1887 Harrison Co. – ...)
  11) **Flossie Drain** (10 Oct 1889 Harrison Co. – 26 Oct 1949 Shinnston)
  12) **Carma Drain** (Aug 1893 Harrison Co. – ...)
 D) **James Drain** (ca.1840 Athens Co. – 14 Jun 1875 Athens Co.)
  = ...; **Phoebe** ... (ca.1841 OH – ...)
  1) **Mary Drain** (ca.1861 Athens Co. – ...)
  2) **Eliza Drain** (ca.1866 Athens Co. – ...)
  3) **Electa Drain** (ca.1871 Athens Co. – 1947)
   = ...; ... **Arnold** (...)
  4) **Margaret Drain** (ca.1875 Athens Co. – ...)
 E) **Eliza Drain** (ca.1842 Athens Co. – ...)
 F) **Charles** Floyd **Drain** (Feb 1845 Athens Co. – 6 Apr 1910 Athens Co.)
  = ...; **Susan Dix** (Nov 1845 OH – ...)
  1) **James Drain** (Mar 1872 Athens Co. – 26 Oct 1909 Athens Co.)
  2) **Elsworth Drain** (Jun 1876 Athens Co. – 29 Oct 1926 Athens Co.)
  3) **Margaret Drain** (Oct 1877 Athens Co. – ...)
  4) **Laura Drain** (ca.1879 Athens Co. – bef.1900)
  5) **Jemima Drain** (Mar 1887 Athens Co. – ...)
  6) **Daniel Drain** (Apr 1888 Athens Co. – ...)
 G) George **Washington Drain** (ca.1847 Athens Co. – ...)
e. **Maj. Gustavus** Savage **Drane** (27 Aug 1789 Prince George's Co. – 16 Apr 1846 Ft. Mifflin, PA[51]) (twin)
= **Margaret Caldwell** (of Mobile, AL) (+1858)
no issue
f. George **Washington Drane** (ca.1790 – ca.1832 Dranesville, VA)
= 23 Jun 1816 Washington, DC; **Anna Maria Dade** (ca.1797 – ca.1855) daughter of Baldwin Dade & Catherine West; =2nd John Farr
I) Anna **Maria** Louisa **Drane** (1822 – 22 Aug 1846 Dranesville[52])

---

[51] Buried at Lauren Hill Cemetery, Philadelphia.

II) **Washington Drane** (...) (+young)
III) **James** Anthony **Drane** (...) (+young)
IV) **Baldwin** Dade **Drane** (8 Sep 1828 Dranesville – 27 Aug 1920 Washington DC[53])
= 20 Jul 1857 Fairfax Co., VA[54]; **Sapphronia Ashford** (Apr 1836 Fairfax Co. – 10 Jul 1909) daughter of Craven Ashford & Ann...
  A) **Fillmore Drane** (ca.1858 MD – aft.1900)
  B) **Annie Drane** (ca.1861 MD – aft.1910)
    = ...; **James Smith** (ca.1863 – ...)
  C) **Samuel** Dade **Drane**[55] (1869 DC – 15 Aug 1916 New York)
  D) Edward **Washington Drane**[56] (ca.1870 DC – aft.1900)
  E) James **William Drane** (Jan 1871 DC – aft.1900)
V) **Anne** Dade **Drane** (ca.1829 – ...)
=...; (her step-brother) **John B Farr** (ca.1820 – ...)
g. **Kinzie Drane** (ca.1791 PA – bef.1870)
see Chapter 12
h. **Stephen Drane** (1795 – 1812) died of dysentery while fighting in War of 1812
i. **Anthony Drane** (1799 – 1851)
see Chapter 13
4. **Walter Drane** (1756 – 1807)
see Chapter 14
5. **Eliza Drane** (...)
6. **Hiram Drane** (ca.1760 Prince Georges Co. – ca.1803)
7. **Benjamin Drane** (ca.1763 Prince Georges Co. – ca.1842 Richmond, GA)
= 2 Feb 1787 Richmond, GA; **Rachel Harris** (ca.1763 – ...)
a. **Jane Drane** (25 Nov 1788 Prince George's Co. – 24 Aug 1847 Washington Co., TN)
= ca.1804; **Chaney Boren** (ca.1770 – 5 May 1834) son of James Boren
8. **William Drane** (1765 – 1847)

---

[52] Buried in Falls Church Episcopal Church Cemetery.
[53] Death certificate lists Andrew J Drane as his father, not George Washington Drane.
[54] Marriage certificate lists James W. Drane as his father.
[55] An actor, he appeared in a few silent films shortly before his death.
[56] Also a performer, he was listed as a "minstrel" with his brother, Sam in a few press reports of the 1890s.

see Chapter 14
9. **Stephen Drane Sr.** (1768 – 1844)
see Chapter 13
10. **Eleanor Drane** (ca.1770 Prince George's Co. – ...)
 = 19 Nov 1792 Prince George's Co.; **George Moore** (ca.1765 – ...)
11. **Ann Drane** (ca.1770 Prince George's Co. – ca.1795)
 = 9 Nov 1790 Prince George's Co.; **Richard** Hall **Lamar** (ca.1758 – ...) son of Robert Lamar & Sarah Hall
12. **Charlotte Drane** (May 1776 Prince George's Co. – ...)
 = 19 Nov 1792; **James Hill** (ca.1776 – ...)

Chapter 6
The Montgomery County Dranes
Including migrations to western Kentucky/Tennessee and to Philadelphia

Part of the land owned by Anthony Drane and his wife, Elizabeth Nichols Drane, was not in Prince George's County. Elizabeth had inherited a parcel in Montgomery County, Maryland, from her parents. It was near the village of Brightwood. Brightwood was later annexed into the District of Columbia, and the name remains as a neighborhood of Washington. The neighborhood is generally reckoned to have Walter Reed Hospital as its northern boundary, and the Nichols-Drane land was situated just off the northeast corner of the present-day Walter Reed complex.

When Elizabeth divided up her land between her sons in 1734, she gave this parcel to eldest son Thomas. Little is known of this senior Thomas Drane. Hand-me-down information is that Thomas's full name was Thomas Osborne Drane, but there is no documentation of this. There is also no obvious source of the name Osborne.

He is believed to have been born about 1735. The age is derived from his position within the family, more than anything else. His date of death is also not known, but he lived to a goodly age, as he was still alive when the 1810 census was taken. His wife's name is believed to be Elizabeth, but this again is handed down information and could easily have gotten confused over the years with other Elizabeths who surrounded him, such as his mother and his daughter-in-law. What is known through census records is that he had four sons, Thomas Offurt, Washington, Anthony, and David.

Thomas Offurt Drane, the eldest of the four brothers, had a curious middle name whose origin is not exactly known. His parents appear in various records along with a George Offurt, who would have been a contemporary in terms of age. It is possible that Thomas's unknown wife may have been a sister of this George Offurt, which would explain giving the name to their eldest son. But Thomas O. could also have been named for a good friend and not a relative.

Thomas Offurt's life is much better recorded than his father's. According to his death certificate, he died on New Year's Day in 1851 at the age of 78, so he was born in 1772. Thomas married twice, first in 1796 to Mary Elizabeth Harding (1778–1838), and second to Sarah Ann Gallagher in 1845. The first marriage took place in Montgomery County, probably at the home of his bride. The eleven children of this marriage were all born in Montgomery County, but sometime after the last one's birth in 1823, the family moved to Logan County, Kentucky.

As the United States expanded west, it had become common practice to open up new territories for homesteading. This meant that anyone who wanted to could go to these new areas and stake a claim on a piece of land on a first-come, first-served basis. The land was typically free, with the caveat that the person claiming the land had to live on it and develop it into something productive, usually a farm. As we will see through the next several chapters, most of the Dranes who originated in Maryland took up this challenge, eventually spreading their family all of the way to the Pacific Ocean.

Thomas O. Drane's farm was near the present-day town of Adairsville in Logan County. His first wife, Mary, died in Adairsville in 1838. Thomas remarried in 1845 to Sarah Gallagher, and they had an additional three children. It would seem the two oldest of these children were born before the marriage. It is possible Sarah was married previously and Thomas Jefferson and George Washington were products of that marriage, but no record of a previous marriage has been found yet. Whether legitimated or adopted, the boys were raised as Dranes. The youngest son, Andrew Jackson, was born well after the marriage, so there is no question of his paternity.

Thomas Offurt Drane died in 1851, leaving his farm to his second son, Walter Harding Drane. The eldest son, Thomas Harding Drane, who was born about 1797, had moved just across the state line to Sumner County, Tennessee, after marrying Melinda Sumner, granddaughter of the county's namesake, Revolutionary War hero Jethro Sumner.

Thomas Harding and Melinda had 12 children over the course of 20 years. There is a thirteenth child listed for them on the 1880 census named Minerva, born in 1861, but that would have meant Melinda had her at the age of 53, which is highly doubtful. Minerva was more likely a granddaughter. It was common practice at the time that, if a teenage daughter became pregnant, and the man involved did not live up to his responsibility, that girl would be hidden until the birth and her mother would claim the child as her own. The timing involved with this birth makes it a prime candidate to be a situation of this nature.

Of their large brood of children, Thomas Harding and Melinda only had two sons, Hugh and Thomas Jarvis. Hugh married Harriett Traughber in 1859, and had three surviving children, all daughters. As an older widower, he married a second time to a lady named Rose Ann, but they had no further issue. Thomas Jarvis Drane married twice, but the name of his first wife is unknown. He brought two small sons to his second marriage to Nancy Matthews in 1865. Thomas J. and Nancy had five children of their own, a boy, Thomas Eldridge, and four daughters. Although Thomas Jarvis Drane was the father of three sons between the two wives, only the youngest, Thomas Eldridge, had children to continue into the 20th century.

It is in this generation that the Civil War interfered with the family. Kentucky was in the Union, and Tennessee was in the Confederacy. Even though the various brothers and cousins lived within a day's ride from one another, the temporary national boundary fell between them. The descendants of Thomas Harding Drane all seemed to want to remain Americans, so they all moved back to Logan County before the war broke out. His brother's family, the descendants of Walter Harding Drane, all stayed in Tennessee.

Talking about the Civil War is as good a time as any to bring up the issue of slavery. The Dranes were slaveowners in Maryland, and this branch continued the practice in Kentucky and Tennessee. After Emancipation was declared in 1863 and made permanent by the 13th Amendment two years later, former slaves found themselves with the dilemma that they now had some rights, but, typically speaking, no surnames. Many slaves adopted the surnames of their last owners as their own.

In northwestern Tennessee, all of the recently freed slaves which had been owned by the Dranes adopted Drane as a surname, creating a significant population of African-American Dranes. There is no evidence of a biological connection between these folks and their previous masters. Sexual liaisons between owner and slave are a popular theme in fictional stories of the slave days. But in reality, it happened very rarely. Most slaveowners convinced themselves slaves were more akin to beasts of burden than people. So they would have considered having sex with them on par with bestiality. When the exceptions occurred, probably most famously with President Thomas Jefferson, the slave owner thought of himself more of an employer than an owner. These situations were typically relationships where both parties were consenting. But since the case of the Dranes seems closer to the former, and there is no evidence of a biological connection, I will not be including those families in this work.

Walter Harding Drane, second son of Thomas Offurt, was born in 1798. He has the distinction of being born in Montgomery County, Maryland, and dying in Montgomery County, Tennessee. In 1825, he married Elizabeth McClure, who was from Clarksville, a town in the Tennessee version of Montgomery County. Walter remained in Clarksville the rest of life, serving as the area's dentist.

Walter and Elizabeth had eleven children, with nine of them surviving to adulthood. Eldest son, William McClure Drane, married Amelia Haddox and with her had eight surviving children, half being sons and half daughters. The youngest of the sons, named Walter Harding after his grandfather, did not leave any children. His eldest brother, Wesley, married and left five daughters. The other boys, Charles Haddox Drane and William McClure Drane Jr., both have descendants thriving through the 20th century.

Walter and Elizabeth's second son, Walter Harding Jr., never married, and the third son, Hugh McClure, left an only daughter. Fourth son, James McClure, died from fever during the Civil War, and fifth son, Edward, left two boys who also never married. The youngest son was the first of a long line of Henry Tupper Dranes that continues to this day. However, most of his descendants were born after 1900.

Thomas Offurt Drane's third son, James Faustus Drane, also moved to the western Kentucky/Tennessee region and settled in Trigg County, Kentucky. However, his line seems to end with his two sons, Charles and Henry. Henry did marry, and to a distant Drane cousin no less—Georgia Drane from Chapter 13—but his only children died in infancy.

The fourth son, John Magruder Drane, remained with the family in Adairsville. He married Louise Boiseau, and they had ten children. Their first two sons died unmarried, but third son, James Haskin Drane, became a doctor and moved across the border to Dyer County, Tennessee, settling in the town of Newburn. His descendants with the Drane name are all through his son John Magruder Drane II. Dr. Drane's younger brother, Robert Wesley Drane, also settled in Newburn, where his descendants still live. The youngest of the brothers, Stonewall Jackson Drane, moved to Texas. His 1952 death certificate lists him as married, but no information about his wife or possible children have been found. If any children did exist, they would not be included anyway, since they would have born after 1900.

Thomas Offurt's fifth son, Wesley, married twice and had nine children between the two wives. His male line descendants, though, are limited to two grandsons, Joe Bates Drane (1881–1955) and Emmett Drane (1879–1975), and their 20th and 21st century descendants.

Another doctor in the family, Dr. Philip Drane, Thomas Offurt's sixth son, set up shop in Sumner County. His male line is believed to be extinct, however the fate of his grandson Philip—born in 1887—is unknown.

The presidentially named children of Thomas Offurt's second wife, Thomas Jefferson Drane, George Washington Drane, and Andrew Jackson Drane, lived out their lives in Logan County. Sadly for Andrew, that was not very long, as he lived to be only six. Thomas Jefferson's family continues to the present, but George's family came a curiously abrupt stop. In his will, probated in 1919, he divided his considerable wealth among his eight surviving children. But he stipulated that if any of them married, they would forfeit their portion of the estate. There is no record of why he made this odd provision, but the children adhered and none of them married, the last dying in 1971.

Little is known of Thomas Offurt's next younger brother, Washington Drane. Family stories say that he went first to Ohio in the early days of its settlement, and then went on to Shelby County, Kentucky. Being born in 1775, he would have been in both locations before adequate recordkeeping had taken hold, so we only have the word of mouth to go by. It is not believed he ever married.

The next younger brother, though, is well recorded. Anthony Drane was born in 1776, and like his brother, Thomas, went to stake out his own land in Kentucky. He didn't go quite as far west and grabbed a plot in Barren County, a couple of counties east of Logan. One may think that Barren County is not an inviting sounding name for farmlands, but in 2007, it was named the "best rural place to live" by *Progressive Farmer Magazine*. Whatever state they found it in, Anthony's family did quite well for themselves, amassing a significant fortune in the process.

Anthony apparently went to Kentucky in about 1804, as his son, Anthony Jr., was born in Maryland in 1803 and daughter, Sabrina, was born in Barren County in 1805. These were just two of the eight children Anthony had with his wife, Catherine Scott, who was known as Kitty.

The eldest son, Richard Keene Scott Drane, died unmarried at the age of 35.

Anthony Drane Jr. lived from 1803 until 1878, and was the owner of a hotel and tavern in Scottsville, in Allen County, Barren County's neighbor. He purchased the land for the hotel in 1830. He married Fannie Settle in 1823, and they had six children, all of whom lived to adulthood. All three of the daughters married, but only one son did, William Anthony. The eldest son, John, served for a time as the town's Postmaster, and the youngest, Zachary, was killed in action in the Civil War fighting for the South.

William Anthony Drane also fought in the War before settling in Glasgow, Kentucky, near his grandfather's place. He married in 1868 to one Valerie Davis, but they appear to have divorced sometime before 1880, something of a rarity for the time. They had two children, Edwin, who never married, and Maurice who lived well into his 80s, remaining in Glasgow the whole time. Maurice's descendants were all born after 1900.

Anthony and Kitty Drane's third son, Judson Scott Drane, added to the land he inherited from his father to become one of the largest landowners, and slaveowners, in Barren County. He and his wife, Louisiana Clayton, had ten children, but three of them died as babies or small children. One of the daughters married a Marcellus Maupin, and they became ancestors of the present-day author, Armistead Maupin, most famous for his *Tales of the City* series.

The eldest surviving son, Eugene, married Rhoda Reeves in 1871. His male descendants are all through his only son, Eugene Jr. Second son, Mark Anthony Drane, and his wife, Agnes Ogilvie, are represented in the present by the heirs of his two sons, Albert and Harry. Although third son, George William, fathered seven children, all of whom lived to adulthood, the male line stopped with his three sons as none of them left children of their own.

Two of them, Richard and Pete, lived in Detroit for a period, where they were barbers.

Anthony and Kitty's youngest son was Thomas Jefferson Drane, a common name to be given Drane boys, regardless of which branch of the family they are in. His male line stops with his only son, Thomas Jefferson Jr., although there are still descendants left through his daughters.

The Philadelphia and Pittsburgh Dranes

The person I have listed as the youngest son of Thomas Drane of Montgomery County, Maryland, is David Drane. There is some controversy if this is where he belongs. His grandson, Frank Condie Drane, was a Drane family researcher in the mid-20th century who was convinced David was a son of Anthony Drane and Ann Smith of Prince George's County, but the evidence makes that impossible. Most notably, Anthony had another son named David, who was ten years older than this one. Furthermore, Frank's grandfather, David, got married in 1801 in D.C. to Elizabeth Leuman, the same year that Anthony's son David married Jean Hayslet in Lexington, Virginia. Both David's had numerous children by their respective wives, so it could not be a case of successive marriages. The two Davids also spelled Drane/Drain differently.

My primary motivation for including Frank's grandfather here is that he was supposedly born in Brightwood. However, there is no documentation of that. Thomas Drane and his family are the only known Dranes in Brightwood at the time, so it makes the most sense that David is one of Thomas's children.

David Drane of Brightwood and his wife, Elizabeth Leuman, had five known children: William, Matilda, Gustavus, Jane, and Alfred. They all married, except Alfred. The other two sons both left the Washington area in the 1830s, moving to different parts of Pennsylvania.

William went to Philadelphia and Gustavus to Pittsburgh.

William Leuman Drane became a newspaperman in Philadelphia, working his way up to editor of the *Public Ledger*. He married twice, his wives being a set of sisters, Mary and Louisa Bonsall, having children by each. While several of his children lived to adulthood, only a few married. His eldest son, also named William, also married twice. He fathered ten children between the two wives, but only two lived past infancy. And of them, only one, Alfred, married. Alfred's only child was a daughter named Emily.

William L. Drane's younger son to marry was the aforementioned Frank Condie Drane. He married Rebecca Snyder in 1892, and they had six children, three boys and three girls. There are still descendants of this family remaining today.

Gustavus Drane moved to the Pittsburgh area around 1835. Four years later, he married Jane Patterson. They would have eight children, but the male line here seems to die out with his sons, as the grandchildren were all girls.

Old David Drane likely died in the 1820s, since that is when he disappears from the census, but his exact date of death is not known. His widow, Elizabeth, continued on to the 1860's, living with her daughter Matilda, who was married to Levi Osborn. Both are buried in Rock Creek Cemetery in Washington, but the cemetery records do not give a date of death or burial.

Thomas Drane (ca.1735 MD – aft.1810 Montgomery Co. MD)
= ...; **Elizabeth** ...[57] (ca.1730 – aft.1772)
a. **Thomas** Offutt **Drane** (1772 Montgomery Co.,. MD – 1 Jan 1851 Logan Co.,. KY)
=1 1796 Montgomery Co.; **Mary** Elizabeth **Harding** (15 Jan 1778 MD – 23 Jun 1838 Logan Co.) daughter of Walter Harding & Mary Murphy
=2 6 Jul 1845 Logan Co.; **Sarah** Ann **Gallagher** (... – 1859) daughter of John Gallagher & Mary Smith; =2nd John Butts
issue of 1st:
I) Thomas **Harding Drane**[58] (ca.1797 Montgomery Co. – aft.1880 Sumner Co.,. TN)
= 3 Apr 1824 Robertson Co.,. TN; **Melinda Sumner** (26 Jan 1808 TN – 31 Jul 1867 Logan Co.)
  A) **America** Emaline **Drane** (1830 TN – 1916 Logan Co.)
  = ca.1847 Logan Co.; **Thomas** Jefferson **Dawson** (14 Jan 1821 – 3 May 1869 Logan Co.)
  B) **Caroline H Drane** (21 Aug 1832 TN – 7 Mar 1915 Adairville, KY)
  =1 7 Nov 1854 Logan Co.; **James S Traughber** (5 May 1829 Logan Co. – 5 Jul 1864 Adairsville)
  =2 ...; **Owen V Ramsey** (20 Oct 1845 Wilson Co.,. TN – 8 Jan 1903 Adairville) son of Richard Ramsey & Lucy Dickerson
  C) **Mary Drane** (ca.1836 TN – ...)
  D) **Elizabeth Drane** (ca.1837 TN – ...)
  E) **Harriet Ellen Drane** (ca.1839 TN – ...)
  F) **Hugh B Drane**[59] (Oct 1840 Logan Co. – ...)
  =1 2 Aug 1859 Logan Co; **Harriett Traughber** (ca.1830 – bef.1892) daughter of John Traughber & Mary Branham
  =2 ca.1892 Logan Co; **Rosanna** ... (Apr 1837 KY – ...)
  issue of 1st:
  1) **Sarah** Jane **Drane** (14 Jan 1864 Logan Co. – 27 Nov 1938 Logan Co.[60])

---

[57] There is no record of Elizabeth's birth name, but there were connections to this family and George Offurt. It is entirely possible Elizabeth was George's sister, explaining how their son got Offurt for a middle name. But this is just a theory.
[58] 1850, 1860 Census: District 1, Logan Co., KY.
[59] 1910 Census: Adairville, Logan Co. KY. living with 2nd wife, Rosa and 1st wife's sister.
[60] Buried Greenwood Cenetery, Adairville, KY.

= ...; Drury **Green Lett** (23 Mary 1859 – 30 Nov 1937 Logan Co.)
  2) **Ella Drane** (ca.1866 – ...)
  3) **Hughanna Drane**[61] (ca.Nov 1869 – aft.1930)
   = 20 Oct 1889 Robertson Co.. TN; **Charles F Price** (... – bef.1930)
 G) Thomas **Jarvis Drane**[62] (ca.1841 Logan Co. – ...)
  =1 ...
  =2 4 Nov 1865 Barren Co.; **Nancy Matthews** (ca.1844 KY – 1924) daughter of W L Matthews & Emerine Buckley
  issue of 1st:
  1) **William T Drane** (ca.1862 KY – ...)
  2) **Henry** Marion **Drane**[63] (28 Feb 1864 KY – 7 Jan 1949 Palestine, TX)
   = ...; **Nancy** ... (ca.1862 – bef.1949)
   no issue
  issue of 2nd:
  3) **Lennie S Drane** (girl) (ca.1867 KY – ...)
  4) **Nora L Drane** (ca.1869 KY – ...)
  5) **Thomas** Eldridge **Drane** (1870 KY- 1920 Grady Co., OK)
   = ...; **Pearl Taylor** (3 Aug 1887 TX – 3 May 1976 Ventura Co. CA) daughter of William Taylor & Nancy Cox
   has issue
  6) **Birdie Drane**[64] (May 1873 KY – ...)
   = 7 Jan 1896 Logan Co. **Samuel C St.John** (Apr 1869 TN – ...)
  7) **Mattie Drane** (ca.1877 KY – ...)
 H) **Olivia Drane** (ca.1844 Logan Co. – ...)
  = 20 Jan 1876; **Arthur Webb** (... – bef.1880)
 I) a daughter (ca.1845 Logan Co. – ...)
 J) **Sarah Drane** (ca.1847 Logan Co. – ...)
  = 12 Oct 1884 Sumner Co.; **Mack Stanfield** (...)
 K) **Augusta Drane** (ca.1849 Logan Co. – ...)
 L) **Mary Drane** (ca.1851 Logan Co. – ...)
 M) **Minerva Drane** (ca.1861 Logan Co. – ...)
II) **Dr. Walter** Harding **Drane** (1 Nov 1798 Montgomery Co. MD – 30 Oct 1865 Clarksville, TN) a dentist

---

[61] 1930 Census: living in Nashville, widowed.
[62] 1880 Census: Schochoh, Logan Co. KY.
[63] 1930 Census: Port Isabel, Cameron Co. TX.
[64] 1900 Census: Davidson Co. TN.

= 18 Oct 1825; **Elizabeth** Jane **McClure** (14 Oct 1808 Montgomery Co., TN – 27 Jul 1889 Clarksville) daughter of Hugh McClure & Sarah Gibson
A) **William** McClure **Drane** (26 Sep 1826 Montgomery Co. – 9 Dec 1909 Clarksville)
   = 29 Sep 1857; **Amelia** Washington **Haddox** (22 Feb 1836 Keysburg, KY – 10 Jun 1906 Clarksville) daughter of Joseph Haddox & Mary Williams
   1) **Olive Drane** (2 Nov 1858 Clarksville – 9 Jan 1919 Clarksville)
      = ...; **Butler Boyd** (...)
   2) **Wesley Drane** (22 Mar 1860 Clarksville – 9 Apr 1943 Clarksville)
      =1 7 May 1885 Montgomery Co.; **Mary** Chapman **Macrae** (1858 – 1901) daughter of Bailey Macrae & Alice Miller
      =2 17 Oct 1903 Clarksville; **Willie** Frances **Elliott** (1880 – 1957 Montgomery Co.) daughter of William Elliott & Lizzie Cooley
      issue of 1st (none by 2nd):
      a) **Alice** Macrae **Drane** (1 Apr 1886 – 1 Sep 1910 Clarksville)
      b) **Mary** Macrae **Drane** (18 Feb 1890 Louisville, KY – 1941)
         = 23 Jun 1909; **Herbert Millsaps** (4 May 1886 Old Trenton, LA – ...) son of Uriah Millsaps & Mary Lockett
      c) **Amelia** Washington **Drane** (1893 – 1985)
         = ...; **William Elliott** (1892 – 1945)
      d) **Myrtle Drane** (6 Mar 1896 Clarksville – 1 Dec 1943 Clarksville)
         = 12 Oct 1915 Montgomery Co.; **Howard Smith** (1889 – 1984)
      e) **Wesley Drane** [a daughter] (11 Jun 1898 Clarksville – 20 Nov 1990 Shreveport, LA)
         = 9 Jun 1919 Clarksville; **Ashton Glassell** (18 Feb 1898 Belcher, LA – Jul 1985 Shreveport)
   3) **Charles** Haddox **Drane** (9 Oct 1861 Clarksville – 3 Nov 1942 Clarksville)
      = 31 Oct 1901 Clarksville; **Lucy** Castner **Gracey** (15 Sep 1877 – 6 Oct 1961 Clarksville) Matthew Gracey & Marion Castner
      has issue
   4) **Louisa Drane** (10 Dec 1863 Montgomery Co. – 12 Aug 1942 Clarksville)

= 31 Aug 1893 Montgomery Co.; **Rev. Primitivo Rodriguez** (1855 – 1909)

　5) **William** McClure **Drane Jr** (23 May 1866 Clarksville – 24 May 1931 Clarksville)
　　= 14 Dec 1899 Montgomery Co.; **Mary** Stacker **Lucket** (4 Jan 1872 Eddyville, KY – 26 Mar 1945 Clarksville) daughter of Thomas Lucket & Maria Gracey
　　has issue

　6) **Maud Drane** (25 Mar 1868 Clarksville – 18 Dec 1954 Clarksville)
　　= 27 Feb 1926 Montgomery Co.; **Elliott Buckner** (...)

　7) **Walter** Harding **Drane** (7 Feb 1870 Montgomery Co. – 20 Jul 1948 Clarksville)
　　= 1910's; **Annie** Henry **Allen** (10 Jun 1881 – 11 Oct 1863 Clarksville)
　　no issue

　8) **Myrtle Drane** (9 Sep 1872 – 31 May 1964) never married

B) **Walter** Harding **Drane Jr** (7 Feb 1828 Clarksville – 28 Dec 1893 Clarksville) unm.

C) **Alice Drane** (8 Nov 1831 – 28 Nov 1832)

D) **Louisa Drane** (24 Dec 1834 Montgomery Co. – 5 Dec 1862 Phillips Co.,. AR)
　= 15 Feb 1859 Montgomery Co; **Capt. John** William **Keesee** (8 Aug 1838 Columbia Co., TN – ... Phillips Co. AR) son of Thomas Keesee & Marie Louise Cross

E) **Hugh** McClure **Drane** (28 Oct 1836 Montgomery Co. – 20 Sep 1878 Clarksville)
　= ca.1868; **Elizabeth Wheeler** (...) daughter of James Wheeler
　1) **Bettie** Wheeler **Drane** (...)
　　= 18 Jul 1895 Montgomery Co.; **George Willig** (...)

F) **Mary Drane** (14 Sep 1838 Montgomery Co. – 29 Jun 1839 Montgomery Co.

G) **Jennie** Elizabeth **Drane** (17 Jul 1840 Montgomery Co. – 9 Mar 1918 Clarksville)
　= 31 Jul 1860 Montgomery Co.; **Robert W Johnson** (...)

H) **James** McClure **Drane** (25 Dec 1842 – 20 Sep 1861 Pocahontas Co.,. (W)VA) died of "camp fever" while on active duty with the CSA in the Civil War

I) **Marian H Drane** (30 Dec 1844 – ca.1878)
　= 14 Jan 1873 Montgomery Co.; **Thomas J Munford** (...)

J) **Edward Drane** (12 May 1848 Montgomery Co. – 31 Jan 1920

Lower Homing, NC) built "Drane-Patch-Catlett" House in Clarksville
=1 29 Aug 1872; **Rosa** Johnson **Flournoy** (31 Jul 1853 – 4 Mar 1876)
=2 2 Apr 1879 Nashville (dv.); **Sarah Eve** (ca.1855 TN – ...) daughter of Paul Eve
issue of 1st:
  1) **Hugh Drane** (1873 Clarksville – 27 Nov 1938 Harriman, TN[65])
issue of 2nd:
  2) **Paul Drane** (ca.1880 Montgomery Co. – aft.1910)
K) **Henry** Tupper **Drane** (31 Dec 1850 Montgomery Co. – 24 Mar 1920 Clarksville)
  = 3 Feb 1874 Kenton, KY; **Elizabeth** Bruce **Thomas** (18 Jun 1851 Clarksville – 12 Jul 1892 Clarksville)
  1) **Laura Drane** (5 Jul 1875 – ...)
    = 20 Nov 1895 Montgomery Co.; **Chiles K Barnes** (...)
  2) Fredonia "**Donie**" **Drane** (14 Feb 1876 – 6 Mar 1945 Birmingham, AL)
    = 19 Apr 1911 Clarksville; **Henry** Tidsnor **DeBardeleben** (2 Jan 1874 – 3 Nov 1948 Birgmingham) son of Henry DeBardeleben & Helen Pratt
  3) **Lewis** Thomas **Drane** (20 Jun 1879 – 1919 New Orleans[66])
    = 1906; **Josephine Becker** (29 Jul 1885 – 1960) daughter of Ferdinand Becker & Mary McGrath
    has issue
  4) **Bettie** Thomas **Drane** (15 Mar 1881 – ...)
    = 7 Feb 1907 Montgomery Co.; **Ferdinand V Becker** (...)
  5) **Henry** Tupper **Drane Jr.** (7 Nov 1883 – 21 Nov 1965 Selma, AL)
    = ...; **Alma Hooper** (7 Aug 1889 – 3 May 1967 Selma)
    has issue
III) **Rachel Drane** (20 Dec 1800 Montgomery Co. MD – 13 Aug 1838 Logan Co.)
  = 13 Dec 1826; **Wiley Holland** (6 Oct 1794 NC – 8 Oct 1878 Madisonville, MS)
IV) **James** Faustus **Drane** (ca.1804 Montgomery Co. MD – ...Trigg Co. KY)
  = ...; **Emily ...** (26 Sep 1816 TN – 2 Aug 1851 Trigg Co.)

---

[65] Single according to death certificate.
[66] Lewis Drane died in Flu pandemic.

A) **Charles H Drane** (ca.1844 – ...)
   = ...; **Sarah A Burradell** (...)
B) **Henry** Clay **Drane** (11 Oct 1845 Trigg Co. – 29 Aug 1872 Choctaw Co. MS)
   = ca.1868; **Georgia** Ann **Drane** (21 May 1848 Choctaw Co. MS – 10 Jul 1901) daughter of Benjamin Drane & Sarah Germany *see Chapter 13*
   1) a child (+inf)
   2) a child (+inf)
V) **Caroline** Harding **Drane** (ca.1806 – 2 Apr 1838)
   = ...; **James Grady** (ca.1806 – ...)
VI) **John** Magruder **Drane** (ca.1808 Montgomery Co. MD – ca.1890)
   = ...; **Louise Boiseau** (ca.1810 KY – ...)
   A) **Martha Drane** (ca.1834 Logan Co. – ...)
   B) **James F Drane** (... – bef.1850 Logan Co.)
   C) **Daniel Drane** (ca.1841 Logan Co. – ...)
   D) **Dr. James** Haskin **Drane** (15 Oct 1843 Adairville, KY – 1931 Dyer Co.,. TN)
      = 1 May 1873; **Eliza** Rebecca **Bobbitt** (28 Aug 1853 – 1904 Dyer Co.) daughter of James Bobbitt & Eliza Province
      1) **Mollie Drane** (ca.1877 – ...)
         = 18 Jul 1912; **Benjamin** Thomas **Roberts** (...)
      2) **Annie** Lou **Drane** (... – 1970 Dyer Co.)
      3) **John** Magruder **Drane** (28 Jul 1882 – 18 Sep 1974 Newbern, TN) TN State Rep 1910-1916
         = 17 Jun 1912; **Lillie Wilson** (19 Mar 1888 – 28 Jul 1968 Newbern, TN)
         has issue
      4) **Joelynn Drane** (15 Sep 1895 Dyer Co. – 29 Jul 1957 Dyer Co.)
   E) **Mildred Drane** (ca.1845 Logan Co. – ...)
   F) **John Drane** (ca.1847 Logan Co. – ...)
   G) **Robert** Wesley **Drane** (25 Jan 1850 Logan Co. – 12 Jul 1888 Dyer Co.)
      =1 2 Dec 1874 Dyer Co.; **Mattie F Fowlkes** (14 Nov 1851 – 1879) daughter of Asa Fowlkes & Elsa ...
      =2 27 Dec 1885 Dyer Co.; **Ella Harvey** (...)
      issue of 1st:
      1) Willie **Clyde Drane** (Sep 1875 Dyer Co. – 1932)
         = 29 Dec 1896 Dyer Co.; **Jettie Johnson** (Dec 1878 Dyer

Co. – 27 Apr 1854 Dyersburg, TN) daughter of George Johnson & Fannie Hurt
has issue
2) **Nellie F Drane** (Nov 1878 Dyer Co. – ...)
issue of 2nd:
3) **Robert** Wesley **Drane** (25 Oct 1886 Florence, AL – 25 Aug 1942 Nashville)
= ...; **Catherine** Willows **Harsson** (14 Apr 1887 – 31 Aug 1853 Florence) daughter of Henry Harsson & Mamie Smith
has issue
H) **Louise Drane** (19 Jan 1858 – 20 Apr 1942 Fulton Co.,. KY)
= 17 May 1878 Dyer Co.; **Bruce Wilkerson** (... – 1919)
I) **Stonewall** Jackson **Drane** (14 Sep 1862 Newburn, TN – 11 Jan 1952 Seymour City, TX[67])
J) **William J Drane** (ca.1864 Dyer Co. – ...)
VII) **Wesley Drane** (1810 Montgomery Co.,. MD – 1880 Madison, MS) a Judge
=1 15 Dec 1836 Warren, MS; **Matilda** Susan **Field** (1818 Dinwiddle Co., VA – 1851 Canton, MS)
=2 26 Sep 1853 Madison Co., MS; **Jerusha** Murdough **Ballard** (1832 NC – ca.1884)
issue of 1st:
A) **Osceola Drane** (1839 Madison Co. – 5 Aug 1861 Mannasas, VA) died of wounds in Civil War
B) **Elizabeth** Collins **Drane** (1841 MS – 1878 New Orleans)
= 22 Nov 1865; **Robert** Lindsey **Moore** (...)
C) **Wesley Drane**[68] (1847 Canton, MS – 1886 TX)
= 20 Oct 1869 Holmes Co., MS; **Elizabeth** Ann **Bates** (6 Jul 1853 Ita Buena, MS – 1 May 1927 Calvert, TX) daugher of Joe Bates & Anna Mitchell
1) **Helen** Wesley **Drane** (25 Oct 1870 Holmes Co. – 26 Apr 1945)
= 14 Jan 1895 Marietta, GA; Sheridan **Sol Smith** (11 Feb 1864 St. Louis, MO – 16 Jan 1935 St. Louis)
2) **Marian Drane** (5 Oct 1875 Kosciusko, MS – 8 Jul 1899 Honey Grove, TX)
= Jun 1895; **Marshall** Albert **Galbraith Jr.** (6 Dec 1871 Honey Grove – 29 Aug 1948 Dallas)

---

[67] Listed as married on his death certificate.
[68] 1880 Census: Goodman, Holmes Co.,. MS living with mother-in-law

3) **Bettie Drane** (1873 – 27 Jul 1878 Goodman, MS)
   4) **Osceola Drane** (14 Jun 1878 Holmes Co. – 13 Mar 1890 Ft.Smith, AR)
   5) **Joe** Bates **Drane** (4 May 1881 Goodman – 18 Nov 1955 Houston)
   = 9 Aug 1905 St. Louis; **Beulah** Willie **Yerkes** (3 Mar 1880 Little Rock – 15 Feb 1967 Houston) daughter of Elias Yerkes & Cora Porter
   has issue
 D) **Matilda S Drane** (1849 – aft.1880)
 E) **Susan S Drane** (1850 – ...)
 issue of 2nd:
 F) **Emmitt B Drane** (1854 – aft.1899)
   = ...
   1) **Emmett Drane** (14 Feb 1879 – 11 Apr 1975 Madison Co.)
   = ...; **Anne Griffin** (14 Mar 1881 – 7 Oct 1970 Madison Co.)
   has issue
 G) **Jennie N Drane** (1856 – aft.1900)
 H) **Helen** Wesley **Drane** (1858 – aft.1880)
 I) **Alma Drane** (1867 – bef.1880)
VIII) **Dr. Philip E Drane** (ca.1811 Montgomery Co.,. MD – ... Sumner Co.)
 = 17 Apr 1839; **Mary Williams** (ca.1828 TN – ...)
 A) **Mary Drane** (ca.1844 Sumner Co. – ...)
 B) **Malvina Drane** (ca.1846 Sumner Co. – ...)
 C) **Lucious Drane** (Jan 1850 Sumner Co. – ...)
   = 2 Jun 1880 Davidson Co; **Clara Shafer** (... – bef.1900)
   1) **Maureen Drane** (Jun 1881 – ...)
   2) **Anne L Drane** (Jan 1885 – ...)
   3) **Philip D Drane** (Mar 1887 – ...)
   4) **Clara L Drane** (Jul 1891 – ...)
 D) **Laura Drane** (ca.1855 Sumner Co. – ...
 E) **James** Walter **Drane** (1856 Sumner Co. – 13 Oct 1924 Gallatin, TN) (twin)
   = ...; **Martha ...** (ca.1867 TN – ...)
 F) **Martha** Pattie **Drane** (1856 Sumner Co. – 20 Jul 19367 Gallatin) (twin)
IX) **Rebecca** Sprigg **Drane** (ca.1814 Montgomery Co.,. MD – 28 Jun 1868 Madison Co. MS)
 = 10 Jun 1841; **Samuel Magruder** (12 Jan 1818 Columbia Co. – 30 Oct 1897 Crystal Springs, VA)

X) **Mary** Harding **Drane** (31 May 1818 Montgomery Co. – 9 Jul 1873 Madison)
= 19 Mar 1842 Madison, MS; **Tullius** Cercero **Tupper** (ca. 1818 – ...)
XI) **Alfred Drane** (ca.1823 Montgomery Co. – aft.1870) unm.
issue of 2nd (may be adopted step-sons):
XII) Thomas **Jefferson Drane** (ca.1841 Logan Co.,. KY – 2 Nov 1915 TX or OK)
=1 ...; **N C** ... (...)
=2 12 Jun 1887; **Martha Freeman** (ca.1857 – ...)
issue of 1st:
  A) **Willie T Drane** (9 Mar 1862 – 25 Jan 1879[69])
  B) **Joseph Drane** (29 Jul 1878 Logan Co. – 11 Nov 1971 Logan Co.
  C) **John** William **Drane** (1882 Logan Co. – 1947)
    =1 ...; **Gabriella Dickey** (...)
    =2 9 Sep 1899 Montgomery Co.; **Lena Dix** (...)
    has issue
  issue of 2nd:
  D) **George** Monroe **Drane** (...)
    = ...; **Belva** Mae **Glass** (...)
    has issue
XIII) **George** Washington **Drane** (16 Dec 1842 Logan Co. – 23 Apr 1919 Logan Co.[70])
=1 ...; **Nancy A McPherson** (18 Jan 1845 – 21 Jan 1928 Logan Co. daughter of William McPherson & Catherine Shepherd; =1st ... Gorham
=2 24 Jun 1897 Logan Co.; **Georgia E Stevenson** (...)
issue of 1st:
  A) **Drusie Drane** (28 Nov 1864 – 13 Jan 1953 Russellville, KY)
  B) John **Wesley Drane** (14 Mar 1867 Logan Co. – 28 Oct 1932 Logan Co.)
  C) **William Drane** (26 Jan 1869 Logan Co. – 6 Apr 1958 Logan Co.)
  D) **Edwin** Booth **Drane** (10 Dec 1870 Logan Co. – 8 Jan 1939

---

[69] Buried in Red River Cemetery, Adairville, KY, with two infant cousins, children of George W. Drane.
[70] The terms of George's Will stripped any of his children of their inheritance if they married. The entire family is buried in Whipporwill Cemetery in Schochoh, Logan Co., with no apparent sign of any of the children having married.

Logan Co.)
   E) a daughter (* & + 28 Sep 1875 Logan Co.)
   F) **Charles Drane** (23 Oct 1876 Logan Co. – 21 Dec 1956 Logan Co.)
   G) a daughter (* & + 10 Feb 1878 Logan Co.)
   H) **Joseph Drane** (29 Jul 1879 Logan Co. – 11 Nov 1971 Logan Co.)
   I) **Ada** May **Drane** (19 Mar 1881 – 13 Nov 1962 Logan Co.)
   J) **Vernon Drane** (22 Mar 1887 Logan Co. – 19 Jul 1912 Logan Co.)
   K) **Ernest Drane** (22 Jul 1889 Logan Co. – 6 Oct 1950)
  XIV) **Andrew** Jackson **Drane** (21 Feb 1849 Logan Co. – 19 Jul 1855 Logan Co.)
 b. **Washington Drane** (ca.1775 MD –...) went to Ohio then Shelby Co,. KY
 c. **Anthony Drane** (1776 Prince Georges Co.,. MD – 30 Oct 1830 Haywood, KY[71])
   = 29 Mar 1792 Prince Ceorge Co; **Catherine Scott** (ca.1775 Prince Georges Co.,[72] – 11 Aug 1855 Barren Co.,. KY) daughter of
Sabritt
   Scott & Martha Clagnett
   I) **Martha Drane** (11 Jan 1793 MD – 6 Feb 1853 Barren Co.)
   = 10 Jan 1822 Barren Co; **Benjamin Leavell** (ca.1790 VA – ...)
   II) **Sarah Drane** (7 Nov 1796 MD – 2 Apr 1843 Barren Co.[73])
   = 5 Sep 1820 Barren Co.; **Hubbard Duff** (3 Oct 1793 – 1845 Barren Co.)
   III) **Richard** Keene Scott **Drane** (17 Aug 1799 MD – 9 Apr 1834 Barren Co.) never married
   IV) **Anthony Drane Jr.** (9 Aug 1803 MD – 7 Feb 1878 Scottsville, KY) owned hotel in Scottsville
   = 9 Oct 1823 Barren Co.; **Frances Settle** (10 Jul 1804 Barren Co. – 1879 Allen Co., KY) daughter of William Settle and Elizabeth Huffman
   A) **Catherine Drane** (9 Jun 1824 Barren Co. – 4 Aug 1863 Barren Co.
   = 22 Dec 1847 Allen Co.; **William Hoffman** (ca.1822 – ...)
   B) **Elizabeth** Ann **Drane** (1826 Allen Co. – 15 Jul 1897

---

[71] Dates of birth and death given by George Turner, husband of a great-granddaughter through female lines.
[72] Death certificate lists age as 80 in 1855.
[73] Buried Parrish Cementery, Goodnight, KY.

Louisville)
= 20 Dec 1850 Allen Co.; **Dr. Charles** Holliday **Alexander** (ca.1826 Allen Co. – 8 Mar 1889 Louisville) son Amzi Alexander & Elizabeth Holliday
C) **John R Drane** (28 Oct 1829 Allen Co. – 22 Feb 1874) one-time postmaster of Scottsville
D) **Mary T Drane** (25 Jan 1833 Allen Co. – ...)
= ...; **Thomas Mansfield** (ca.1833 – ...)
E) **William** Anthony **Drane**[74] (1843 Allen Co. – ...) served in the CSA army
= 7 Jun 1868 Barren Co. (dv.1880); **Valerie** Sophia **Davis**[75] (ca. 1834 – ...)
 1) **Edwin B Drane**[76] (ca.1875 – ...)
 2) **Maurice** Lynn **Drane** (15 Apr 1879 Glasgow – 1 Dec 1967 Glasgow)
  = ...; **Mary** Emily **Depp** (1885 – 29 Mar 1953 Glasgow) daughter of Henry Depp & Laura Settle
  has issue
F) **Zachary** Taylor **Drane** (19 Jun 1845 Allen Co. – 17 Oct 1864) a Private in the CSA army
V) **Sabrina Drane** (25 Aug 1805 Barren Co. – 21 Mar 1837 Barren Co.) dunm.
VI) **Judson** Scott **Drane** (4 Aug 1807 Barren Co. – 26 Feb 1868 Barren Co.)
= 1 Dec 1845 Barren Co; **Louisiana Clayton** (12 Jun 1826 Barren Co. – 15 Aug 1894 Haywood) daughter of John Clayton & Lucinda Dodd
A) **Sabrina** Scott **Drane** (8 Jan 1847 Barren Co. – 31 Aug 1909 Barren Co.)
= 6 Nov 1869 Glasgow, KY; **Christopher** Thompkins **Ellis** (27 Oct 1935 Barren Co. – 23 Aug 1913 Glasgow) son of George Ellis & Fannie Wheeler
B) **Josephine Drane** (11 Apr 1848 Barren Co. – 1 Oct 1918 Smith's Grove, KY)
=1 11 Jul 1864; **Marcellus H Maupin** (ca.1845 – ...)
=2 ...; David **Lee Crain** (ca.1845 – ca.1910)
C) **Richard** Kane **Drane** (7 Jan 1850 Barren Co. – 20 Jun 1860

---

[74] 1880 Census: Living single as a clerk.
[75] 1880 Census: listed as Divorced and with her two sons in Glasgow, Barren Co., KY.
[76] 1930 Census: Living in Washington DC and single.

Barren Co.)
D) **Eugene Drane** (2 Apr 1852 Barren Co. – 11 Feb 1935 Barren Co.)
= 22 Nov 1871 Barren Co; **Rhoda** May **Reeves** (8 Dec 1852 TN – 17 Aug 1906 Haywood) daughter of William Reeves & Jemima Ritter
  1) **Lula Drane** (21 Mar 1873 Haywood – 22 Feb 1910 Haywood)
  2) **Mamie** Belle **Drane** (30 May 1875 Haywood – 19 Jun 1911 Glasgow)
     = **Nathaniel Settle** (7 Feb 1869 – ...)
  3) **Lallah** Page **Drane** (29 Aug 1878 Haywood – 22 Feb 1954 Haines City, FL)
  4) **Eugene Drane Jr.** (28 Dec 1886 Haywood – 2 Apr 1970 Exeter, CA)
     =1 23 Nov 1910 Glasgow; **Bettie Edmunds** (...)
     =2 5 Nov 1913 Carrollton, KY; **Victoria Coombs** (22 Dec 1885 Glasgow – 14 Nov 1972 Linsay, CA) daughter of Henry Coombs & Eugenia Witt
     has issue
E) **Frederck Drane** (24 Jan – 14 Feb 1854 Barren Co.,. KY)
F) **Mark** Anthony **Drane** (26 Apr 1855 Barren Co.,. KY – 2 Mar 1919 Charleston, MO)
= 24 Oct 1877 Charleston; **Agnes Ogilvie** (26 Oct 1857 Wolf Island, MO – Jan 1948 Charleston) daughter of Sam Ogilvie & Sally McElmurry
  1) a child (+inf)
  2) **Albert H Drane** (4 Dec 1880 Charleston – 22 Nov 1950 Cole Co.)
     = ca.1905; **Pearl Stafford** (ca.1885 MO – ...) daughter of ... Stafford & Ida ...
     has issue
  3) a child (+inf)
  4) **Mable Drane** (Sep 1885 Charleston – ...)
     = bef.1910; **Garland Noland** (ca.1882 MO – ...)
  5) a child (+inf)
  6) **Harry J Drane** (Oct 1888 Charleston – ...)
     = ca.1915; **Alura ...** (ca.1895 MO – ...)
     has issue
G) **George** William **Drane Sr.** (19 Mar 1857 Barren Co. – 2 Feb 1931 Glasgow)

= 16 May 1889 Scottsville; **Hattie** Bright **Steenbergen** (7 Jul 1867 Barren Co. – 26 Jan 1932 Louisville) daughter of William Steenbergen & Elizabeth Gillock

1) **Sarah** Nevell **Drane** (2 Dec 1890 Barren Co. – 9 Mar 1981 Glasgow)
= 23 Dec 1913; **Ebley** Clay **Peden** (6 May 1880 Barren Co. – 6 Mar 1963 Barren Co.) son of Alonzo Peden & Mary Adams

2) **Florence** Parrish **Drane** (22 Jan 1893 Barren Co. – 11 Feb 1979 Barren Co.)
= ca.1918; **Warner** Lacy **Settle** (5 Apr 1881 Barren Co. – ...) son of Thomas Settle & Josie ..

3) **Nellie** Grant **Drane** (1 Feb 1895 Barren Co. – 19 May 1942 Glasgow)
= 25 Dec 1919; **Rice** Chism **Read** (19 Mar 1886 – 6 Dec 1960 Glasgow) son of James Read & Ann Sims

4) **Judson** Scott **Drane** (13 Feb 1897 Barren Co. – 19 Oct 1962 Glasgow)
= 17 Dec 1920; **Hallie** Mae **Jordan** (22 Sep 1899 Barren Co. – 7 Feb 1990 Glasgow) daughter of Louis Jordan & Francis Ellis
no issue

5) **Richard** Kane **Drane** (23 Mar 1899 Barren Co. – 31 Jan 1970 Glasgow) lived a while in Detroit; a barber
= ca.1928; **Mabel M Shircliff** (27 Apr 1897 MI – 13 May 1980 Glasgow)
no issue

6) **Clara** Lee **Drane** (30 May 1906 Barren Co.,. KY – 7 Oct 1993 Louisville)
=1 31 Nov 1925 Jefferson, IN (dv.ca.1935); **James** Milton **Williams** (14 Oct 1904 Barren Co. – 26 Jul 1950) son of Milton Williams & Junia Pritchard
=2 7 Jun 1936 Jefferson, IN; **Charles** Louis **Bearden** (12 Aug 1910 – 29 Oct 1968 Atlanta) son of Edgar Bearden & Sarah Sumner

7) George William "**Pete**" **Drane Jr.** (21 Aug 1908 Barren Co. – 19 Oct 1948 Detroit) a barber
= 11 Jul 1936 Jefferson, IN; **Lucy B Wathen** (18 Jan 1906 Henderson, KY – ...) daughter of John Wathen & Mary Moore
no issue

H) **Harriet Drane** (* & + Dec 1857 Barren Co.)

I) **Lucy** Belle **Drane** (3 Mar 1859 Barren Co. – 27 Mar 1940

Smith's Grove)
   =1 17 Nov 1881 Barren Co; **Charles** Nathan **Allen** (ca.1855 – ...)
   =2 ...; **Richard B Allen** (ca.1857 – ...)
  J) **Rosa Drane** (3 Dec 1860 Barren Co. – 16 Feb 1901 Barren Co.
   = 16 Jul 1879 Jefferson; **Henry** Buckner **Trabue** (19 Mar 1856 Barren Co. – 7 Nov 1938 Barren Co.) son of Benjamin Trabue & Lelia Anderson
VII) **Margaret Drane** (14 Apr 1811 Barren Co. – 11 Jun 1830 Barren Co.) unm
VIII) **Thomas** Jefferson **Drane** (1813 Barren Co. – ca.1849 CA) died in the gold rush
   = 27 Jan 1838 Barren Co; **Mary Williams** (ca.1815 Barren Co. – ...)
  A) **Elizabeth Drane** (ca.1839 – ...)
   = 19 Mar 1857 Glasgow; **John R Williams** (ca.1831 – ...)
  B) **Catherine S Drane** (ca.1841 – ...)
   = 19 Oct 1859 Glasgow; **J.B. Benedict** (ca.1839 – ...)
  C) **Thomas** Jefferson **Drane** (ca.1843 – ...)
   =1 4 Nov 1865 Glasgow; **Frances Matthews** (...)
   =2 10 Mar 1872 Glasgow; **Catherine Fisher** (ca.1856 – ...)
   issue of 1st:
   1) **Bettie Drane** (ca.1867 – 23 May 1937 Bowling Green, KY)
    = ...; **John** Allen **Andrews** (...)
  D) **Margaret Drane** (ca.1844 – ...)
   = 1 Dec 1859 Glasgow; **Thomas W Hart** (ca.1837 – ...)
 d. **David Drane** (ca.1780 – btw.1820/30[77]) corporal in DC militia in War of 1812
  = 11 Aug 1801; **Elizabeth** Mary **Leuman** (ca.1788 – btw. 1860/70)[78]
  I) **William** Leuman **Drane** (22 Feb 1811 Montgomery Co. MD – 27 May 1881 Philadlephia, PA) moved to Philadelphia ca.1830
   =1 ca.1833 Philadelphia; **Mary Bonsall** (ca.1811 – 22 Jan 1842 Philadelphia)
   =2 ca.1845 Philadelphia; (his sister-in-law) **Louisa Bonsall** (ca.1811 PA – 7 Jan 1852 Philadelphia) =1st ... Solomon
   issue of 1st:
   A) **William Drane** (ca.1834 – ...)

---

[77] Both David and Elizabeth are buried in Rock Creek Cemetery, but the cemetery records do not give burial dates for them.
[78] 1850 Census: Living with daughter, Matilda Osborn, in DC.

=1 ...; **Cora** Cecilia ... (ca.1843 Philadelphia – 29 Jan 1871 Philadelphia)
=2 ca.1874; **Caroline** ... (ca.1855 PA – 27 Feb 1896 Philadelphia)
issue of 1st:
1) **Francis B Drane** (1861 Philadelphia – 3 Jun 1862 Philadelphia)
2) **William L Drane** (ca.1863 Philadelphia – 22 Apr 1900 Philadelphia) unm.
3) **Henry Drane** (Nov 1865 Philadelphia – 12 Apr 1866 Philadelphia)
4) **Alfred** Osbourne **Drane** (ca.1868 Philadelphia – ...)
   = 1896; **Louisa Louderback** (Aug 1877 Philadelphia – ...) daughter of Frank Louderback & Sarah ...
   a) **Emily Drane** (May 1897 Philadelphia – ...)
issue of 2nd:
5) **Nina Drane** (ca.1875 Philadelphia – ...)
6) **Robert Drane** (2 – 3 Jun 1877 Philadelphia)
7) **Ralph Drane** (* & + 8 Jun 1878 Philadelphia)
8) **Charles Drane** (Nov 1882 Philadelphia – 25 Jun 1883 Philadelphia)
9) **Paul** Snyder **Drane** (12 – 13 Oct 1885 Philadelphia)
10) **Herbert Drane** (Jun 1887 Williamsburg, PA – 21 Mar 1889 Philadelphia)
B) **Louisa** Jane **Drane** (ca.1837 Philadelphia – 27 Aug 1853 Phildelphia)
C) **Dr. Henry** Gustavus **Drane** (ca.1841 Philadelphia – 7 Mar 1866 Philadelphia) unm.
issue of 2nd:
D) **Alfred Drane** (Dec 1843 Philadelphia – 26 Jun 1844 Philadelphia)
E) **Margaret C Drane** (May 1845 Philadelphia – 19 Mar 1846 Philadelphia)
E) **Frank** Condie **Drane** (ca.1848 Philadelphia – ...)
   = 5 Jun 1872; **Rebecca** Moore **Snyder** (...)
   1) Maude Isobel "**Bessie**" **Drane** (ca.1874 – ...)
   2) **Frank** Condie **Drane Jr.** (ca.1877 – ...)
   3) **Edwin** Snyder **Drane** (ca.1880 – ...)
      = 29 Sep 1905; **Jessie Rainsby** (...)
   4) **Mabel** Elise **Drane** (Mar 1885 Philadelphia – 8 Aug 1886 Philadelphia)

5) **Walter** Gordon **Drane** (ca.1886 – ...)
6) **Marie Drane** (ca.1891 – ...)
II) Matilda **Ann Drane** (17 Dec 1811 Montgomery Co., MD – ..
= 12 Apr 1838 Washington, DC; **Levi Osborn** (...)
III) **Gustavus** Leuman **Drane** (7 Dec 1813 Montgomery Co. – 1867) moved to Pittsburgh area 1835
= 1839 Allegheny Co., PA; **Jane Patterson** (ca.1820 Ireland – ...)
A) **David Drane** (ca.1838)
B) **Elizabeth Drane** (ca.1843 – 1866) unm.
C) **Mary Drane** (ca.1845 – ...)
D) **William Drane** (Nov 1848 – ...)
 = ...; **Agnes ...** (ca.1847 PA – bef.1900)
 1) **Edith Drane** (ca.1879 Allegheny Co. – ...)
E) **Annie Drane** (...)
F) **Matilda Drane** (...)
G) **Charles Drane** (... – 1896) never married
H) **Henry** McClellan **Drane** (Apr 1861 – 1909)
 = ...; **Mary ...** (...)
 1) **Jane Drane** (Nov 1872 – 11 Aug 1873)
IV) **Jane Drane** (...)
 = **Hezekiah Davis** (... – 1858)
V) **Alfred Drane** (ca.1822 – 22 Dec 1879 Washington, DC) unm.

Chapter 7
The Central Kentucky Dranes
Including a migration to Boone County, Missouri

The remainder of this book will follow the numerous lines of descent from James Drane (1715–1787) of Prince George's County and his two wives, Elizabeth Tyler and Elizabeth Piles.

The senior-most line is that of his eldest son, Thomas, whose mother was the former Elizabeth Tyler. Thomas was born in either very late 1750 or in 1751, according to his death certificate which states he was 77 years old when he died in Marion County, Kentucky, in October, 1828. His wife, Martha Wells, died six months earlier.

Thomas and Martha moved their family to Kentucky in 1806 or 1807. The approximate date is known because his daughter Eleanor was born in 1806 in Maryland, but his daughter Martha was born in December, 1807, in Kentucky. Their first home in Kentucky was in Washington County, in the middle of the state. However, they later moved to neighboring Marion County after a short period.

Thomas and Martha had eleven children, all of whom lived to adulthood, an amazing feat for a frontier family. Of the eleven, all except son Richard married. Another son, Stephen, married, but he and his wife remained childless. Initially, it looked like this would be a family of all boys, as Martha gave birth to six of them in a row. However, when the girls started coming, they also did so in a stream, starting with twins, Elizabeth and Nancy, in 1803. They were followed by Eleanor and Martha, who were previously mentioned. In order of their births, they became Mrs. Isaac Pearce, Mrs. John Allen Prewitt, Mrs. Richard Brody, and Mrs. Meredith Prewitt. This family saw several cases of a set of siblings marrying another set of siblings. John Allen Prewitt and Meredith Prewitt were brothers, and their sister, Sarah, also married one of the Dranes. Furthermore, Richard Brody's sister, Bernadetta, married the youngest of the Drane siblings, James, the only boy to be born after the string of girls.

Thomas named his first son Walter after one of his own younger brothers. Walter was still living in Washington County when he married his first wife in 1807. Her name was Rachel Givens. Walter and Rachel had only three children, Thomas, Mary, and James. The younger son, James, married, but his only child, Sarah, died young.

Rachel passed away in 1857. A year later, her 70-year old widower, Walter, married a woman 22 years his junior, Jane Parent. It is not clear if Parent was her maiden name or the name of a previous husband. As she was 48 at the time, the latter is more likely. Given their ages, it is obvious Walter and Jane did not have any children together.

Walter's elder son, Thomas Givens Drane, who was born in 1809, moved a little further west to Hardin County, where he married Polly Crume. Thomas and Polly made up the difference for his brother not having any surviving children. They had nine children, seven of whom made it out of childhood. Compared to many in his family, Thomas did not live a long life, dying at age 56, but it was about the average lifespan for the area and for the time. By contrast, his widow lived to be 93, moving with their eldest daughter, Sarah McGuffin, to Oklahoma in the late 1800s.

Thomas's eldest son, another Walter, had quite the adventurous marital record. His first wedding was in the mid-1850s to Susan Paul, but she lived only another five years. We will see the Paul name a couple more times as other members of that family married junior branches of this line. Walter married a second time, around 1864, to Emily Prudence Harrell. She seems to have used Emily for all legal purposes, but was generally known as Prudy to her family and friends. That marriage ended in divorce in the 1870s. Wife number three, Susan Tucker, walked down the aisle with Walter in 1881, only to be dumped in 1890. Susan was apparently set aside for a mistress, Elizabeth Westbrook. Walter, perhaps being a little gun-shy by now, never formally married Elizabeth, but lived in a common-law situation with her for a few years in the early 1890s. Walter left Elizabeth behind when he made the trek with some of his brothers to the West Coast. There he married his last wife, Isabelle, in about 1896. They are buried together in Coquille, the Oregon town where they made their home. He died there in 1914, at the age of 79. His widow lived another thirteen years.

Through all of this, Walter racked up a total of nine children through four of the five wives. The only one not to have any was his common-law wife, Elizabeth. Before her death, first wife Susan gave birth to two sons, Pressley Harrison and Elmore. Pressley was blinded by an accident while in his 40s. He and his wife, Mary Dennis, had three children, William, Etta, and Walter. All three married after 1900 and left issue. Elmore's children were born right around the turn of the 20th

Century. They had several daughters, but only one son, Paul, who was still unmarried in the 1930 census.

Walter and his second wife, Prudy Harrell, had four children together, all boys, whom she continued raising after their divorce. The youngest son, Moses, only lived to be thirteen. The three older boys, James, Alvin, and William, all married, their children continuing on into the 1900s. Alvin's wife was interesting in that her name was Susan Paul, the same as his father's first wife. The two Susans were aunt and niece to one another.

Walter and Susan Tucker's two boys, Joseph and Charles, also married after 1900, both leaving further descendants. It was not until his last child was born, a son with his last wife, Isabelle, that he named one after himself. Walter Jr., born in 1897, died in 1957, and as a bachelor it would seem. He is buried in the same plot with his parents.

Thomas and Polly's second son was his namesake, but avoided being a Junior by having a different middle name: Walter. He also moved to Oregon, where he lived and died in Coos County. He married Emma Hamblock after getting there. They had two children, a daughter who died in infancy, and Elmore Frederick Drane, who served two terms as Mayor of Bandon, Oregon, and was known by his middle name. Frederick's death was a strange affair. He somehow managed to drive off the end of a pier into a river, but was not found for another two days. It was never fully determined if this was an accident or a suicide. He left no children.

Thomas Walter's next younger brother, James, eventually joined him in Oregon, but stopped in Missouri for a while along the way. His five children with wife Molly Gilbert were all born in Missouri or Kansas and seem to have remained there. Molly died in childbirth with the last baby, who also perished. James quickly remarried to Anna Hook McLaughlin, herself also a widow. James and Anna did not have children together, but Anna had had some with her first husband, Sam McLaughlin. The male line of his family became extinct in 1967, with the death of James's childless son, Buck; his real name was Alvin. Buck's elder brother, Louis, had two daughters. Thomas and Polly's youngest son, Philip, followed much of his family to Oregon, but he, too, left only daughters, so the Drane name does not continue in the Beaver State.

Stephen Drane was the second, but a childless, son of Thomas Drane and Martha Wells. Their third son, George, moved around in central Kentucky quite a bit during his life. But his wanderings were contained to the tri-county area of Hardin, Grayson, and Breckinridge Counties. George married twice, first to Julia Whitley, who appears to have died around 1820, and then to Polly Lawrence in 1821. George and Polly only had one child, Joseph, who moved to Mississippi and remained childless. By his first wife, however, George left eight children, including four daughters of which almost nothing is known and two sons of which only a little is known. The middle two sons, James and Judson, each married and had children, but they do not show up on the census records and any details besides the birth of these children remain a mystery.

The eldest son, Thomas Jefferson Drane, left a better trail to follow. He married twice. He divorced his first wife, Susannah Keith, after five years of marriage. After the divorce, Susannah and her two children lived with her parents. Her son was named Joseph, and there is no evidence that he had any children. Susannah's daughter had the very unusual name of Endamile. Not surprisingly, after her marriage, she was always known simply as Mrs. Bench.

Three years after the divorce, T.J. Drane married Margaret Thurman and moved southward, until finally ending up in Baton Rouge, Louisiana. Thomas and Margaret had at least two children of their own. The gaps between their wedding and the births suggest there were likely more that died in infancy. Their son, Robert, lived with his sister, Margaret, all of his life, which ended in 1935 at the age of 77. This suggests he may have had some medical or mental condition that prevented him from living on his own. He never married.

George Drane's youngest son with his first wife, Julia, was William Whitley Drane. He and his wife, Martha Baird, had a total of thirteen children, but four of them died young. Of the remaining children, four were boys who would continue the name.

Eldest son, William Henry Harrison Drane, moved his family to Holmes County, Mississippi, where most of his seven children were born. He and his wife, Elizabeth Bunnell, had two surviving sons. The elder was named Gallie Walton Drane. Gallie was probably short for Gallatin, the middle name of his uncle, but it always appears as Gallie in the records of his life. Gallie's younger brother was William Emerson Drane. Both men married after 1900 and left issue.

William Whitley Drane's second son was Albert Gallatin Drane, named for the congressman and Secretary of the Treasury whose name was very prominent in pre-Civil War politics. Albert and his wife, Katherine Henry, had eight children, including three sons, Marvin, Joseph, and Louis, who married and had children of their own. As Albert's children were born in the 1880s and '90s, their issue would all be born after 1900. Albert moved his family to Florida around the turn of the century.

Albert's next younger surviving brother was Charles Monroe Drane. Although he and his wife, Maggie Follin, had five children, they were all daughters, so the Drane name did not go any further in this line. The youngest brother, Louis, married Henrietta Just, the daughter of German immigrants, and they left three children, one of which was son Albert to carry on the name.

The fourth son of Thomas and Martha, was the life-long bachelor Richard. The fifth son, Anthony, moved to Columbia, Missouri, which is in Boone County, right after his marriage to Mercy Lawless. Anthony and Mercy had nine children, beginning with the oddly-named twins, Esafane and Parthena. They were followed by two more sisters, but consecutively this time.

Anthony's eldest son, George Thomas Drane, married twice, but only had children with his first wife, Sarah Fenton. His male line ended, though, with his son, Joseph William, who died in 1923, leaving two surviving daughters.

The senior line still existing in Columbia descends from Davis Clark Drane, Anthony and Mercy's second son. He married Anne Elizabeth Goslin in 1861. They had eight children, but only one son who still has male line descendants living, Joseph Walter Drane. Joseph Walter was generally known as Honesty Drane. Of his five children, three are sons whose marriages all took place after 1900.

The only remaining male line from this Missouri branch is through youngest son, Joseph Drane. He was married to Lucinda Goslin, Elizabeth's sister. He had an elder son, Fielden, but he and his wife, Carrie Morgan, did not have children. The younger son, Thomas Emmett, married Irene Elliott. Their children were born in the 20th Century.

The sixth son of Thomas Drane and Martha Wells is Joel Thomas Drane. After the family moved to Kentucky, he eventually made his home in Breckinridge County, a neighboring county to Hardin and Grayson. His five children would make their homes between Hardin and Breckinridge Counties.

Joel married Sarah Prewitt, a sister to John and Meredith, in 1820. They named their eldest son Meredith Prewitt Drane, after his double uncle. He and his wife, Sarah Burch, had ten children, including four sons, Joel Thomas II, John Robert, Meredith, and Lee Andrew. The youngest was always known as Bunk. All of these families remained in central Kentucky except for John Robert Drane, who moved his family to Ripley County, Missouri, near the end of the 19th century.

Joel and Sarah's second son, James Drane, married Phoebe Smith. Like James's parents, they also had four boys and a daughter. The eldest and the youngest sons, Clinton and Oscar, never married. Clinton died in the 1918 influenza pandemic, but Oscar lived on to 1929. The other two sons, unusually named Millis and Merida, both married, but it is not known if Merida left descendants or not. If he did, they would have been born after 1900.

Third son, Alvin, married Phoebe's sister, Theodocia Smith. Four of their six surviving children were sons who all married and left descendants. There was also an infant who perished. The four boys, Clarence, Vessie, Solomon, and Cleveland, all remained in Breckinridge County with their families. The second son, Vessie, had a most peculiar name. It is not known where it came from, but it does not appear to be a nickname, as it is the name listed on his death certificate and his tombstone.

Joel and Sarah's youngest son, Joel Clelland Drane, married Elizabeth Harned, but their male line became extinct in 1985 with the death of a grandson. One of their daughters, Belle, married her first cousin, the aforementioned Millis Drane.

The most junior line of this family is that of James Drane, Thomas and Martha's youngest child, who was born in 1808. As previously noted, he married Bernadetta Brody in 1829. They had five sons, two of whom, Joe and James, never married. Eldest son Elijah married twice, but his only child died in infancy. The remaining sons, George and Henry, each married and remained in Breckinridge County with their families.

Thomas Drane (ca.1751 Prince Georges Co., MD – 27 Oct 1828 Marion Co., KY)
= 4 Feb 1786 Prince Georges Co., MD; **Martha Wells** (ca.1770 – 9 Apr 1828 Marion Co.) daughter of George Wells
a. **Walter Drane** (1788 Prince George Co., MD – ...)
  =1 13 Aug 1807 Washington Co., KY; **Rachel Givens** (btw. 1772/1777 – 22 Dec 1857 Hardin Co.)
  =2 7 Mar 1858 Hardin Co[79].; **Jane Parent** (1810 Nelson Co., KY – ...)
  issue of 1st (none by 2nd):
  I) **Thomas** Givens **Drane** (22 Mar 1809 – 1865 Hardin Co.)
    = 10 Nov 1831 Hardin Co., KY; Mary (**Polly**) **Crume** (29 Sep 1813 – 19 Nov 1906 Blair, OK) daughter of William Crume & Susanna Jones
    A) **Sarah** Emmaline **Drane** (10 Nov 1833 KY – 17 Oct 1906 Blair, OK)
      = 19 Mar 1854 Hardin Co. KY; **Halen McGuffin** (1813 – 1890) son of Samuel McGuffin & Sarah ...
    B) **Walter Drane** (22 Sep 1834 KY – 17 Mar 1914 Coquille, OR[80])
      =1 ...; **Susan Paul** (ca.1838 – 28 Mar 1860) daughter of Thomas Paul & Mary Taylor
      =2 ca.1864 (dv.) Emily **Prudence Harrell** (29 Sep 1847 – 16 Jan 1921) daughter of Moses Harrell & Catherine Duncan
      =3 21 Feb 1881 (dv.1890) **Susan** Janet **Tucker** (Nov 1846 – 1928 Pine, MO) daughter of James Tucker; =1st John Hay
      =4 (common law from 1890) **Elizabeth Westbrook** (...)
      =5 ca.1896; **Isabelle ...** (1851 – 1927[81])
      issue of 1st:
      1) **Pressley** Harrison **Drane** (30 Apr 1857 Leitchfield, KY – 5 Apr 1943 Mt. Hebron, KY) blinded by an explosion in his 40s
        = ...; **Mary** Jane **Dennis** (25 Sep 1864 – 8 Feb 1948) daughter of John Dennis & Nancy Woodruff
        a) **William** Thomas **Drane** (11 Apr 1884 Grayson Co. – 6 Sep 1952 Leitchfield)
          = 19 Nov 1905 Grayson; **Viola Richardson** (14 Dec 1889

---

[79] Marriage certificate confirmed Walter's date of birth. Sources giving a date of death for him in 1834 are clearly incorrect.
[80] Col. in KY Calvary according to Tombstone.
[81] Buried with Walter at Masonic Cemetery, Coquille, OR.

Grayson Co. – 6 Dec 1989 Leitchfield) daughter of James Richardson & Amanda Conder
has issue
 b) **Etta** Lillian **Drane** (29 Mar 1886 – 14 Jan 1968 Grayson Co.)
 =20 Mar 1904 Grayson, KY; **Sye** Wesley **Dennis** (12 Jun 1880 Hart Co., KY – 16 May 1968 Grayson Co.) son of Bud Dennis & Nancy Huff
 c) **Walter** Elliott **Drane** (ca.1892 – ca.1961)
 = ...; **Emily** Ann **Mattingly** (28 Apr 1895 Grayson Co. – 6 Mar 1952 Grayson Co.) daugher of John Mattingly & Rebecca Miller
has issue
2) **Elmore Drane** (Mar 1859 Hardin Co. – ...)
= ca.1893; **Wessie Jones** (Jun 1875 KY – ...) daughter of ... Jones & Belle ...
 a) **Una Drane** (Oct 1894 Hardin Co. – ...)
 b) **Ina Drane** (Mar 1899 Hardin Co. – ...)
 c) **Paul Drane** (ca.1902 Hardin Co. – ...)
 d) **Juanita Drane** (ca.1904 Hardin Co. – ...)
issue of 2nd:
3) **James** Robert **Drane** (3 Feb 1867 Eveleigh, KY – 25 Jan 1954 Leitchfield)
= 23 Aug 1900 Grayson; Susan (**Sudie**) **Eveleigh** (29 Sep 1867 Bloomfield, IN – 20 Feb 1920 Breckenridge Co., KY) daughter of William Eveleigh & Katharine Duncan
has issue
4) **Alvin H Drane** (14 Jan 1868 Eveleigh, KY – 5 Jan 1933 Grayson)
= 26 Oct 1890 Grayson, KY; **Susan Paul** (26 Oct 1870 Grayson – 1948)
 a) **Marvin Drane** (19 Aug 1896 Grayson – 3 Aug 1959)
 = ...; **Anna** Mae **Glasscock** (ca.1891 – ...) daughter of Samuel Glasscock & Ida Langley
 has issue
5) **William** Thomas **Drane** (24 Aug 1869 – 15 Jun 1943 Leitchfield)
= 1 Nov 1891; **Amy E Adams** (9 May 1869 – 8 Jan 1956 Leitchfield) daughter of James Adams & Laura Barnes
 a) **Nova J Drane** (18 Nov 1892 – 6 Sep 1970 Hardin Co.)
 = 11 Jan 1914; **Hubbard Conklin** (1889 – 21 Mar 1960) son

of Robert Conlin & Elizabeth Mattingly
- b) **Carl** Bryant **Drane** (18 Oct 1896 Grayson, KY – 5 Oct 1982 Leitchfield)
  = 21 Apr 1918; **Naomi Houk** (5 Feb 1899 – 2 May 1989 Grayson Co.)
  no issue
- 6) **Moses** Lloyd **Drane** (7 Nov 1873 – 30 Sep 1888 Grayson[82]) issue of 3rd (none by 4th):
- 7) **Joseph Drane** (11 Apr 1885 Pine, MO – 10 May 1965 Pine[83])
  = 1 Aug 1909; **Alice Tipton** (25 Oct 1890 Hardin Springs, KY – 9 Nov 1970 Jefferson City, MO) daughter of John Tipton & Nancy Johnson
  has issue
- 8) **Charles** Naylor **Drane** (27 Mar 1890 Butler Co., MO – 17 Jul 1954 Ripley Co.)
  = ...; **Mima** Artemicia **Looney** (20 May 1886 – 8 Dec 1986 Ripley Co.) daughter of William Looney & Caldonia Simmons
  has issue
  issue of 5th:
- 9) **Walter L Drane** (16 Sep 1897 –25 Jun 1977 Portland, OR[84])
- C) **Martha** Ann **Drane** (21 Oct 1836 Hardin Springs, KY – 17 Feb 1914 Jackson Co., OK)
  = ca.1859; **Capt. Samuel Sands** (ca.1810 – ca.1890)
- D) **Rachel** Catherine **Drane** (29 Nov 1837 Breckenridge Co., KY – 4 Jan 1925 Ellis Co., OK)
  = 26 Feb 1857 Hardin Springs, KY; **Hiram Leslie** (6 Feb 1832 KY – 16 Sep 1890 Girard, OK) son of Peter Leslie
- E) **Burnetta Drane** (24 Jun 1841 Hardin Springs, KY – ...)
- F) **Thomas** Walter **Drane** (23 Oct 1844 Hardin Springs, KY – 28 Aug 1917 Greer, OR) lived in Coos Co., OR
  = 30 Dec 1885 OR; **Emma Hamblock** (14 Feb 1858 MO – 28 Sep 1947 Coquille, OR)
  - 1) Elmore **Frederick Drane** (27 Oct 1886 Parkersburg, OR – 4 Nov 1935 Bandon, OR[85]) served two terms as Mayor of

---

[82] Date of birth and name of mother given in obituary in Grayson County Gazette 26 Oct 1888.
[83] Buried Pine Cemetery, Pine, MO, with much of his family.
[84] Buried Willamette National Cemetery, Clackamas, OR.
[85] Died by driving off a pier. Was found a few days later.

Bandon
= 16 Aug 1914; Bandon, **Maude Newton** (Sep 1882 – 29 May 1986 Santa Rosa, CA)
no issue
2) **Mary** Cora **Drane** (31 Jan – 6 Apr 1889 Parkersburg, OR)
G) **James** N **Drain**[86] (9 Dec 1848 Hardin Springs, KY – 11 Jun 1902 Coquille, OR)
=1 6 Jul 1869 Cherokee Co., KY; Mary (**Molly**) **Gilbert** (1843–1880) daughter of Samuel Gilbert & Elizabeth Daughtery; =1st
... Reardin
=2 aft.1880; **Anna Hook** (...) daughter of ...; =1st Samuel McLaughlin
issue of 1st (none by 2nd):
1) **Louis C Drane** (1870 MO – 1940 Zincite, MO)
=1 ...; **Minnie** Mae **Pierce** (...)
=2 ...; **Isabelle** ... (...) =2nd ... Earl
issue of 1st (none by 2nd):
a) **Madelyn** Alice **Drane** (18 Feb 1892 Zincite, MO – ...)
=1 **Frank Bock** (...)
=2 **Clifford Gallops** (...)
=3 **James van Zant** (...)
b) **Gladys** Dora **Drane** (...)
=1 **Raymond Weideman** (...)
=2 **Joseph Chumley** (...)
=3 **... Harris** (...)
2) **Olive L Drane** (1872 KS – ...)
= 18 May 1888 Sabastian, KS; **George Roddin** (...)
3) Alvin (**Buck**) **Drane** (27 Dec 1873 KS – 21 Feb 1967[87])
= 12 Nov 1894; **Elizabeth Mahollan** (...)
4) Martha Salina (**Mattie**) **Drane** (5 Apr 1877 Galena, KS – 5 Aug 1961 CA)
= 19 Jan 1898; (her first cousin) **James** Walter **McGuffin** (12 Jan 1863 Breckenridge Co., KY – 13 Oct 1947 CA) son of Halin McGuffin & Sarah Drane
5) a child (b & d.1880)
H) **Silas H Drane** (15 Jun 1852 Hardin Springs, KY – bef.1860)
I) **Philip** Elmore **Drane** (23 Oct 1854 Hardin Springs, KY – 27 Oct 1931 Coquille, OR) moved to Oregon 1873

---

[86] Appears to be the only member of this line to use the Drain spelling. 1880 Census: Coffeyville, Prince George Co., KS.
[87] Buried in Union Chapel Cemetery, Galena, KS.

=1 1877 Coos Co., OR; **Isabelle W Smith** (ca.1851 CA – aft.1925) daughter of Joseph Smith & Hannah Hambrock; =1st Russell Pike
=2 ca.1929; **Ada C. Goldsborough** (... – 29 Nov 1931) =1st ... Currer; =2nd Thomas Barklow
issue of 1st (none by 2nd):
   1) **Mary Drane** (Feb 1878 – 26 Jul 1958 Indianapolis, IN)
      = **Benjamin** Franklin **Lawrence** (...) some-time editor of the *Indianapolis Star*
   2) **Julia Drane** (Oct 1880 – ...)
      = **E E Johnson** (...)
II) **Mary Drane** (ca. 1810 – ...)
= 30 Dec 1833 **John Pilburn** (1833 – ...)
III) **James Drane** (1812 – ca.1880)
= ...; **Martha Durham** (...)
   A) **Sarah Drane** (ca.1858 Hardin Co. – ...)
b. **Stephen Drane** (ca.1788 Prince George Co., MD – ...) living in Breckenridge Co., KY 1830
= 3 Dec 1818 Washington Co., KY; **Nancy** Pearce **Lawless** (ca.1793 – ...)
no issue
c. **George** Thomas **Drane** (27 Aug 1789 Prince George Co., MD – aft.1840) living in Breckenridge Co. KY 1840
=1 ...; **Julia Whitley** (ca.1795 – bef.1821)
=2 9 Jan 1821 Washington Co., KY; **Polly Lawrence** (ca.1789 –...)
issue of 1st:
I) **Martha Drane** (...)
II) **Mary Drane** (...)
   = **... Stone** (...)
III) **Julia Drane** (...)
   = **... Gibson** (...)
IV) **Sarah Drane** (...)[88]
V) **Rev. Thomas** Jefferson **Drane**[89] (30 Nov 1813 Lebanon, KY – 16 Oct 1895 Baton Rouge, LA[90])
=1 6 Feb 1831 Hardin Co., KY (dv.1836); **Susannah Keith** (1815 – 1883) daughter of Benjamin Keith & Ruamy Waters

---

[88] In a letter from her niece to another researcher, Sarah was said to have married a Presbyterian minister and had two sons, the elder of whom also became a minister.
[89] 1880 Census: Polk Co. NE.
[90] Buried in Roselawn Memorial Park, Baton Rouge, LA.

=2 29 May 1838 Marion Co., KY; **Margaret** Ann **Thurman** (11 Feb 1819 England – 12 Mar 1889[91])
issue of 1st:
A) **Joseph Drane** (ca.1832 – ...)
   = 10 Sep 1854 Meade Co.; **Sarah Herrington** (...)
   issue ?
B) **Endamile Drane** (ca.1833 KY – ...)
   = 20 Aug 1854 Meade Co.; **Ferdinand Bench** (...)
   issue of 2nd:
C) **Margaret** Ann **Drane** (4 Aug 1846 KY – 8 Nov 1924 Baton Rouge, LA)
   = ca.1863; **George H Tichenor** (12 Apr 1837 – 14 Jan 1923 Baton Rouge)
D) **Robert L Drane** (7 Mar 1858 TN – 6 Mar 1935 Baton Rouge)
VI) **James S Drane** (...)
= ...
A) **Emily Drane** (May 1857 KY – ...) (twin)
B) **Harriet B Drane** (May – Dec 1857 KY) (twin)
C) **Samuel Drane** (Feb 1858 KY – ...)
D) **Harriet Drane** (15 Jul 1859 KY – ...)
VII) **Judson S Drane** (...)
= ...
A) **Nelson Drane** (12 Jan 1855 Barren Co. – ...)
B) **Eliza Ann Drane** (15 Sep 1855 Barren Co. – ...)
C) **Seth Drane** (23 Dec 1857 Barren Co. – ...)
VIII) **William** Whitley **Drane** (ca.1816 Barren Co. – ...)
   = **Martha** Jane **Baird** (ca.1826 – ...)
A) **George** Christopher **Drane** (+ inf)
B) **Christopher** Columbus **Drane** (+ inf)
C) **Mary** Jane **Drane** (ca.1840 KY – bef.1915)
   = **Daniel** Slaughter **Fouchee** (... – bef.1915)
D) **William** Henry Harrison **Drane**[92] (6 Feb 1842 Louisvillie, KY – 1 Jun 1905 Holmes Co., MS[93])
   = 18 Feb 1868 Louisville; Susan **Elizabeth Bunnell** (1851 KY – 1903 Holmes Co.)
   1) **John W Drane** (ca.1870 KY – ...) [possibly +young]
   2) **Elnora** Catherine **Drane** (25 Nov 1878 Bowling Green, KY – 16 Mar 1905 Holmes Co.)

---

[91] Buried in Roselawn Memorial Park, Baton Rouge, LA.
[92] 1880 Census: Hardyville, Hart Co. KY.
[93] Buried in Mitzpah Cemetery, Durant, MS.

3) **Gallie** Walton **Drane Sr.** (25 Jul 1880 Louisville – 1951 Holmes Co.)
= 1911; **Rowena Bankhead** (1887 – 1976) daughter of Thomas Bankhead & Minnie Verner
has issue
4) **Burdie Drane** (20 Sep 1884 Holmes Co. – ...)
5) **William** Emerson **Drane** (14 Mar 1885 Louisville – 1951 Delaware Co., PA)
= 12 Dec 1923 Philadelphia; **Lenora Evans** (31 Aug 1890 Philadelphia – 1976 Swainton, NJ)
has issue
6) **Henrietta Drane** (6 Jan 1887 Louisville – May 1969 Jones Co., MS)
7) **Viola Drane** (Apr 1890 Durant, MS – ...)

E) **Albert** Gallatin **Drane**[94] (11 Feb 1845 – 4 Aug 1918 FL[95])
= 9 Oct 1880 Glasgow, KY; **Katherine Henry** (ca.1850 – 24 Oct 1909 St. Petersburg, FL) daughter of James Henry; =1st ... Depp
1) **Samuel R Drane** (Jul 1882 – 16 Aug 1935)
2) Charles **Marvin Drane** (Dec 1883 – 5 Feb 1945 New Orleans)
= ...; **Marie Alberte** (...)
3) **Ida** May **Drane** (Dec 1885 – ...)
= 12 Sep 1906 Glasgow; **C L Lutz** (...)
4) **Sallie** Mattie **Drane** (Jun 1886 – ...)
= ...; **B B Hagan** (...)
5) **Edith W Drane** (Jan 1888 KY – ...)
= ...; **Walter Johnson** (...)
6) **Nellie B Drane** (Mar 1890 – ...)
= ...; **Harold Pascoe** (...)
7) **Joseph** Russell **Drane** (16 Mar 1893 KY – 20 May 1976 St. Petersburg)
= ...; **Estelle Coachman** (1894 – 1980)
has issue
8) **Louis** Edwin **Drane** (4 Apr 1895 Glasgow, KY – 14 Dec 1865 Savannah, GA)
= 26 Sep 1921 Isle of Hope, GA; Clifford Jane (**Martha**) **Washington** (16 Jan 1904 Savannah – 13 Feb 1934 Savannah) daughter of ... Washington & Leonora Byrd

---

[94] 1880 Census: with brother in home of John Leach, Barren Co. KY.
[95] Buried in Royal Palm South Cemetery, St. Petersburg, FL.

has issue
F) **Martha** Jane **Drane** (ca.1847 KY – bef.1915) dunm.
G) Virginia Crittenden (**Birdie**) **Drane** (ca.1849 KY – aft.1915)
 = 16 Jul 1872 Glasgow; **L P Beck** (...)
H) **George** Washington **Drane** (Feb 1852 Barren Co. – ...)
I) Arabella (**Belle**) Rogers **Drane** (Mar 1853 KY – aft. 1915)
 = **Elizer Warder** (...)
J) **Clelland Drane** (15 Jun 1854 Barren Co – ...)
K) **Charles** Monroe **Drane** (ca.1855 Grayson Co., KY – ...)
 = 14 Sep 1892; **Maggie M Follin** (20 May 1871 – ...) daughter of William Follin & Virginia Neel
 1) **Lorena Drane** (14 Jun 1893 – ...)
 2) **Lalla E Drane** (12 Sep 1894 – ...)
 3) **Stella M Drane** (4 Jul 1896 – ...)
 4) **Hazel G Drane** (Apr 1898 – ...)
 5) **Virginia Drane** (...)
L) James **Louis Drane** (14 Aug 1856 Grayson Co. – aft. 1915)
 = ca.1876; **Henrietta Just** (Feb 1862 KY – ...)
 1) **Birdie Drane** (Jun 1880 Louisville – ...)
 2) **Edith Drane** (Sep 1882 Louisville – ...)
 3) **Albert Drane** (Mar 1896 Louisville – ...)
M) **Ida** May **Drane** (ca.1859 KY – ...)
 = aft.1880; **Richard Rolling** (...)
issue of 2nd:
IX) **Joseph N Drane** (ca.1827 – aft.1880)
 = 21 Sep 1848; **Cecilia Cully** (29 Jun 1824 Mumfordville, KY – 28 Dec 1886[96] Holmes Co.)
 no issue
d. **Richard Drane** (ca.1790 VA – aft.1850)
e. **Anthony Drane** (14 Jul 1791 Prince George Co. – 10 Oct 1875 Harrisburg, MO[97])
 = 2 Sep 1822 Washington Co. KY; **Mercy Lawless** (8 Jan 1800 KY – 31 Jul 1885 Boone Co. MO)
 I) **Esifane Drane** (13 Sep 1823 Boone Co. – 1855 Knox Co.) (twin)
 = 8 Nov 1841 Boone Co.; **David March** (ca.1818 KY – 1870 Knox Co. MO) son of Absalam March & Elizabeth Brandenburg
 II) **Parthena Drane** (13 Sep 1823 Boone Co. – 24 Oct 1901 Audrain Co.) (twin)

---

[96] Buried in Durant Cemetery, Holmes Co., MS.
[97] Buried in Bethlehem Cemetery, Harrisburg, MO.

= 8 Nov 1841 Boone Co.; **Nicholas Long** (19 Jan 1819 MO – 12 Sep 1909 Audrain Co. MO) son of Daniel Long & Elizabeth ...

III) **Salina Drane** (22 Oct 1825 Boone Co. – 26 Jan 1874 Boon Co.)
= 10 Jun 1847 Boone Co.; **James** Harvey **Petty** (... – 1860's[98])
= ...; (her brother-in-law) **Perry Petty** (...)

IV) **Sarah** Adeline **Drane** (5 May 1831 Boone Co. – 3 Oct 1910 MO)
= 4 Nov 1847 Boone Co.; **James Fenton** (5 Jun 1820 Fleming Co., KY – 5 Feb 1869 Boone Co.) son of William Fenton & Lucinda Stice

V) **George** Thomas **Drane** (4 Oct 1834 Boone Co. – 29 Jan 1919 Boone Co.)
=1 12 Mar 1857 Hinton, MO; **Sarah** Ann **Fenton** (1 Aug 1839 Boone Co. – 17 Jul 1886 Boone Co.) daughter of Caleb Fenton & Lettice Foster
=2 ca.1888; **Mary** ... (Mar 1845 KY – ...)
issue of 1st (none by 2nd):
  A) Joseph **William Drane** (11 Aug 1858 Boone Co. – 20 Feb 1923 Boone Co.)
   = 30 Jun 1879 Hinton, MO; **Julie Purcell** (2 Oct 1853 KY – 22 Feb 1929 Boone Co.) daughter of Cyrus Purcell & Charlotte Temple
   1) **Mattie Drane** (25 Oct 1880 – Mar 1970)
     = ...; **Cliff Ketchum** (...)
   2) a daugher (b & d.9 May 1882 Boone Co.)
   3) **Mamie Drane** (27 Oct 1886 – Mar 1977 St. Louis, MO)
     = ...; **Deck** Lemie **Long** (...)
  B) **Lettice Drane** (12 Oct 1860 Harrisburg, MO – 22 Jul 1934 MO)
   = 10 Oct 1876 Hinton; **James** Andrew Jackson **Watson** (31 Jan 1836 Dearfield, VA – 10 Dec 1940 Harrisburg)
  C) **Salina** Dorsey **Drane** (13 Jul 1863 Boone Co. – 21 Feb 1932 Boone Co.)
   = 12 Oct 1882 Boone Co.; **George** Washington **Denham** (11 Nov 1848 Rocheport, MO – 21 Jan 1929 Columbia, MO) son of Samuel Denham & Catherine Toalson

VI) Davis **Clark Drane** (10 Oct 1836 Boone Co. – 12 Jul 1922 Boone Co.)
= 4 Apr 1861 Boone Co.; Anne **Elizabeth Goslin** (27 Oct 1839

---

[98] Killed during a Civil War prisoner exchange.

Boone Co. – 25 Dec 1915 Boone Co.) daughter of Rueben Goslin & Mary Davenport

A) **James** Newton **Drane** (1 Jan 1863 Boone Co. – 2 Dec 1938 Monroe Co., MO)
= 25 Dec 1890; **Anna** Florence **Tinder** (13 Aug 1867 Andrews Co., MO – 24 May 1910 Monroe Co.) daughter of James Tinder & Eliza Thompson
  1) **Myrtle Drane** (8 Aug 1893 – 12 Oct 1949)
    = ...; **Roy** Francis **Rumans** (...)
  2) **Estelle Drane** (8 Feb 1900 – 1976 Mobley, MO)
    =1 ... (dv.1926); ... **Riley** (...)
    =2 ...; ... **Thompson** (...)
    =3 ...; ... **Milby** (...)
    =4 ...; **Roscoe Ornburn** (...)

B) **Mecy Drane** (13 Jul 1864 Boone Co. – 19 Aug 1937)
= 6 Nov 1884 Hinton; Andrew **Bluford Fenton** (12 Sep 1862 Boone Co. – 25 Mar 1932 Boone Co.) son of William Fenton & Lucinda Stice

C) **Mary Drane** (1867 Boone Co. – shortly after Sept 1915)
  =1 ...; **Judson Lyons** (...)
  =2 ...; **Price Buckler** (...)

D) Joseph Walter (**Honesty**) **Drane** (25 Mar 1869 Boone Co. – 20 Mar 1948 Boone Co.)
= ca.1898; Carrie **Effie Little** (22 Apr 1871 – 13 Jan 1950 Centralia, MO) daughter of Josiah Little & Nancy Elliott
  1) **Winnie** Ruth **Drane** (30 Sep 1899 Boone Co. – 28 Mar 1998 Boone Co.)
    = 20 Feb 1919 Columbia, MO; **John** Wesley **Bell** (23 Jul 1891 Rocheport, MO – 13 Mar 1970 Columbia, MO) son of John Bell & Osie Potts
  2) **Joseph** Clark **Drane** (2 Nov 1901 Boone Co. – 22 Aug 1975 Boone Co.)
    = 20 Nov 1920; **Mary** Francis **Dinkle** (3 Dec 1903 – 12 Jun 1999 Boone Co.) daughter of Thomas Dinkle & Belle Smith
    has issue
  3) **Oren** Glenn **Drane** (7 Oct 1903 Boone Co. – 29 Dec 1990 Boone Co.)
    = 23 Oct 1921; **Anna Semon** (22 Nov 1902 – 5 Dec 1990 Boone Co.) daughter of William Semon & Lydia McKinley
    has issue
  4) Mary Ethel (**Jean**) **Drane** (6 Nov 1905 Boone Co. – 17 Jun

2003 Boone Co.)
   = Jun 1933; **Samuel** Emerson **Rees** (4 Jul 1902 – 13 Dec 1996 Boone Co.) son of Thomas Rees & Eliza Gladwell
  5) James **Edgar Drane** (3 Nov 1907 Boone Co. – 29 Apr 2004 Boone Co.)
   = 1 Oct 1934 Fulton, MO; **Mary** Margaret **Norvell** (13 Nov 1907 – 16 Nov 1990 Boone Co.) daughter of John Norvell & Sarah Stevens
   has issue
 E) **Honor Drane** (23 Oct 1873 – 21 Jul 1874)
 F) **Benjamin Drane** (15 Mar 1874 – 19 Nov 1877)
 G) **Maude Drane** (9 Jan 1876 Boone Co. – 14 Jun 1966)
  = 1900; **George W Potter** (...)
 H) **Cora Drane** (Nov 1877 – aft.1939)
  = ...; **Benjamin** Thomas **Goslin** (20 Oct 1874 – 16 Mar 1943) son of Benjmain Goslin & Mary West
VII) **James** R **Drane** (1839 Boone Co. – 1866 Alton, IL) served in the CSA Calvary, died as a POW
VIII) **Dicy** E **Drane** (4 Oct 1842 Boone Co. – 5 Sep 1873 Boone Co.)
  = 9 Nov 1865 Howard Co., MO; **Francis Dejarnette** (1830 Boone Co. – 1932) son of Isaac Dejarnette & Mahala Boyce
IX) **Joseph** W **Drane** (27 Oct 1844 Boone Co. – 1 May 1916 Boone Co.)
  = ca.1869; **Lucinda Goslin** (3 Mar 1846 Boone Co. – 4 Feb 1923 Boone Co.) daughter of Rueben Goslin & Elizabeth Davenport
 A) **Fielden** David **Drane** (3 Aug 1870 Boone Co. – 8 Apr 1931 Kansas City, MO)
  = ...; **Carrie** Martha **Morgan** (23 Aug 1876 Boone Co. – 20 Jul 1953 Kansas City) daughter of William Morgan & Lucy Peacher
  no issue
 B) **Mary** Alice **Drane** (25 Aug 1876 Boone Co. – 26 Jan 1968 Boone Co.)
  = ...; **Harry H Keithley** (25 Aug 1876[99] MO – 10 Jan 1918 Mobley) son of Thomas Keithley & Julia Meade
 C) Thomas **Emmett Drane** (15 Apr 1878 Boone Co. – 8 Jun 1954 Boone Co.)
  = 2 Aug 1909 Boone Co.; **Irene Elliott** (21 Sep 1884 Boone

---

[99] According to their joint tombstone, both Mary and Keith were born on the same day: 25 Aug 1876.

Co. – 27 Aug 1969 Boone Co.) daughter of Fielden Elliott & Sophia Hofstetter
has issue

f. **Joel** Thomas **Drane** (4 May 1797 Prince George Co. – 17 Oct 1846 Breckinridge Co.)
= 4 Sep 1820 Washington Co.; **Sarah Prewitt** (28 Feb 1800 VA – 6 Jul 1869 Breckinridge Co.)

I) **Meredith** Prewitt **Drane** (9 Jan 1824 Hardin Co. – 1 Feb 1907 Breckinridge Co.)
= ca.1849; **Sarah Burch** (18 Jan 1830 – 8 Jan 1901)

A) **Ruanne** Catherine **Drane** (26 Sep 1850 Breckinridge Co. – 28 Jun 1899 Grayson Co.)
= 21 Aug 1871 Hardin Co.; **Jerry** Wellington **Calvert** (22 Sep 1850 Hardin Co. – 1 May 1925 Hardin Co.) son of Elijah Calvert & Hannh Litsey

B) **Bernetta Drane** (ca.1853 – ca.1870)

C) **Joel** Thomas **Drane** (8 Feb 1855 Breckinridge Co. – 20 Sep 1905)
= ca.1874; **Sarah** Jane **Gregory**[100] (Mar 1857 KY – ...)

1) **Hollis Drane** (Nov 1877 Breckinridge CO. – ...)
= ...; **Nannie ...** (ca.1885 – ...)
no issue

2) **William** Robert **Drane** (2 Apr 1880 Hudson, KY – 5 Sep 1944 Louisville)
= 3 Aug 1898 Constantine, KY; **Pearl McGuffin** (3 Aug 1880 Constantine – 2 Apr 1954 Louisville)

a) **Wilma Drane** (12 Jul 1899 Hudson, KY – 17 Jun 1967 Dallas, TX)
= ...; **Stephen** George **Steimer** (20 Jun 1896 Beaver Falls, PA – ...)

3) **Arthur Drane** (Oct 1882 Breckinridge Co. – ...)
4) **Thurman Drane** (Jan 1884 Breckinridge Co. – ...)
5) **Owen Drane** (Jul 1887 Breckinridge Co. – ...)
6) **Vernon Drane** (Oct 1893 Breckenridge Co. – ...)
7) **Hobert Drane** (Oct 1897 Breckinridge Co. – ...)

D) **John** Robert **Drane**[101] (2 Feb 1856 Hardin Co., KY – 3 Mar 1940 Doniphan, MO)
= ca.1878; **Martha** Jane **Stone** (26 Jun 1856 Hardin Co. – 2 Jan

---

[100] According to the 1900 Census, Sarah had had 9 children, 8 of whom were then alive.
[101] 1880 Census: Hudsonville, Breckinridge Co.

1941 Bardley, MO)
1) **Pearl Drane** (ca.1879 Breckinridge Co., KY – ...)
2) **Elijah** Lee **Drane** (13 Sep 1888 – 4 Jan 1950)
   = ...; **Ida Kelly** (24 Dec 1887 – 19 Jun 1965)
   has issue
3) **Clifford** Ellis **Drane** (24 May 1895–8 Sep 1970 Ripley Co.)
   =1 ...; **Della** Leona **Drew** (1 Aug 1898 IL – 26 Jan 1922 Ripley Co.) daughter of George Drew & Emma Duncan =2 aft. 1922; (his sister-in-law) **Naomi** Ruth **Drew** (1 Jan 1908 – 12 Nov 1972) daughter of George Drew & Emma Duncan; =1st ... Stone
   has issue
4) **John Drane** (1898 – 1963)
   = ...; **Carrie** Lee ... (1905 – 1966)
   has issue
E) **Elina Drane** (ca.1857 – aft.1860)
F) **Della Drane** (ca.1859 – aft.1860)
G) **Meredith Drane** (Jun 1863 KY – 1940 Hardin Co., KY)
=1 ...; ...
=2 24 Jan 1894; Samira **Alice Perry** (5 Apr 1873–21 Jan 1903)
=3 ca.1906; **Viola** ... (ca.1872 – ...)
issue of 1st :
1) **Neppie Drane** (Apr 1886 Breckinridge Co. – ...)
issue of 2nd:
2) **Homer Drane** (Oct 1896 Breckinridge Co. – 16 Jun 1955 Hardin Co.)
3) **Ida Drane** (Feb 1899 Breckinridge Co. – ...)
4) **Sudie** Ethel **Drane** (5 Aug 1900 Breckinridge Co. – 30 Apr 1970 Grayson Co.)
   = ...; Charles Kendrick (**Bud**) **Harris** (28 May 1894 Grayson Co. – 6 May 1964 Grayson Co.) son of John Harris & Mary Collard
issue of 3rd:
5) **Gilbert Drane** (ca.1907 Breckinridge Co. – ...)
H) Lee Andrew (**Bunk**) **Drane** (16 Jul 1865 Hardin Co. – 22 Feb 1948 Hardin Co.)
= 6 May 1900 Hardin Co.; **Mattie McDonald** (5 May 1872 Hardin Co. – 4 May 1943 Hardin Co.)
has issue
I) Minerva **Sarah Drane** (ca.1867 – ...)
J) **Ellen Drane** (ca.1873 – ...)

II) **Susan Drane** (1828 KY – ...)
III) **James R Drane** (14 Dec 1834 KY – 21 Jul 1911)
  = 14 Jan 1859 Breckinridge Co.; **Phoebe Smith** (Oct 1841 KY – ...)
  A) **Clinton Drane** (9 Jul 1860 KY – 4 Apr 1918)
  B) **Millis Drane** (May 1862 KY – 1944 Breckinridge Co.)
    =1 3 Apr 1882 Breckinridhe Co.; **Margaret Carman** (...)
    =2 ca.1891; (his first cousin) Celina **Belle Drane** (Mar 1872 – 1945 Breckinridge Co.) daughter of Clelland Drane & Elizabeth Harned *see below*
    issue of 1st:
    1) **Charles Drane** (Dec 1884 KY – ...)
      = 12 Jul 1906 Breckinrdige Co.; **Estella West** (...)
      has issue
    2) **Clint Drane** (Aug 1885 KY – ...)
      = ...; **Ivy Probus** (ca.1892 KY – ...)
      has issue
    issue of 2nd:
    3) **Cova Drane** (Aug 1893 Breckinridge Co. – 1974)
      = 20 Jul 1910 Breckinridge Co.; **Charles West** (1882 – 1976)
    4) **John Drane** (Jun 1898 Breckinridge Co. – ...)
  C) Daniel **Merida Drane** (ca.1864 KY – 1938 Breckinridge Co.)
    = ...; **Viola Keesee** (1869 – 16 Jun 1951 Breckinrdige Co.) daughter of William Keesee & Jane Prewitt
    issue ?
  D) **Sarah Drane** (1868 KY – ...)
    = 7 Sep 1884 Breckinridge Co.; **Alfred Carman** (1860 – ...)
  E) **Oscar Drane** (21 Feb 1871 KY – 16 Jan 1929) unm.
IV) **Alvin Drane** (Oct 1836 Marion Co., KY – bef.1910)
  = 14 Jan 1869 Breckenridge Co., KY; **Theodocia Smith**[102] (Jan 1850 KY – 2 Sep 1918 Breckinrdige Co.) daughter of John Smith & Polly Milam
  A) **Della Drane** (1870 KY – 1961 Breckenridge Co.)
  B) **Clarence Drane** (Oct 1871 KY – 21 May 1950 Breckinridge Co.)
    = aft.1900; ... (+bef.1910)
    has issue
  C) **Vessie Drane** (5 Jun 1873 KY – 22 May 1953 Breckinridge Co.)

---

[102] According to the 1900 Census, Theodocia had a 7th child who was dead by that time.

= ca.1898; **Palestine** ... (1870 – 1961)
1) **Victor Drane** (1 Oct 1898 – Oct 1970 Kansas City, MO)
   = ...; **Fanny Dyer** (...)
   has issue
2) **Verbal Drane** (...) [dau]
   = ...; **Cline Bruner** (...)
3) **Hallie Drane** (...)
   = ...; **Alvin Patterson** (...)
4) **Rhua Drane** (...)
   = ...; **Harold Dyer** (...)
5) Kirby (**Jack**) **Drane** (25 Mar 1907 – Dec 1964)
   = ...; **Clara Lucas** (...)
   has issue
6) **Bob Drane** (7 May 1908 Breckinridge Co. – 28 Mar 1980 Breckinrdige Co.)
   = 6 Oct 1924; **Vitula Meador** (5 Mar 1910 – 2 Oct 2002 Garfield, KY) daughter of George Meador & Eliza Elliott
   has issue
7) **Edna Drane** (...)
   =1 ...; **Roy West** (...)
   =2 ...; **William Henninger** (...)
8) **Coleman Drane** (16 Apr 1910 – 13 Apr 1984)
   = ...; **Gladys Dyer** (...)
   has issue
D) **Effie Drane** (Mar 1876 KY – ...)
E) **Solomon Drane** (15 Oct 1881[103] KY – ...)
   = 6 Feb 1907 Breckinridge Co.; **Mattie Fentress** (ca.1892 – ...)
   has issue
F) **Cleveland Drane** (22 May 1884 KY – ...) served in World War I
   = 19 Dec 1904 Breckinridge Co., KY; **Celia Smiley** (1886 – ...) daughter of A.A. Smiley & Belle ...
   has issue
V) Joel **Clelland Drane** (4 May 1840 Breckinridge Co., KY – 16 Feb 1900)
   = 11 Jul 1867 Breckinridge Co., KY; **Elizabeth Harned** (3 Jul 1850 Breckinridge Co. – 11 Feb 1892) daughter of John Harned & Elizabeth Duncan
   A) Celina **Belle Drane** (ca.1870 KY – 1945 Breckinridge Co.)

---

[103] Solomon and his brothers Vessie and Cleveland signed up for military the same day: 12 Sep 1918 to fight in World War I.

    = ca.1891; **Millis Drane** (1862 – 1944)
see above
  B) **Essie Drane** (ca.1873 KY – ...)
    = ca.1898; **John Lymes** (Aug 1853 IL – ...)
    issue by...:
    1) **Henry Drane** (Jul 1893 Breckinridge Co. – ...)
  C) Martha **Parthenia Drane** (2 Oct1875 Breckinridge Co. – 14 Jun 1922 Hardin Co.)
    = ...; William **Howell Nall** (8 Nov 1861 Hardin Co. – Dec 1940 Hardin Co.) son of John Nall & Frances Neff
  D) James **Lee Drane** (3 Jan 1877 – 23 May 1961)
    = 13 Sep 1899 Grayson Co.; **Alverder Ford** (16 Apr 1874 – 2 Feb 1966 Hardin Co.)
    has issue (male line extinct 1985)
  E) **Elizabeth Drane** (ca.1878 KY – ...)
g. **Elizabeth Drane** (ca.1803 Prince George Co. – ...)
  = 26 Apr 1820; **Isaac** Brody **Pearce** (ca.1810 – ...)
h. **Nancy Drane** (1803 Prince George Co. – 18 Jul 1878 Grayson Co.)
  = 13 Sep 1821 Washington Co.; John **Allen Prewitt** (ca.1800 – ...)
i. **Eleanor Drane** (ca.1806 Prince George Co. – ...)
  =18 Dec 1923 Washington Co.; **Richard Brody** (...)
j. **Martha Drane** (13 Dec 1807 Hardin Co. – 23 Mar 1861 KY)
  = 13 Aug 1829 Washington Co.; **Meredith Prewitt** (26 May 1805 – ...)
k. **James Drane** (14 Sep 1808 Hardin Co. –15 Jan 1894 Hardin Co.)
  = 10 Aug 1829 Washington Co.; **Bernadetta Brody** (14 Jun 1812 Washington Co. – 22 Jul 1882) daughter of Thomas Brody & Rebecca Clarke
  I) **Elijah Drane** (Nov 1831 KY – 1916 Hardin Co.)
    =1 ca1854; **Sarah ...** (Nov 1832 KY – ...)
    =2 9 Mar 1910 Grayson Co.; **Mary Paul**[104] (ca.1849 – ...) daughter of Thomas Paul & Mary Taylor
    A) a child (+ young)
  II) **Joe Drane** (ca.1835 KY – ...)
  III) **George** William **Drane** (Apr 1837 KY – 1922 Hardin Co.)
    = ca.1861; **Sidney Hurley**[105] (Jul 1839 KY – 1922 Hardin Co.) daughter of Isaiah Hurley & Elizabeth Carter

---

[104] Mary was the sister of Susan Paul, Walter Drane's first wife.
[105] According to the 1900 Census, Sidney had 5 children, 4 of when were then still alive.

  A) **William Drane**[106] (ca.1872 Hardin Co. – ...)
  B) **Lulla Drane** (Mar 1874 Hardin Co. – ...)
    = 5 Dec 1900 Grayson Co.; **I. L. Milner** (ca.1862 – ...)
  C) **James Drane** (ca.1877 Hardin Co. – ...)
  D) **George Drane** (Feb 1881 Breckinridge Co. – ...)
    = 8 Jul 1903 Breckinrdige Co.; **Mary** Elizabeth **Shrewsbury** (ca.1882 KY – ...)
    has issue
  E) **Nettie Drane** (Oct 1886 Breckinridge Co. – ...)
IV) **Henry Drane** (Feb 1843 KY – ...)
=1 ca.1872; **Mary** ... (ca.1856 KY – ...)
=2 6 Dec 1893 Breckinrdige Co.; Mary **Ann Carman** (Nov 1849 KY – ...)
issue of 1st (none by 2nd):
  A) **L K Drane** (a son) (ca.1873 Breckinridge Co. – ...)
  B) **Clarence Drane** (ca.1875 Breckinridge Co. – ...)
  C) **Clinton Drane** (ca.1879 Breckinridge Co. – ...)
  D) **Effie Drane** (Nov 1881 Breckinridge Co. – ...)
V) **James Drane** (ca.1845 KY – ...)

---

[106] Listed as widowed in 1910 Census and living with parents.

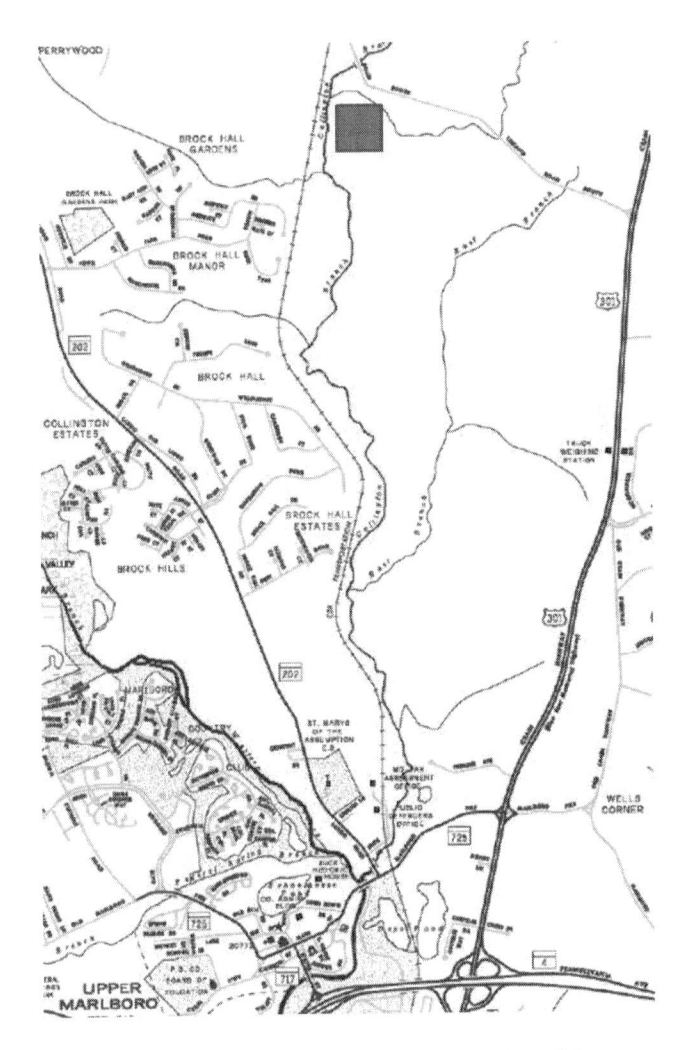

Shaded area shows approximate location of the
Drane plantation called "Greenfield"

William Reason Drain (1876-1959) and his wife,
Eva (Holder) Crabtree Drain (1877-1960)
Courtesy Carol Draine Herr

An illustration of the Battle of Dranesville, Virginia (1861)
Source: Harper's Weekly Jan. 11, 1862

Gordon Holliday Drane (1890-1957)
courtesy idrane.com

Anthony Drane (1791-1875)
Courtesy idrane.com

Davis Clark Drane (1890-1954) and his wife,
Mima Artemicia (Looney) Drane (1886-1986)
Courtesy idrane.com

Hiram Drane (1823-1907)
courtesy idrane.com

Hiram Alanson Drane (1872-1961) and his wife (facing camera),
Anna (Masterson) Drane (1879-1969) ca.1959
Courtest idrane.com

Robert Leroy Draine (1878-1970)
Courtesy idrane.com

Richard Lamar Drane (1798-1886)
Courtesy idrane.com

James Erasmus Drane (1836-1933), his wife Mary (Shaw) Drane
(1830-1915), and their children,
(L-R) John, Richard, Myra, James Jr., and Susan (on father's lap)
Courtesy idrane.com

Edward Kemper Drane (1842-1918)
Courtesy idrane.com

Bert Frances Drain (1877-1933)
Courtesy Shellie Hess

Rev. Robert Brent Drane Jr. (1851-1939)
Courtesy Blount Researcher at findagrave.com

Harry Raymond Drane (1875-1936), his wife Minnie (Cornell) Drane (1884-1936), and their 10 surviving children (clockwise from upper left): Paul, Virginia, Mary, Hazel, Bill, Harry, Helen (my grandmother), Charmaine, Elinor (Chinkie), Lawrence
Courtesy Jean Wardingley

George Washington Drain (1867-1957)
Courtesy Ruby Casto

Rep. Herbert Jackson Drane (1863-1947)
Congressman 1917-1933
Courtesy U.S. Congressional Archives

Howard Judson Drane (1877-1951)
Courtesy Tami Campbell

Chapter 8
The Accident, Maryland, Dranes
Including migrations to South Dakota, Montana, California, Arizona, Texas, Missouri, and North Carolina

The town of Accident, Maryland, situated in Garrett County in the western-most tip of that state, was founded in approximately 1801 by William Lamar and his brother-in-law, James Drane. This James was the son of James Drane of Prince George's County and his wife, Elizabeth Tyler. He was born in 1753 and is reckoned as the first permanent resident of Accident. His home, a log and frame house, still remains there and is listed on the National Register of Historic Places. As for the town, it is not much bigger now than it was then. The 2000 Census gives the population as 353.

James married William Lamar's sister, Priscilla, in 1789, while still living in Prince George's County. All but the youngest two of their children were born there. The descendants of their eight children are some of the best-recorded in the entire Drane family, largely thanks to the prominent place that James and Priscilla held in the society of western Maryland. Despite this prominence, all of this family eventually moved to other parts of the country. The last Drane to remain in the Accident area was one of their granddaughters, who died in the 1930s as an 80-something-year-old spinster.

James, who had fought in the War for American Independence, received the land as a War Grant. War Grants were plots of land, usually in undeveloped areas, that the federal government handed out to veterans of the American Revolution and of the War of 1812. James seems to have gone there with the intention of starting a tobacco plantation, but the climate was not suited for this crop. Therefore, he became a farmer of vegetables and grains.

The eldest of James's children, Thomas Lamar Drane, lived from 1789 to 1874. He was a lifelong bachelor and served in the War of 1812. During this war he had a front row seat for one of this country's great historic moments. He was at Fort McHenry during the bombardments from the British which inspired Francis Scott Key to write the Star Spangled Banner.

The North-Central Plains Dranes

The second son, James Drane III, was one of the first to leave Accident. While still there, he married Margaret Frazee. In the summer of 1845, he moved his family to Missouri, where the last of his seven children was born. But James did not remain in Missouri. He turned his eyes to mostly unexplored areas around the headwaters of the Mississippi. He lived for a short time in Nebraska and Iowa, working his way up to Wisconsin, where he died in 1863, only three months after his wife.

James and Margaret's children were generally spread across the path James took during his wanderings, with some going even further westward. The eldest son, Hiram, also settled in Wisconsin, living there until his death in 1907. He married but left no children. The second son, Robert, remained unmarried, dying in northern California in 1892. The third son, George Washington Drane, also never married. After the Civil War, where he fought for the Union, he settled in South Dakota, near his younger brother's family. The two daughters, Harriet and Priscilla, stayed in the central part of the country. Harriet, who married Alason Corson, lived out her life near her parents in Wisconsin, and Priscilla moved around Wisconsin, Illinois, and Nebraska with her husband, John Dunn.

Although Jonathan Drane was the fourth son of James and Margaret, he was the first to leave descendants. In 1871, he married Mary Fisher, and they moved to Red Bluff, in the middle of northern California. They had two sons, Hiram and John, but only Hiram fathered any children. He remained in Red Bluff, while John moved southward to the Los Angeles area.

The youngest child of James and Margaret was Thomas Marion Drane. Born in Missouri in 1846, Thomas fought in the Civil War for the Union before settling down with first wife, Mary Harris. In the 21 years that they were married, they had eight children. A few years after Mary's death, Thomas remarried, this time to Eva Sproul, a widow who was 21 years his junior. Thomas and Eva had seven more children. While raising his children, Thomas mostly lived in Iowa and Nebraska, but later in life, moved to Montana. He took Eva and several of their children there with him. He died at the age of 79 in Ridge, a small town in southwest Montana.

Of Thomas's fifteen children, nine were sons, eight of whom married and left descendants. The ninth, Harris Drane, died at the tender age of four. All of the sons married after 1900, except the eldest, Thomas Marion Drane Jr. He went with his father to Montana and settled in Powderhorn County, in the town of Broadus. He and his wife, Lena Irish, left nine children. However, only two of the four sons married. Thomas Marion Jr. is the ancestor of Larry David Drane, the owner of idrane.com, the most comprehensive website covering the Drane family on the internet.

The Marion County, Missouri, Dranes

George Drane, the third son of James and Priscilla Drane of Accident, was one of the sons who moved to Marion County, Missouri. However, his line was cut short by the trip. After the death of his wife, Eliza Hoye, he and his children went by covered wagon to western Pennsylvania and then proceeded by raft down the Ohio River. While en route, both of his sons, James and William, became ill and died unmarried shortly after arriving at his brother's, Richard's, house in Palmyra, Missouri. George's daughter, Maria, produced his only grandchildren with her husband, Benjamin Bishop.

The brother they went to in Missouri, Richard, was two years younger than George, being born in 1798. He followed a similar path as George, but a few years earlier, going to Missouri in about 1839. While still in the Accident area, Richard married Susie West, the daughter of a local judge, Erasmus West. Richard and Susie had seven children. Only two of the three sons married. The middle boy, Richard Henry Drane, served in the Confederate Army before joining his elder brother in the westward migration to Arizona.

The Arizona and Houston Dranes

James Erasmus Drane, eldest son of Richard and Susie, was born in Maryland, went to Missouri with his parents, but returned east as a young man, going to Massachusetts. It was while there he married Mary Shaw, and then returned to Missouri. Towards the end of the 19th century, James and Mary moved, with their surviving children and his brother, Richard Henry, to Phoenix, Arizona. Their male line continues in Arizona through their sons, James Erasmus Jr. and John Angier. Their third son, Richard Lamar, left an only daughter.

James Erasmus Drane Sr.'s younger brother, Edward Kemper Drane, also took his family to new territories. He and his wife, Mary Smith, remained in Missouri for the births of all ten of their children, but then moved the lot of them to Houston, Texas. From there, the family spread to cover a swath from Houston to San Antonio. Of these ten children, the male lines continue on through sons Edward Kemper Jr., Francis Marion, Hugh Nelson, and Philip Brooks, all of whom married after 1900. There was a fifth son, Joseph Lamar, who lived to be 71, but never married.

Marien Drane, fifth son of James and Priscilla of Accident, married Maria Hoye, sister of Eliza. They were the parents of two children. Marien and Maria also moved to Missouri, but Maria never took to the place and when she fell terminally ill, Marien returned with her to Accident, leaving his then grown children in Missouri. Six months after Maria's death in 1848, Marien took a new wife, Mary Chambers. They would have five more children, most of whom died young, and none of whom ever married. Their one surviving daughter, Mariah, lived into the 1930s, and became the last Drane in Accident, Maryland, a town founded by her grandfather, James, more than 130 years previously.

Of Marien's children who remained in Missouri, one was a son, Capt. Richard Drane. He began his adult life serving in the Union Army, working his way up to the rank of Captain during the Civil War. Before the war, he married Eleanor McCandless. They had four children, one of whom was the only son, Edward. He never married. Since his date of death is unknown, it is possible he died young.

Richard and Eleanor had a daughter named Ellen, but she was called Nellie. Nellie Drane Kettering, as she was known after her marriage, was quite the colorful figure. In the 1920s, faithfully believing the legends of Sir

James Anthony Drane and his close kinship to Lord Baltimore, attempted to sue the federal government for compensation of the Drane lands "confiscated to build Washington, D.C." Of course, the case was quickly dismissed for reasons explained in Chapter 1, but the theater that surrounded Nellie during this time is worth a mention. She visited the White House in 1924, wishing to show Pres. Calvin Coolidge what she claimed was a land grant from Lord Balitmore to "his cousin," Sir James Anthony Drane. Cool Cal was not home at the time—perhaps he was fishing—and Nellie never publicly displayed this valuable piece of evidence. But it all made for entertaining newspaper copy during a period when coverage of a president who rarely spoke in public was leaving a lot of blank space on the front page.

The Wilmington, North Carolina, Dranes

The next to youngest son of James and Priscilla of Accident, Robert, has been something of a mystery. Most accounts of the family simply say he "went west," and no further information is given. However, there is another Robert Drane who does not fit in the family where most researchers try to put him.

Robert Brent Drane, who would eventually move to North Carolina and have a family there, was born in 1800, the same year as the Robert born to James and Priscilla. Most researchers call him the son of the Anthony Drane of Prince George's County and his wife, Ann Smith, but this cannot be true. When dedicating the plaque that covers Anthony and Ann's grave, their son, Capt. Anthony Drane, stated he was their youngest son, and he was born before Robert Brent. Furthermore, Capt. Anthony was born in December, 1799, and Robert Brent was born in January, 1800, making it a biological impossibility for them to have the same mother.

Given that Robert Brent and Robert of Accident were born in the same year—the Accident Robert's exact date is not recorded—and that Robert Brent has traditionally been misplaced in the family, and that nothing else is known about Robert of Accident, I see good circumstantial evidence that Robert Brent and Robert of Accident are the same person. Furthermore, Robert Brent is believed to be born in Prince George's County, as is James's and Priscilla's son, Robert. However, this information could possibly be an assumption tied to the misplaced belief that Robert Brent's parents were Anthony and Ann of the same county.

One more clue is Robert Brent's marriage. He married in Massachusetts. Although the two events are separated by 35 years, the only other Maryland Drane to even be found in Massachusetts is from this family and would be a nephew to Robert Brent, assuming he is indeed a son of James and Priscilla.

I would be remiss if I failed to point out a second possibility. Robert Brent Drane was clearly named for Robert Brent, a man of prominence in the portions of Montgomery County that became the District of Columbia, and served as Washington's first mayor. The Brentwood Estates, town, and neighborhood are all named for him. Because of their close association with this area, it would be reasonable to think Robert B. Drane belongs with the Montgomery County Dranes, from Chapter 6. There is one place in that family where he could fit: as a son of Thomas Offurt Drane and Mary Harding. For that to be true it would mean that Mary had a child (Robert) in January, 1800 and another (Rachel) in December of the same year. While that is possible, it does not seem very likely, especially considering the more ample spacing of the rest of Thomas's and Mary's children. Furthermore, none of the pretty well documented accounts of Thomas O.'s descendants mention another son.

Weighing the two options, I am more inclined to believe Robert Brent belongs with the Accident line rather than the Montgomery County line. But the reader should be aware I am quite prepared to be wrong on this point if more evidence is ever found to the contrary.

After questioning his correct parentage, the rest of Robert Brent Drane's life is well recorded. As a young man, he went to Massachusetts to pursue an education in divinity, ultimately achieving a doctorate degree in the discipline. While there he married Augusta Endicott, whose family came over on the *Mayflower*, and includes the first governor of the Massachusetts Bay Colony. He served as an Episcopal minister in several parishes, working his way southward as time went on. He returned to Maryland with his new bride and their two sons, Richard Hooker and Henry Martyn, were both born in Hagerstown, in Washington County. The fact that he settled in a neighboring county to Garrett also lends credence to the connection to the Dranes of Accident.

In about 1840, Robert moved his family to North Carolina, settling in Wilmington, where he served as a minister the rest of his life. Augusta died in 1847, and Robert remarried in 1851. His new wife was Catherine Parker. They had at least two more children, Robert Brent Jr. and a daughter, Marian.

Richard Hooker Drane married Martha Watson in 1850, but they do not appear to have had any children. Richard's date of death is not known, but he does not appear on any census after 1850, so he may have died shortly after marrying Martha.

Henry Martyn Drane was born in Hagertown in 1832. He served in the Confederate Army, rising to the rank of Colonel. As the war broke out, he married Virginia Lloyd, and returned to a life with her in Wilmington after the surrender. He died in 1908, after which, Virginia moved to Macon, Georgia, to live with their youngest child.

Henry and Virginia had five children, one of whom, probably son Henry, died young, according to the 1900 census. The other two sons, Salter Lloyd, who was named for Virginia's father, and George Thomas, both married, their children being born after 1900. Lloyd, as the elder son was known, lived most of his life in Florida, dying in Jacksonville in 1926. George and his wife, Mary Bacot, moved to Macon, taking his mother with them.

Robert Brent Drane Jr. followed his father into the clergy. He, too, was an Episcopal minister, serving most of his career in Edenton, in northeastern North Carolina. He married Maria Skinner in 1878, and they had seven children. Only the eldest son, Brent Skinner, has a male line of descendants still living. The second son, Frank Parker, became a doctor, and the youngest son, Frederick Blount, went into the "family business," becoming a preacher. After years of missionary work with the Eskimos in northern Alaska and the Yukon territory, he became the rector of St. Paul's church in Monroe County, North Carolina. Robert's and Maria's youngest daughter, Marian, was the wife of U.S. Senator Frank Graham who served in the late 1940s.

James's and Priscilla's youngest son, William, lived into his 90s but never married. Late in life, he joined his nephews who went to Phoenix.

James Thomas **Drane** (Aug 1753 Prince Georges Co. – 27 Jun 1828 Accident, MD[107]) son of James Drane & Elizabeth Piles
= 18 Feb 1789 Prince Georges Co., MD[108]; **Priscilla Lamar** (ca.1770 Prince Georges Co. – 26 Feb 1836 Accident[109]) daughter of Robert Lamar & Sarah Hall

  a. **Thomas** Lamar **Drane** (1789 Prince Georges Co. – 1874 Hoyes, MD[110]) dunm.[111] Fought in the War of 1812 as a private. Was present at the bombardment of Fort McHenry.

  b. **James Drane** (1793 Prince Georges Co. – Jun 1863 Monroe, WI) = ca.1820; **Margaret Frazee** (ca.1802 Accident, MD – 4 Mar 1863 Monroe) daughter of Jonathan Frazee & Margaret Friend

    I) **Hiram Drane** (1823 Accident – 1907 Monroe)
= 16 Mar 1858 Green Co., WI; **Sarah Miller** (1824 – 1891 Monroe) daughter of Jacob Miller & Barbara ...; =1st A.B. Cunningham
no issue

    II) **Harriet Drane** (19 Nov 1824 Accident – 11 Nov 1909 Monroe) = 1848; **Alanson Corson** (25 Dec 1808 Somerset Co., NE – 24 Jun 1892 Monroe)

    III) **Priscilla Drane** (25 Dec 1828 Accident – 21 Aug 1911 Burwell, NE)
= 3 Jan 1854 Green Co.; **John Dunn** (3 Jan 1832 Girard, PA – 8 Oct 1872 Winslow, IL) son of Joseph Drane & Elizabeth Barber

    IV) **Robert** Leroy **Drane** (1834 MD – 7 Oct. 1892 Red Bluff, CA[112]) dunm.

    V) **George** Washington **Drane** (15 Jun 1836 Sanlick Hill, MD – 29 May 1920 Hot Springs, SD) fought in Civil War for the Union; dunm.

    VI) **Jonathan Drane** (10 Feb 1845 MD – 1 Mar 1902 Red Bluff, CA[113])

---

[107] Date of death from his tombstone. Buried in the Lutheran cemetery in Accident, MD.

[108] Prince George's Co. Marriage Records.

[109] Calendar of Wills, Allegany Co. MD.

[110] Tombstone gives year of death. Buried in the Methodist cemetery, Hoyes, MD.

[111] Jevne, Louise Priscilla Armstrong. *Drane Families of Maryland and Some Descendants.*

[112] Robert Drane is buried at Oak Hill Cemetery, Red Bluff, CA.

[113] Jonathan & Mary Drane are buried at Oak Hill Cemetery, Red Bluff, CA.

fought in Civil war for the Union
= 1 Jan 1871 Waverly, IA; **Mary** Louise **Fisher** (5 Dec 1854 – 22 Mar 1889 Red Bluff)
   A) **Hiram** Alanson **Drane** (21 Jul 1872 IA – 14 Mar 1961 Tehama Co. CA)
   = 8 Jan 1902 Red Bluff, CA; **Anna Masterson** (17 Jan 1879 MO – 21 Jan 1969 Tehama Co.)
   has issue
   B) **John Drane** (4 Nov 1873 – 8 May 1940 Alturas, CA)
   = 12 Jun 1920; **Nettie** Riede **Leonard** (18 Sep 1886 – May 1981 Los Angeles, CA)
   no issue
VII) **Thomas** Marion **Drane** (12 Apr 1846 Honeywell, MO – 12 Sep 1925 Ridge, MT) fought in the Civil War for the Union
=1 16 May 1868 Shell Rock, IA; **Mary** Elizabeth **Harris** (11 Sep 1849 Grundy Co., IA – 18 Nov 1889 Spring View, NE) daughter of John Harris & Mary Wilcox; =1st Silas Holbrooke
=2 5 Mar 1892 Springview, NE; **Eva** Olivia **Tyler** (19 Sep 1865 Belvedere, IL – ... Jasper Co., MO) daughter of Harlow Tyler & Susannah DeWolf; =1st Theodore Sproul
issue of 1st:
   A) **Margarette** Maryette **Drane** (11 Nov 1871 Waverly – 10 Dec 1947 Lynch, NE)
   = 10 Oct 1888 Springview, NE; **Charles** Harrison **Stewart** (Oct 1851 May Co., MO – 1934 Lynch) son of William Stewart & Caroline Smith
   B) **Thomas** Marion **Drane Jr.** (20 Dec 1872 Waverly – 30 Nov 1949 Broadus, MT)
   = 13 Nov 1897; **Lena** Helen **Irish** (11 Feb 1878 Clark, WI – 3 Jun 1957 Belle Fourche, SD) daughter of Frank Irish & Urania Reynolds
      1) **Morton** Dewey **Drane** (21 Apr 1898 Jameison, NE – 10 Apr 1965 Broadus)
      2) **Daisy Drane** (20 Dec 1899 Jamison, NE – 4 Jun 1985 Aurora, Co.)
      = **Frank** Thomas **Brunner** (23 May 1897 Rapid City, SD – 11 Jun 1960 Denver, Co.)
      3) **Everett Drane** (21 Feb 1902 NE – Oct 1910 NE)
      4) **Adeline** Florence **Drane** (29 Jan 1906 Jameison – Jan 1977 Billings, MT)
      =1 31 Jul 1925 Deadwood, SD (dv.); **Paul Knie** (3 Jan 1895 –

Oct 1979 Missoula, MT)
=2 9 Jan 1935; **Dewey Stewart** (5 May 1898 – Nov 1962 MT)
5) **Elsie Drane** (5 Sep 1908 – 25 Mar 1996 Prescott, AZ)
=1 **Ed Parks** (...)
=2 **Stanley Holt** (...)
6) **Earl Drane** (27 May 1911 Jameison – 14 Aug 1996 Miles City, MT)
= 14 Apr 1934 Broadus; **Hazel** Christine **Camper** (8 May 1913 Dillon Mill, VA – 15 May 1995 Broadus) daughter of Waldo Camper & Renie Bowman
has issue
7) **Dorothy Drane** (31 Jul 1913 Belle Fourche – ...)
= **Fred Mackaben** (4 Apr 1905 Union, IL – ...) son of Fred Mackaben & Anna Wenaky
8) **Merle** Melvin **Drane** (4 Oct 1915 – Nov 1972 Garfield Co., MT)
=1 **Elaine** Reva **Burley** (...)
=2 19 May 1934 Belle Fourche; **Georgia** Ellen **Jones** (...)
has issue
9) **Frances** Helen **Drane** (26 Jun 1919 Ridge, MT – 11 Dec 2003 Gillette, WY)
= 28 May 1936 Belle Fourche; **Roy** Bruce **West** (15 Aug 1912 Rocky Point, WY – 22 Jun 1994 Gillette) son of William West & Sylvia Jones
C) **Harris Drane** (3 Jul 1876 Waverly – 9 Aug 1880 Waverly)
D) **Robert** Leroy **Draine** (1 Jan 1878 Waverly – 26 Apr 1970 Sturgis)
= 6 Apr 1906 Bassett, NE; **Myrtle** Frances **Irish** (22 Feb 1885 Simon NE – 9 Sep 1964 Sturgis) daughter of Al Irish & Isabelle Pendleton
has issue
E) **George** Henry **Draine** (9 Aug 1881 Waverly – 24 Sep 1937 Appleton, MN)
= 3 Oct 1910 Milan, MN; **Inga** Elvira **Smith** (16 Mar 1886 Chicago, IL – Jun 1976 Missoula) daughter of Harry Smith & Hannah Sorensen
has issue
F) **Florence** Effie **Drane** (3 Apr 1884 Waverly – 10 Jul 1964 Allsworth, NE)
= Jan 1905 Fairfax, SD; **Cyrus** Osborn **Snider** (11 Aug 1869 Carthage, IL – 10 Aug 1932 Keyapaha Co., SD) son of

Hamilton Snider & Mary Aleshire
- G) **Lillian** Belle **Drane** (6 Apr 1885 Carnes, NE – 25 Nov 1965 Sturgis)
= 5 Nov 1900 Crofton, NE; **William** Alva **McKee** (1875 MN – 12 Dec 1952 Valentine, NE) son of William McKee & Hannah Wells
- H) **Herbert** William **Draine** (25 Oct 1889 Carnes – 1 Jun 1970 Sheridan, WY)
=1 18 Jan 1909 Belle Fourche; **Amanda** Ann **Blaylock** (6 Sep 1890 OR – 5 Feb 1924 Miles City)
=2 9 Dec 1924 Broadus; Mildred (**Flossie**) **Slayton** (11 Jul 1902 – 27 Mar 2001 Spokane, WA) =1st Wilkerson
has issue
issue of 2nd:
- I) **Susan** Priscilla **Draine** (26 Dec 1893 Carlock, NE – 27 May 1951)
= ...; **James** Louis **McKee** (27 Aug 1891 Carlock – 3 Feb 1955) son of William McKee & Hannah Wells
- J) **James** Harrison **Draine** (10 Mar 1895 Springview – Oct 1982 Wood, SD)
=1 Mar 1915 Winner, SD; **Alice** Facitta **Horton** (... – 1917) daughter of Isaac Horton & Lucinda ...
=2 **Esther Burnham** (b.18 Nov 1917 Naper, NE) daughter of Ivy Burnham & Mayse Dickerson; =1st Vernon Brown
has issue
- K) **Walter** Leslie **Draine** (16 Sep 1897 Keyapaha Co. – 20 Jun 1977 Portland, OR)
= ...; **Maud Frazer** (...)
has issue
- L) **Joseph** McKinley **Draine** (27 Jul 1900 Burton, NE – 25 May 1976 Sandpoint, ID)
= 11 Jul 1930 Ranch Creek, MT; **Ella Ragland** (9 Mar 1915 – 20 Oct 1999 Boise, ID) daughter of George Ragland & Grace Hopkins
has issue
- M) **Albert** Benjamin **Draine** (10 Feb 1903 Gregory Co., SD – 16 May 1976 Sandpoint, ID)
=1 **Daisy** Margaret **Bocock** (...) daughter of Thomas Bocock & Flossie O'Neal
=2 18 Aug 1923 Sundance, WY; Irma **"Willie" Williams** (21 Dec 1902 – 29 Sep 1934 Miles City) daughter of Benjamin

Williams & Mary Richards *has issue*
- N) **Adolphia** Neomia **Draine** (14 Jul 1905 Burton, NE – ca.Dec 1972 Dayton, OR)
  = **Paul Otto** (...)
- O) **Adha** Jane **Draine**[114] (8 Jun 1909 Burton – 18 Aug 1988 Lewis and Clark Co., MT)
  =1 22 Nov 1927 Broadus (dv.); **Ernest Alderman** (17 Dec 1896 Strausburg, PA – 1948 Belle Fourche) son of George Alderman & Martha Fish
  =2 28 Oct 1947; **Ernest Errand** (...)

c. **George** Washington **Drane** (1795 Prince Georges Co. – 1845 Marion Co., MO)
= 31 Mar 1821 Cumberland, MD[115]; **Eliza Hoye** (10 Jan 1803 Accident – 28 Jan 1828 Accident) daughter of William Hoye & Eleanor Slicer
- I) **James** Anthony **Drane** (13 Jul 1823 – ca.1850 Palmyra, MO[116])
- II) **Maria Drane**[117] (11 Feb 1825 Accident – 19 Jan 1884 Monroe City, MO)
  = 14 Apr 1857 Sharpsburg, MO; (her 1st cousin) **Benjamin** Caleb **Bishop** (1 Oct 1831 Smithburg, MD – 11 Jul 1894 Monroe City) son of Elijah Bishop & Ann Hoye
- III) **William Drane** (8 Jan 1826 – ca.1850 Palmyra)

d. **Richard** Lamar **Drane**[118] (16 Feb 1798 Prince Georges Co. – 16 Apr 1886 Blackburn, MO)
= 4 Feb 1833 Frederick Co., MD; **Susan** Johnson **West** (6 Dec 1804 – 6 Mar 1890 Blackburn, MO) daughter of Erasmus West & Eleanora Belt
- I) **Ellen** West **Drane** (24 Oct 1834 Allegany Co., MD – 1917 Phoenix, AZ)
  = 24 Jan 1869 Saline Co., MO; **Goodrich Wilson** (24 Nov 1818 Barter Hill, VA – 10 Jun 1890 Malta Bend, MO) son of Matthew Goodrich & Elizabeth Trent

---

[114] Adha is an Indian name which means "light."
[115] Marriage license is dated 31 Mar 1821.
[116] James and his brother, William, became ill during the trip to Missouri and died at the home of their uncle, Richard Drane.
[117] Hoye, Charles E. *The Hoyes of Maryland.* After the death of her parents, Maria lived with her uncle, Richard Drane, near Palmyra, MO. It was at Richard's home where James and William, Maria's brothers, both died.
[118] 1880 Census: Elmwood, Saline Co., MO.

II) **James** Eramus **Drane** (8 Feb 1836 Allegany Co. – 1933[119] Phoenix)
= Dec 1863 Bridgewater, MA; **Mary Shaw** (2 Apr 1840 MA – 13 Dec 1915 Mesa, AZ)
  A) **Myra Drane** (a.1870 – Blackburn) +young
  B) **Dr. James** Eramus **Drane Jr.** (11 Aug 1872 Blackburn[120] – 24 Dec 1947 Phoenix)
    = 27 Nov 1901 Mesa, AZ; **Edith Abell** (24 Jun 1878 MI – 8 Aug 1958 Phoenix) daughter of Wilbur Abell
    has issue
  C) **John** Angier **Drane** (Apr 1875 MO – 1956 Maricopa Co. AZ)
    =1 ...; **Etta Gardner** (22 Dec 1880 MI – 22 Dec 1906 Phoenix)
    =2 ...; (his sister-in-law) **Ella Gardner**[121] (22 Dec 1880 Mi – 12 Dec 1975 Mesa)
    has issue
  D) **Richard** Lamar **Drane** (Sep 1878 Saline Co. – ... Menlo Park, CA)
    = **Leah Brown** (...)
    has issue, an only daughter
  D) **Susan** West **Drane** (Sep 1886 Blackburn – ... Eureka Springs, MO) dunm.
III) **Eliza** Hillary West **Drane** (28 Apr 1838 Allegany Co. – 1917 Phoenix[122]) (twin) dunm.
IV) **Priscilla** Elizabeth **Drane** (28 Apr 1838 Allegany Co. – 15 Jan 1913 Oakland, CA) (twin)
= 18 Jun 1857 Hunnewell, MO; **Dr. Edward** Nathan **Garrard** (ca.1833 – 18 Mar 1904 Phoenix)
V) **Richard** Henry **Drane** (20 Sep 1840 Marion Co. – 1910 Phoenix) served in the CSA Army; dunm.
VI) **Edward** Kemper **Drane** (20 Mar 1842 Marion Co. – 29 Mar 1918 Lincoln Co., Co.) served in the Union Army
= 21 Dec 1870 Lexington, MO; **Mary** Fry **Smith** (3 May 1851 Malden, (W)VA – 31 Dec 1923 Long Beach, CA) daughter of

---

[119] "Soldier of Revolution Honored" *The Glade Star* (Accident, MD) 3 Jun 1943. Give 1932, but the AZ death index list his death as 1933.
[120] "Soldier of Revolution Honored" *The Glade Star* (Accident, MD) 3 Jun 1943.
[121] The Gardner sisters were twins. Etta died in childbirth with her only child.
[122] Eliza, her brother Richard, and their uncle William Drane are all buried in Greenwood Memorial Laen Cemetery in Phoenix, AZ.

Robert Smth & Sarah Ruffner
A) **Roberta** Ruffner **Drane** (18 Oct 1872 Saline Co. – ca.1950 Houston, TX)
= **Rev. David** Griffin **Gunn** (...) served in the CSA Army
B) **Edward** Kemper **Drane Jr.** (24 May 1874 Saline Co. – 30 Sep 1931 Houston)
=1 (dv); **Lillian Wilson** (...)
=2 **Mary** Elizabeth Clifford **Stevens** (4 Aug 1888 West Point, MS – 25 May 1959 Houston) daughter of John Stevens & Frances Gibson =1st ... Hecker
has issue
C) **Francis** Marion **Drane** (28 Jan 1876 Blackburn – 21 Aug 1938 Ft. Worth, TX)
=10 Feb 1908 Cleveland, OH; Mary **Grace Humphrey** (30 Apr 1882 Columbus, OH – 6 Aug 1963 Ft. Worth) daughter of John Humphrey & Catherine Cowdell
has issue
D) **Eliza** West **Drane** (20 Mar 1878 Blackburn – 11 Jul 1961)
= **Ralph Goddard** (...)
E) **Elizabeth** Madeline **Drane** (12 Mar 1880 Blackburn –)
=1 **Robert Hiller** (...)
=2 **Ernest** Orlando **Moss** (...)
F) **Sarah** Evelyn **Drane** (... – ca.1940 St. Louis)
=1 **Otto A Schroer** (...)
=2 **Douglas Webber** (...)
G) **Hugh** Nelson **Drane** (6 Jan 1884 Blackburn – 23 Dec 1961 San Antonio, TX)
= 15 Jan 1908; **Jane** Velura **Humphrey** (4 Jul 1885 Columbus – 1968 San Antonio) daughter of John Humphrey & Catherine Cowdell
has issue
H) **Mary** Alice **Drane** (11 Feb 1886 Blackburn – ca.1971)[123]
=1 **... Fairbanks** (...)
=2 **Dr Charles Morrow** (...)
=3 **Edwin Taylor** (...)
I) **Joseph** Lamar **Drane** (15 Nov 1889 Blackburn – 30 Aug 1960 San Antonio) never married
J) **Philip** Brooks **Drane** (5 May 1893 Blackburn – Sep 1978 Hardin Co., TX)
=1 **Katherine** Mayo **Richardson** (... – 1933)

---

[123] Mary Drane had no issue by any of her husbands.

=2 **Marie** Alberta **Peterson** (...) =1st ... Jones
has issue
VII) **John Drane** (...) +young
e. **Marien Drane** (1 Feb 1799 Prince Georges Co. – 8 Apr 1883 Garret Co.[124])
=1 23 Mar 1824 Allegany Co.; **Mary Ann Hoye** (13 Oct 1805 – 28 Apr 1848 Accident) daughter of William Hoye & Eleanor Slicer
=2 26 Oct 1848 Macheny, MD; **Mary** Ann **Chambers** (1822 MD – ...) daughter of William Chambers
issue of 1st:
I) **Priscilla** Ann **Drane** (7 Feb 1825 Accident – 1905 Clarence, MO)
= ...; **Dr. William Feazel** (...)
II) **Capt. Richard Drane** (2 May 1833 Accident – 1880 Hannibal, MO) served in the Union Army; postmaster of Hannibal, MO 1877-1880
= 24 Mar 1857 Allegany Co. **Eleanor McCandless** (1836 – 1871)
  A) **Priscilla** Lamar **Drane** (3 Nov 1858 Hannibal – 1892 Monmouth, IL)
    =23 Dec 1880; **Frank Martin** (... – 20 Jun 1888)
  B) **Eliza Jane (Tupie) Drane** (31 Jan 1860 Hannibal –... Palmyra)
    = **Thaddeus Ray** (...) Sheriff of Marion Co., MO
  C) **Ellen (Nellie) Drane** (4 Apr 1862 Hannibal – ...)[125]
    =1 (dv.) **William Kittering** (...)
    =2 ... **Pascoe** (...)
  D) **Edward Drane** (1864 Hannibal – ...)
issue of 2nd.[126]
III) **William Drane** (29 Oct 1849 – ...)
IV) **Eliza Drane** (9 Apr 1851 – 15 Oct 1853)

---

[124] Death Notices. *The Mountain Democrat.* – Apr 1883.

[125] Nellie Kittering Pascoe claimed to have in her possession a deed showing the grant of land from Lord Baltimore to the Drane Family in Prince George's Co. MD. It was supposedly in her possession in July 1924 when she visited the White House. It is unclear if she showed it to anyone. This trip to the White House was part of a civil suit Nellie brought against the federal government for compensation for the use of the old Drane plantation for the building of parts of Washington, DC. The case was dismissed for lack of evidence, which is not surprising, since the Drane plantation was not in the part of Maryland ceded to the District of Columbia.

[126] None of Marien Drane's children by his second wife ever married.

V) **Mariah Drane** (1854 – ... Accident)[127]
VI) **Mary Drane** (...)
VII) **Isabel Drane** (1858 – ...)
f. **Rev. Robert** Brent **Drane** (9 Jan 1800 Prince George's County – 15 Oct 1862 Wilmington, NC[128]) an Episcopal minister at Wilmington, NC since ca.1840
=1 12 Apr 1828 Salem, MA; **Augusta Endicott** (27 Jul 1807 Danvers, MA – 7 Jul 1847 Wilmington, NC) dau of Moses Endicott & Anna Towne
=2 1850; **Catherine Parker** (ca.1817 NC – aft.1880) dau of Theophilus Parker & Mary Toole
issue of 1st:
  I) **Richard** Hooker **Drane** (15 Feb 1829 Hagerstown, MD – ...)
    = 26 Nov 1850 Washington Co. MD; **Martha Watson** (...)
  II) **Col. Henry** Martyn **Drane** (10 Aug 1832 Hagerstown – 10 Sep 1908 Wilmington, NC[129]) served in the CSA Army
    = 1861; **Virginia Lloyd**[130] (21 Jan 1835 – 25 Dec 1912 Macon, GA) daughter of Salter Lloyd & Eliza Brown
    A) Salter **Lloyd Drane** (Oct 1861 Wilmington – 11 Sep 1926 Jacksonville, FL)
      = ...; **Alma** ... (ca.1879 NC – ...)
      has issue
    B) **Kate Drane** (1863 – ...)
    C) **Eliza** Brown **Drane** (1865 – ...)
    D) **Henry Drane** (1870 – ...)
    E) **George** Thomas **Drane** (1874 Bladen, NC – 6 Jan 1910 Macon, GA)
      = 7 Dec 1899 LA; **Mary** Louise **Bacot** (Oct 1879 SC – 1952)
      has issue
  III) **Mary Drane** (ca.1843 NC – ...)
issue of 2nd:
  IV) **Rev. Robert** Brent **Drane Jr.** (15 Dec 1851 Wilmington – 29 Oct 1939 Durham, NC[131]) Episcopal minister in Edenton, NC
    = 13 Nov 1878; **Maria** Louisa Warren **Skinner** (13 Nov 1859 Edenton, NC – 24 Dec 1921 Edenton) dau of Tristrim Skinner &

---

[127] The last of the Dranes to live in Garrett Co., MD.
[128] Buried at Oakdale Cemetery, Wilmington, NC with first wife.
[129] Buried at Oakdale Cemetery.
[130] According to the 1900 Census, one of Henry and Virginia's children was already dead.
[131] Buried at St. Paul's Episcopal Churchyard, Edenton, NC with wife.

Eliza Harwood
- A) **Brent** Skinner **Drane** (9 Sep 1881 Edenton – 1948 in NC)
  = 29 Dec 1908 Charlotte, NC; **Florence Thomas** (9 May 1885 Wilmington – Feb 1973 Tarboro, NC) dau of Jordan Thomas & MariePrince
  has issue – male line extinct 1944
- B) **Eliza** Harwood **Drane** (15 Sep 1883 – 30 Jul 1973 Orange Valley, NC)
  = 9 Jun 1910 Edenton; **Joseph** Cheshire **Webb Jr.** (11 Oct 1879 – 13 Apr 1932) son of Joseph Webb & Mary Hill
- C) **Frank** Parker **Drane** (16 Sep 1885 Edenton – 28 Apr 1918 Charlotte, NC) a doctor
- D) **Robert Drane** (Dec 1887 – ...)
- E) **Rev. Frederick** Blount **Drane** (1 Aug 1890 – 18 Jan 1982 Edenton[132]) Missonary to Alaska & Yukon 1915-1926. Rector of St.Paul's, Monroe Co., NC 1929-1958
  = ...; **Rebecca** Bennehan **Wood** (28 Jul 1892 – 26 May 1984 Edenton) daughter of Frank Wood & Rebecca Collins
  no issue
- F) **Katherine** Parker **Drane** (Dec 1897 – ...)
  = ...; **B.H. Perry** (...)
- G) **Marian Drane** (21 Dec 1899 Edenton – 27 Apr 1967 New York, NY)
  = 21 Jul 1932; **Sen. Lt. Frank** Porter **Graham** (14 Oct 1886 Fayetteville, NC – 16 Feb 1972 Chapel Hill, NC) son of Alexander Graham & Katherine Sloan; Lt. in WWI, Pres. of Univ of NC 1930-1949, US Senator 1949-1950
- V) **Marian Drane** (Dec 1853 Wilmington – ...)
- g. **Elizabeth** Ann **Drane** (16 Oct 1802 Allegany Co. – 12 Jun 1842 Allegany Co.)
  = 30 Jul 1830 Allegany Co.; **William Browning** (14 Nov 1804 Great Glades, MD – 27 Jun 1879 MD) son of Meshach Browning & Mary McMullen
- h. **William Drane** (5 May 1805 Allegany Co., MD – 22 Jun 1899 Phoenix) dunm.

---

[132] Buried at St. Paul's.

Chapter 9
The Pittsylvania County, Virginia, Dranes
Including migrations to Forsyth County, North Carolina, and Daviess County, Missouri

As noted in Chapter 5, Anthony Drane of Prince George's County had several sons, many of whom founded their own branches of the Drane family. The eldest of these was William Hezekiah Drane, who was generally known as Hezekiah. The only place the first name shows up is on his marriage records to his two wives. Notably, all of the sons by Anthony and his first wife, whose identity is not known, have biblical names from the Old Testament. In the next two chapters we will meet Hezekiah's brothers, David and Isaac.

Hezekiah left his father's home at a young age. It is not known when he traveled to Pittsylvania County, in southern Virginia, but he was there by October 1793 when he married his first wife, Nancy Smith. Using a best estimate for his date of birth, Hezekiah would have been 21 or 22 at this time. Nancy would be dead within a decade, leaving her husband with at least five surviving children. As was common practice in that day, Hezekiah quickly remarried to give his children a new mother, and picked another lady named Nancy. Her family name was Earls. There is no record of Hezekiah and this second Nancy having any more children.

The marriage records of all of the five children do still exist. The three daughters, Sally, Martha, and Polly, married Joseph Brimm, James Oakes, and William Yearbrey, respectively. The two sons, Peter Hezekiah and Thomas, each had large families and they form the two branches of this line.

The Winston-Salem Dranes

The elder brother, like his father, was known by his middle name, Hezekiah. He married Nancy Tifflin in Brosville, the small village in Pittsylvania County where the family lived. Of their eight children, five were daughters, and one of the sons died in infancy. The elder surviving son, Thomas Smith Drane, married three times, but his only child was a daughter. His third marriage was a little controversial, not only because of the 30 year gap in their ages, but also because, as a child, she had been placed in his care as a ward after the death of her parents.

Thomas's younger brother, Peter Tifflin Drane, was born about 1835. After serving in the Confederate Army during the Civil War, he settled in central North Carolina, a few miles south of the current city of Winston-Salem. After arriving there, he married Phoebe Long. Peter and Phoebe had six surviving children, plus a little boy who died at age two. Peter was a cobbler by profession and worked until his death in 1894. His widow lived on another decade. After initially living in Davidson County, Peter moved his family closer to town, settling in Clemmons, which is today a suburb of Winston-Salem.

The eldest son, William, is the only one who married before 1900. His brother, James, also left issue, but after the turn of the century, and the remaining brother, Thomas, never married. William married twice, the first wife being his cousin, Cora Long. It is not clear if Cora died or if they divorced, but after their only child, Emma was born in 1890, William married again. His second wife was Minnie Jones, and she would give him another eleven children. Four of the five sons, Paul, Alfred, Dewey, and Glenn, married and have several descendants in the Winston-Salem area living today.

The Daviess County Drains

Thomas, the younger son of the senior Hezekiah, remained in Pittsylvania County while his father was still alive, but then took his family to Gallatin, in Daviess County, Missouri, on the banks of the Missouri River. He married Susan Shackleford in 1831, and they would have at least nine children, but only two would marry. The remainder mostly died young. Thomas and Susan moved to Missouri in the mid-1830s, which must have been difficult with three children, all under the age of six. It appears to be during this migration that the name changed to the Drain spelling. It is the only spelling recorded for them in Missouri.

The eldest of these children was a daughter named Deidamia. She and her husband, Andrew Blakely, would provide her parents with half of their grandchildren. The other half came from her brother, and long-time next-door neighbor, William.

William Drain was born in August 1835, shortly before the move to Gallatin. He married Cynthia Richesson, after returning from the Civil War, in 1866. They had a total of five children, but three died young, including a daughter named Deidamia for her aunt. In time, William, Cynthia, and the surviving kids moved to Audrain County. While it may be tempting to attach some significance to the similarity in the names Drain and Audrain, there appears to be no connection. The county was named for Col. James Audrain who was a commander in the War of 1812, and later a Missouri legislator.

William's two surviving children, William Thomas and Bert Francis, each married, but only William fathered any children. His descendants continue to live in the town of Mexico in Audrain County. However, Bert did raise two step-children, the kids of his second wife, Mrs. Manerva Quall Edwards. He was a railroad worker until his death after being struck by a train while working in 1933.

William **Hezekiah Drane** (bef.1772 – bef.1850)
=1 10 Oct 1793 Pittsylvania Co., VA; **Nancy Smith** (... – bef.1802)
=2 3 Apr 1802 Pittsylvania Co; **Nancy Earls** (...)
issue of of 1st (none by 2nd):
I) Peter **Hezekiah Drane** (ca.1794 – 18 Apr 1864)
 = 21 Dec 1820 Pittsylvania Co.; **Nancy** Allen **Tifflin** (ca.1794 Pittsylvania Co. – 16 Dec 1859 Pittsylvania Co.)
  A) **Thomas** Smith **Drane** (ca.1824 Brosville, VA – bef. 1912) Sgt. in CSA
  =1 31 Dec 1845 Pittsylvania Co.; **Nancy Burnett** (ca.1824 – bef.1850) daughter of Thomas Burnett & Cenna Dallas
  =2 12 Dec 1850 Pittsylvania Co.; **Missouri** Ann **Davis** (ca.1830 Pittsylvania Co. – bef.1880) daughter of ... Davis & Frances ...
  =3 22 Apr 1882 Pittsylvania Co.; **Nancy B Dalton** (ca.1854 – ...) daughter of Martin Dalton & Ruth Thompson
  issue of 2nd (none by 1st):
   1) **Eliza Drane** (ca.1852 Pittsylvania Co. – ...)
  B) **Elizabeth** Ann **Drane** (ca.1828 Brosville – ca.1885)
  = 16 Dec 1842 Pittsylvania Co.; **Thomas** Parnell **Green** (23 Dec 1817 Brosville – ca.1882) son of John Green & Sally Clark
  C) **Mary** John **Drane** (ca. 1832 Brosville – 5 Jan 1897 Brosville)
  = 12 Jan 1850 Brosville; **John** Baily **Green** (20 Nov 1819 Brosville – 20 Feb 1899 Pittsylvania Co.) son of John Green & Sally Clark
  D) **Joseph Drane** (b. & d.ca.1834 Brosville)
  E) **Peter** Tifflin **Drane**[133] (ca.1835 Brosville – 19 Oct 1894)
  = ...; **Phebe Long** (17 Mar 1849 Davidson Co. NC – 1903) daughter of Daniel Long & Mary Doty
   1) **William Drane** (5 Aug 1869 Davidson Co. – 18 Aug 1925 Clemmons, NC)
   =1 ...; **Cora Long** (...)
   =2 ...; **Minnie** Elizabeth **Jones** (18 Mar 1875 Forsyth Co. NC – 18 Feb 1941 Clemmons)
   issue of 1st:
    a) **Emma** Martha **Drane** (4 Dec 1890 – 5 Mar 1917 Winston-Salem, NC)
     = ...; **Pleasant** Arthur **Reich** (30 Aug 1887 NC – 16 Jan 1959 Winston-Salem)
    issue of 2nd:
    b) **Martha Drane** (Nov 1895 Clemmons – ...)

---

[133] 1880 Census: Clemmonsville, Davidson Co. NC.

c) **Paul** Tifflin **Drane** (8 Nov 1896 Clemmons – 2 Feb 1958 Winston-Salem)
= ...; **Carrie** Lee **Loggins** (1916 – ...)
has issue
d) **William Drane** (Nov 1898 Clemmons – ...)
e) **Alfred Drane** (1900 Clemmons – 1931)
= ...; Vera **Maria Wood** (...)
has issue
f) **Elizabeth Drane** (ca.1903 Clemmons – ...)
g) **Lula Drane** (ca.1905 Clemmons – ...)
= ...; **Junius Cochran** (...)
h) **Lillie** Julie **Drane** (ca.1908 Clemmons – ...)
= 26 Dec 1931 Henry Co. VA; **John** Howard **Carver** (18 Jan 1909 – ...) son of Manual Carver & Fleta Veach
i) **Hazel Drane** (ca.1911 Clemmons – ...)
j) **Dewey** Edward **Drane** (17 Oct 1912 Clemmons – 20 May 1980)
= ...; **Alice** Josephine **Stipe** (5 Nov 1913 Winston-Salem – 17 Oct 1938 Winston-Salem) daughter of H.W. Stipe & Nannie Neely
issue ?
k) **Lucille Drane** (ca.1915 Clemmons – ...)
l) **Glenn** Robert **Drane** (3 Aug 1919 Clemmons – 23 Sep 2001 Stokes Co. NC)
= ...; **Fannie Jones** (14 Oct 1918 – 15 Apr 2007)
has issue
2) Mary **Elizabeth Drane** (12 Feb 1873 Davidson Co. – 13 Feb 1908 Clemmons)
= ...; ... **Taylor** (...)
3) **Thomas Drane** (ca.1876 Davidson Co. – ...)
4) **James Drane** (20 Mar 1880 Davidson Co. – 9 Dec 1945 Durham, NC)
= ...; **Eula Churchill** (12 Jul 1886 – 18 Sep 1978)
has issue
5) **Charles Drane** (1884 – 1886)
6) **Anne Drane** (Apr 1888 Davidson Co. – ...)
7) **Emma Drane** (July 1894 Clemmons – ...)
F) **Nancy Drane** (ca.1836 Brosville – Mar 1891)
= 3 Feb 1852 Pittsylvania Co.; **George** Jackson **Green** (28 Apr 1828 Brosville – ca.1890) son of John Green & Sally Clark

G) **Martha** William **Drane**[134] (20 May 1840 Brosville – bef. 1936)
      = 31 Mar 1861 Pittsylvania Co.; **Absalam Haynes** (ca.1840 Pittsylvania Co. – bef.1900)
   H) **Lucy Drane** (ca.1846 Brosville – ...)
II) **Sally Drane** (...)
   = 26 Jan 1822 Pittsylvania Co; **Joseph Brimm** (...)
III) **Martha Drane** (...)
   = 19 Dec 1825 Pittsylvania Co; **James Oakes** (...)
IV) **Polly Drane** (...)
   = 27 Dec 1827 Pittsylvania Co.; **William Yearbrey** (...)
V) **Thomas Drain** (ca.1800 Pittsylvania Co. – aft.1860 Gallatin, Daviess Co. MO)
   = 3 Dec 1831 Pittsylvania Co; Nancy **Susan Shackleford** (ca.1805 VA – bef.1860 MO)
   A) **Deidamia Drain** (Sep 1832 Pittsylvania Co. – aft.1900 Lone Tree, KS)
      = 8 Dec 1853 Daviess Co., MO; **Andrew Blakely** (Jul 1831 London, KY – aft.1900 Lone Tree)
   B) **William Drain** (Jul 1834 Pittsylvania Co. – 1928 Pleasantville, IA)
      = 13 Dec 1866 Daviess Co.; **Cynthia** Ann **Richesson** (2 Jun 1848 Warren Co. IA – 29 Jun 1935 Mexico, MO) daughter of Michael Richesson & Arathusa Farrington
      1) **Deidamia Drain** (ca.1868 Daviess Co. – bef.1900)
      2) a child (+ bef.1900)
      3) **William** Thomas **Drain** (17 Oct 1872 Daviess Co. – 18 Aug 1951 Audrain Co. MO)
         = ...; **Elizabeth Brundage** (1882 – 1956)
         has issue
      4) a child (+bef.1900)
      5) **Bert** Frances **Drain** (29 Jun 1877 Audrain Co. – 6 Jun 1933 Pike Co. MO)
         =1 1900; **Frances** ... (May 1882 MO – ...)
         =2 22 Dec 1916; **Manerva** Angeline **Qualls** (27 Aug 1889 Audrain Co. – 22 Feb 1976 Fulton, MO) =1st James Edwards
         no issue
   C) **John Drain** (ca.1835 VA – aft.1860 Cass Co., NE)
      = 17 Jul 1855 Halifax Co., VA; **Mary Walthall** (ca.1825 VA –...)
   D) **Perry Drain** (ca.1839 MO – 1860s)
   E) **Allison Drain** (ca.1841 MO – ...)

---

[134] Lived with her widowed sister-in-law, Phoebe in 1900 census.

F) **Nancy Drain** (ca.1844 MO – ...)
G) **Pocahontas Drain** (ca.1847 MO – ...)
H) **Celestia Drain** (Sep 1850 MO – aft.1920) (twin)
I) **Reason Anthony Drain** (5 Sep 1850 MO – 28 Feb 1927 Mexico, Missouri) (twin) unm.

Chapter 10
The Rockbridge County Drains
Including migrations to the Ohio River Valley and to Colorado

So far in this book, I have challenged several notions that people researching the Drane family have taken for granted. In each case, I have tried to show the sources, or in some cases, the lack of sources, to support each conclusion I have drawn. One of these notions I have challenged, without much support so far, is that Anthony Drane of Prince George's County had an unknown wife prior to Ann Smith. This chapter is where we will discuss the family members whose records have drawn me to this conclusion.

The Drains of Rockbridge County, Virginia—and that is the spelling they mostly used—was founded by David Drain. David is my direct ancestor. When researching my own ancestry, I found it reasonably easy to get back to David, but not to his ancestors. Not until comparing notes with a second cousin I didn't know I had and who lived remarkably close to me, in Colorado.

David disappears from the Virginia censuses between 1840 and 1850, at a time when he would have been in his 70s, so it was easy to assume he died. But that was not the case. He packed up his wife and two of his sons, and the lot of them moved to Illinois. But why move to Illinois when in his 70s? Because the U.S. government gave him free land there.

David Drain received a War Grant of land in what became Warren County, Illinois. But he did not serve in any war to receive this land. His brother, Stephen, did, and Stephen named David as his heir. Stephen's military records from the War of 1812 are the key to linking this all together. Stephen entered the military as a minor and therefore needed the signature of his father. This approval document clearly shows Stephen's father to be Anthony Drane of Prince George's County. The only adult Drane named Anthony living in Prince George's County at the beginning of the War of 1812 was the one who was married to Ann Smith. So this establishes that Stephen, born in 1795, well after the marriage of Anthony to Ann Smith, is definitely their son.

The next document in the same war records is the one signed by Stephen designating his heir in the event he died on active duty, which is exactly what happened. He designated David Drain of Rockbridge County his heir, noting that David was his brother. Hezekiah would have been dead by this time, so David was the eldest surviving brother, a natural selection for a young, single soldier to make. Furthermore, Stephen joined a Virginia regiment rather than a Maryland one, suggesting maybe he went with David when the latter moved to Virginia. This nomination of his brother David as heir proves that David is a child of Anthony.

However, this becomes a conflict between David and Ann Smith. David was born in 1772; this is documented by his death record and supported by all of the censuses he is recorded in. Anthony and Ann Smith did not marry until 1778; their marriage record survives. Furthermore, Anthony's son, Hezekiah, is older than David. So this can only mean that Anthony had a wife before Ann. This first marriage would have taken place in approximately 1770. During the Revolution, many records were destroyed, and it appears this is what happened in Prince George's County. Sadly, Hezekiah and David's mother is, therefore, lost to history.

Just to rule out one other possibility—it was not common in colonial times, but did occasionally happen that a couple would have children before getting married. This could not be the case with Anthony, Ann, and his older sons. Ann's date of birth is recorded on her death record as 1761. This means she would have only been ten when Hezekiah was born and eleven when David was born. As it was, she was only seventeen when she married Anthony, so she is clearly not Hezekiah; and David's mother.

Having established David's place in the family, he removed himself from their presence pretty early on. He was in Rockbridge County, which was in the center of what was then Virginia—after West Virginia broke away, it became the new western edge of Virgina—by 1801, when he married 16-year-old Jean Hayslet, whose family had already been there for a decade or so.

David and Jean settled near the town of Lexington, which then was not much more than a wide spot in a road that wasn't even built yet. He was a farmer all of his life. They had seven children who lived long enough to appear in some record somewhere. But there are several gaps in their ages, suggesting there likely were a few children who died young.

Not much is known about David's life in Lexington, except that he left it in the early 1840s to claim the land which should have gone to his brother Stephen. Stephen had died while on active duty during the War of 1812, not from any military action, but from dysentery. However, because of his service, he, or his heir in this case, was entitled to the War Grant of land.

The land given out by the government, as was usually the case, was in a newly opened and undeveloped area. This parcel sat in the western part of Illinois, in the area that "bulges out" to the west if one is looking at a state map. The land was not prime real estate by any means. The Mississippi River was several miles away and there were no nearby streams or creeks. Farming on this piece of brick was no easy task, and the family would sell the land after David's death.

I found it remarkable that David would move, in his mid-70s, to what was then the untamed west. But he must have been a man of great of stamina, because he lived nearly 20 more years once he got there. At his death in December 1863, David was 91 years old, an age almost unheard of in those days. His wife, Jean, had died seven years earlier at age 71.

David and Jean took their eldest and youngest sons, John and David, to Illinois with them. John married there in 1845, to Abigail Rounds. Abby was John's second wife. When arriving in Illinois, he had a daughter, Thankful, who was born in 1824. Thankful died unmarried in 1848. John and Abby's only children were a set of twins who also died at young ages.

The exact date of the family's westward relocation is not known, but the earliest recorded event for them in Warren County was David Jr.'s 1842 marriage to Lucinda Meachum. It also was not recorded what path the family took from Virginia to Illinois, but it probably involved going down the Ohio River a large part of the way. This idea is reinforced by the fact that David and Lucinda named their first child Cincinatus. Cincinnati, Ohio, must have made quite the impression on the young David, Cincinatus was followed by two more brothers, Andrew Hayslet and William.

David Drain Jr. worked in the import/export business and used the nearby Mississippi River as his connection to the rest of the world. It was while on a trade mission to South America that David died, in 1850, while at sea near Panama. His widow, Lucinda, remarried to Alfonso Smith.

Cincinatus Drain married Harriet Baldwin in 1863. Their only child, a daughter named Orpha, married Frank Earle of Rhode Island, and they settled in Kansas.

Andrew Hayslet Drain married Virginia Wornam, and they had four sons, James, Edwin, Ralph, and Dale. Edwin and Dale died unmarried. James made a career of the military, ultimately being appointed General. Most of his children were daughters, his one son, James Jr., married, but died childless in 1993.

William Drain and his wife, Almira Ray, are the ancestors of the Drains who still remain in the western bulge of Illinois. They had a total of twelve children, which included five sons, who would each leave descendants, all of whom were born after 1900.

David Drain's and Jean Hayslet's second son, Lorenzo, lived to adulthood, but not much more. He died as a young adult while the family was all still in Rockbridge County. The third son, William, remained in Lexington with his wife, Ann Armstrong. They had eight children before his death in 1859.

When the South seceded from the Union, Ann found herself a proud American who suddenly was no longer in the United States. Many Virginians found themselves in this same predicament, prompting the state to split in half, the western portion being readmitted to the Union as the State of West Virginia, in June, 1863. Ann, and several other residents of Lexington, still found themselves on the wrong side of the dividing line, so had to move their families into the new state.

Ann and her children apparently wanted to make sure they were well inside the Union's borders because they moved to the far side of West Virginia, settling in Parkersburg on the Ohio River. By this time, her elder children had already married and the two eldest daughters, Mary and Caroline, chose to remain with their husbands' families in Lexington. One son, John Roland, made himself a black sheep in his mother's eyes by actually joining the Confederate Army. He was killed in action in the Battle of Chancellorsville in 1863.

The move from Confederate State to Union State also seems to have prompted a change in the spelling of the family name. After arriving in Parkersburg, the name seems to have been spelled Drane very regularly, with one notable exception, which will be discussed shortly.

When the smoke of the War cleared, Ann was left with four surviving sons, who were all with her in Parkersburg: Robert, Lewis, James, and William. Each of these sons had numerous children, and the Drane male lines in Parkersburg today all come from these brothers. Ann lived on another 25 years after the war.

The only lines of the family to leave Parkersburg come from the eldest son, Robert. He married Elizabeth Anderson in 1859, and they had a total of ten children, but only two of the sons would have children of their own.

The elder of these sons was William Henry, who was always called Pete. He left home at an early age and really did not look back. His nieces and nephews always said they were never told about what caused him to leave, but they were left with the impression he essentially ran away as a teenager. And he ran far. He stopped running when he got to Kansas, working the farming circuit in the south central area of the state. There he he took up the Drain spelling and married Maude Cary, and with her had seven children. The whole family moved to Pueblo, Colorado, near the turn of the 20th century, and most of their descendants still live in the southern part of that state.

Pete's younger brother, Harry, also left Parkersburg, but he seemed to have done so to find a better job. He moved to East Liverpool, Ohio, which sits in the corner of Ohio where it meets Pennsylvania and West Virginia, along the Ohio River. In the 1890s, East Liverpool became a Mecca for the pottery and porcelain business, and it was in this industry that Harry made his living. He fell in love with one of the artisans who hand painted his plant's creations, Minnie Cornell. Harry seems to have had some difficulty with the proper arrangement of the cart and the horse, but luckily figured it out in time to say "I do" with Minnie just hours before the midwife was telling Minnie to "push!" with their first child. They had a total of fourteen children, but four of them died as babies. The next to youngest child became my grandmother in the 1960s.

The remaining son of David and Jean, James Anthony Drain, would be the only one to have descendants still living in the Lexington, Virginia, area. James married twice, and to two women named Nancy. His first wife, Nancy Standoff, was the mother of all of his children. He married his second wife, Nancy Porter Black, when they were both older and were both widowed.

James and Nancy Standoff had eight children, only two of whom were daughters. Of the six sons, William and David died unmarried, the latter dying of typhus while serving in the Confederate Army. The eldest son, Allen James, lived from 1833 to 1906 and fathered three children, all boys, with his wife, Margaret Riley. Margaret's brother Walter and sister Julia would also marry into this branch of the Drain family. Only the two elder sons of Allen and Margaret married and left descendants, all born after 1900.

Allen's younger brother, John, married Sarah Jane Moore. Jane, as she was generally known, was a second cousin to her husband. Her maternal grandfather was a brother to Jean Hayslet, John's grandmother. John and Jane continue to be represented in Rockbridge County by the descendants of their only son, James Anthony and his wife, Emma.

The next son of James Drain and Nancy Standoff was Andrew Jackson Drain. He married Sarah Potter in 1869, and went on to have fourteen children with her. Five of their children were dead by 1900, none of whom married. Of the remaining nine, the present day male-line descendants come from only two, Andrew Robert and Charles Gilbert. Each of their families were formed right around the beginning of the 20th century. The youngest surviving son of Andrew and Sarah had an unusual name. His given name was Napoleon, which was not so unusual for the day, as he was born during the Second Empire's reign in France, but his nickname was Pelican. It seems to be a childhood play on the given name, but it stuck and was the name he was known by until his death in 1965. He never married—or would that be mated?

James's and Nancy's youngest son, Charles, married Julia Riley, Margaret's younger sister. Their nine children include five sons who married, but one of those lines has since died out and another is unclear if they had children. If they did, it would have been well into the 20th century. One son, Stuart, and his wife both died prematurely, leaving a small son to be raised by Charles and Julia. This boy, Robert, died unmarried in 1976.

David Drain (1772 Prince George Co. – 9 Dec 1863 Warren Co. IL)
= 1801 Rockbridge Co. VA; **Jean Hayslet** (1785 – 1856) daughter of Andrew Hayslet & Martha ...
I) **John Drain** (ca.1803 Rockbridge Co. – ...)
=1 ...;
=2 19 Jun 1845 Warren Co. IL; **Abigail Round** (ca.1818 NY – ...)
issue of 1st:
  A) **Thankful J Drain** (Jul 1824 – 20 Nov 1848 Knox Co.) dunm.
issue of 2nd:
  B) **William Drain** (1849 IL – ...) (twin)
  C) **George E Drain** (1849 IL – 16 Oct 1855 Knox Co. IL[135]) (twin)
II) **Lorenzo Drain** (ca.1804 – btw.1820/50) unm.
III) **William Drane** (ca.1808 – ca.1859 Rockbridge Co.)
= 18 Apr 1834 Rockbridge Co.; **Ann Armstrong** (ca.1808 – ca.1880 Parkersburg, WV) daughter of Robert Armstrong & Rhoda ...
  A) **Mary** Estaline **Drane** (3 Jan 1832 Rockbridge Co. – 27 Feb 1901 Rockbridge Co.)
  = 16 Mar 1856 Rockbridge Co.; **John** James **Mays** (3 Oct 1839 Amherst Co., VA – 5 Feb 1896 Rockbridge Co.) son of John Mays & Susan ...
  B) **Robert** William **Drane** (1836 Rockbridge Co.– 10 Sep 1890 Parkersburg)
  = 3 Feb 1859 Rockbridge Co.; **Elizabeth** Jane **Anderson**[136] (1840 Rockbridge Co. – 1921 Roller Mills, WV) daughter of Thomas Anderson & Rosanna Tetherly
    1) **Emma Lou Drane** (ca.1860 – bef.1936)
    = 10 Apr 1881 Wood Co.; **William** Jackson **Ruble** (3 Oct 1859 Wood Co. – 18 Dec 1934 Parkersburg, WV[137])
    2) **Jennie Drane** (1863 – 1913)
    = ... **Stevens** (...)
    3) William Henry (**Pete**) **Drain** (9 Dec 1868 Parkersburg – 25 Nov 1938 Pueblo, Co.)
    = 18 Oct 1921 Anthony, KS; **Maude** Florine **Cary** (18 Jan 1877 – ...) daughter of William Cary & Elizabeth Trumble
      a) **Gertrude** Elizabeth **Drain** (18 Mar 1892 Harper Co., KS – 21 Mar 1930 Harper Co.)

---

[135] Buried in Hunt Cemetery, Saint Augustine, Knox Co. IL.
[136] 1900 census lists Elizabeth as having 10 children, all of whom were still alive.
[137] Buried in Mount Olivet Cemetery, Parkersburg, WV.

  =1 25 Dec 1909 Pueblo; **Orvis Farmer** (...)
  =2 ...; **Joe Hundley** (...)
 b) **Ethel** Lena **Drain** (18 Feb 1894 Harper Co. – 21 Nov 1950 Pueblo)
  = 15 May 1912 Pueblo; **George Webster** (10 Sep 1888 Chicago – 24 Nov 1968 Pueblo)
 c) **Raymond** Roy **Drain** (3 Mar 1896 Harper Co. – Nov 1975 Salida, Co.)
  = 26 Aug 1916; **Nellie Dunlap** (16 Jan 1898 – 11 Oct 1992 Canon City, Co.)
  has issue
 d) **Riley** Arthur **Drain** (23 Mar 1898 Harper Co. – 16 Feb 1958 Pueblo)
  =1 8 Sep 1918 Pueblo; **Minnie** Marie **Dunlap** (15 Aug 1900 Pueblo – 29 Aug 1929 Pueblo)
  =2 ...; Emma (**Peggy**) **Martinez** (...)
  has issue
 e) **Melvin** Lewis **Drain** (14 Oct 1900 Barber Co., KS – 16 Feb 1957 Sterling, Co.)
  = 12 Apr 1922 Colorado Springs, CO; **Mildred** Pearl **Lenehan** (30 Nov 1905 Newkirk, OK – 26 Jan 1948 Pueblo) daughter of James Lenehan & Essa Smith
  has issue
 f) **Oscar** Grove **Drain** (21 Jul 1905 Harper Co. – 13 Sep 1968 Pueblo)
  = 21 Mar 1925 Colorado Springs; **Ina Inman** (31 May 1907 Independence, KS – 28 Jun 1993 Colorado Springs) daughter of Joseph Inman & Minnie ...
  has issue
 g) Vernon William (**George**) **Drain** (3 Aug 1910 Pueblo – 12 Mar 1951 Pueblo)
  = 3 Sep 1935; **Rosita Sutton** (22 Sep 1915 Tampico, Mexico– ...)
  has issue
4) **Sarah** Frances **Drane** (1869 Parkersburg – bef.1936)
 = 22 Jan 1889 Parkersburg, **William** Henry **Meeks** (...)
5) **Julia** Florence **Drane** (1872 Parkersburg – bef.1936)
 = 16 Jun 1896 Parkersburg; **Herbert** Stanford **Lowther** (8 Oct 1871 Ritchie Co. WV – 12 Nov 1944 Orlando, FL)
6) **Harry** Raymond **Drane** (7 Mar 1875 Parkersburg – 20 Oct 1936 East Liverpool, OH)

    = 15 Oct 1902 East Liverpool; **Minnie** Mae **Cornell** (22 Jul 1884 Parkersburg – 22 Jul 1936 East Liverpool) daughter of Robert Cornell & Leona Brown
    has issue[138]
  7) **Thomas Drane** (1877 Parkersburg – bef.1936)
    = 13 Mar 1908 Parkersburg; **Alice Smythe** (ca.1879 – ...)
  8) **Rosa Drane** (Nov 1879 – aft.1936)
    = ... **Charles Hannon** (...)
  9) **Mary** Esther **Drane** (15 May 1885 Parkersburg – 6 Jan 1962 East Liverpool)
    = 10 Oct 1906 Beaver Co. PA; **James Bolles** (1884 – 1917)
  10) **Maud Drane** (... – after 1936)
    = ...; ... **Miller** (...)
C) **Caroline Drane** (ca.1838 – ...)
  = 19 Feb 1857 Rockbridge Co.; **Andrew Moore** (...)
D) **George Drane** (ca.1839 – bef.1860)
E) John **Roland Drane** (ca.1840 Rockbridge Co. – 13 Jan 1863 Richmond, VA) died of wounds in Civil War, fought for the CSA
F) **Susan Drane** (ca.1843 – ...)
G) William **Lewis Drane** (1845 – ...)
  = 29 Jun 1873; Elizabeth **Jerushia Strader** (... – 1909 Wood Co., WV)
  1) **Earl Drane** (...)
  2) **William** Isaac **Drane** (...)
  3) **James** Franklin **Drane** (16 Nov 1875 Waidsville, WV – ...)
    = 4 Dec 1894; **Viola** Mary **Spurgeon** (1 May 1877 – ...)
    a) **Mary** Elizabeth **Drane** (9 Jan 1896 – bef. 1989)
      = **Marion Gray** (3 Mar 1880 – ...)
    b) **William** Ira **Drane** (10 Jun 1899 Dodderidge Co., WV – 14 Feb 1989 Auburn, WV[139])
      = 25 May 1923; **Myrtle** Lora **Tingler** (3 Apr 1899 – ...)
      has issue
    c) **Carrie** Etta **Drane** (29 Dec 1901 – bef.1989)
    d) **Gen. Holden Drane** (13 Feb 1908 – 17 Apr 1965 Auburn, WV[140])
      = 29 Oct 1932 Pennsboro, WV; **Lela** Mae **Lusk** (13 Dec 1906 – 20 Jan 1994 Auburn)

---

[138] Harry Drane & Minnie Cornell were the great-grandparents of the author.
[139] Obituary in *Ritchie Gazette* 16 Feb 1989.
[140] Buried in Auburn Community Cemetery, Ritchie Co., WV.

  e) **Ella** Vera **Drane** (28 Jan 1912 – bef.1989)
   = **Marvin** Noel **Watson** (...)
  f) Carl **Wade Drain**[141] (28 Jan 1914 – 6 Nov 1990 Spraggs, PA)
  g) **Harold** Wesley **Drane** (15 May 1916 – 6 Oct 1991 Parkersburg)
  h) a son (...)
 4) **Jessie Drane** (26 Feb 1879 Ritchie Co. WV – 29 Nov 1964 Fremont, WV)
  = 11 Sep 1898 Gilmer Co. WV; **Jefferson** Lee **Flesher** (7 Oct 1869 – 26 Dec 1945) son of William Flesher & Eliza Spurgeon

H) **James** Matthias **Drane** (Mar 1846 Rockbridge Co. – 1903 Wood Co.)
=1 ...
=2 23 Sep 1880 Wood Co.; **Mary Frances Wigal** (Sep 1850 – 1917 Wood Co.)
issue of 1st:
1) **Charles** E **Drain** (25 Jul 1875 – 20 Dec 1941 Wood Co.[142]) dunm.
issue of 2nd:
2) **Amanda Drain** (1 Nov 1882 Wood Co. – aft.1941)
 = ...; ... **Corbin** (...)
3) James **Henry Drain** (5 Jan 1884 Wood Co. – 18 Nov 1932 Parkersburg[143])
 = ca.1908; **Ina** Irene **Mayhew** (4 Apr 1887 Mineral Wells, WV – 18 Dec 1958 Mineral Wells) daughter of Thomas Mayhew & Catherine Teeters
 has issue
4) **Susan Drain** (...)
 = ...; ... **Shears** (...)

I) **William** Andrew **Drain** (15 May 1849 Rockbridge Co. – 25 Jul 1923 Parkersburg[144])
= ...; Alma **Rebecca Marlowe** (Jun 1849 Wood Co. – 30 Mar 1924 Parkersburg)
 1) **George** Keever **Drain** (Oct 1881 – ...)
  = 22 Dec 1904 Wood Co.; Violetta (**Lettie**) **Jackson** (ca.1885 –

---

[141] Wade's siblings seem to have used the Drane spelling, but Carl is Drain according to the Social Security database.
[142] Buried Ruble Cemetery, Wood Co., WV.
[143] J Henry & Ina are buried in Ruble Cemetery, Wood Co. WV. He was killed by a falling tree.
[144] Buried Creel Cemetery, Davisville, WV.

 ...)
 has issue
 2) **Amanda Drain** (ca.1883 – ...)
  = 21 Apr 1902 Wood Co.; ...
 3) **Capatola** Vanlura **Drain** (Feb 1884 – ...)
  = 29 Oct 1902 Wood Co.; **Stonewall Jackson** (ca.1880 – ...)
 4) Joseph **Frederick Drain** (Aug 1886 – ...)
  = ca.1909 Wood Co.; **Inez ...** (ca.1893 – ...)
 5) **William Drain** (May 1893 – ...)
  = **Rosa ...** (ca.1893 – ...)
 has issue
J) **Julietta Drain** (ca.1850 – ...)
IV) **James** Anthony **Drain** (ca.1809 – 8 Mar 1889 Rockbridge Co.)
=1 26 Oct 1831 Rockbridge Co.; **Nancy Standoff** (ca.1810 – bef.1876)
=2 1876; **Nancy Porter** (Jun 1827 – ...) daughter of William Porter & Mary ... =1st ... Black
issue of 1st (none by 2nd):
A) **Allen** James **Drain** (17 Mar 1833 Rockbridge Co. – 8 Jan 1906 Rockbridge Co.)
 = 17 May 1880 Rockbridge Co.; **Margaret Riley** (1859 Albemarle Co., VA – aft.1910 Rockbridge Co.) daughter of Andrew Riley & Annie Flint
 1) **David** Floyd **Drane** (15 Mar 1881 Rockbridge Co. – 12 Sep 1939 Rockbridge Co.)
  = 28 Apr 1904 Rockbridge Co.; **Lula** Belle **Carter** (1869 Rockbridge Co. – ...) daughter of Nicholas Carter & Mary Ford
  has issue
 2) **Samuel H. Drain** (Sep 1887 Rockbridge Co. – bef.1930)
  = ...; **Mattie ...** (1889 VA – ...)
  has issue
 3) **John F Drain** (23 Nov 1889 Rockbridge Co. – bef.1900)
B) **William Drain** (ca.1834 – bef.1889)
C) **David C.C. Drain** (1836 Rockbridge Co. – 29 Oct 1861 Staunton, VA[145]) died of typhus while serving in the CSA army
D) **John F Drain** (23 Nov 1839 Rockbridge Co. – 23 Nov 1889 Rockbridge Co.)
 = 31 Dec 1866 Rockbridge Co.; Sarah **Jane Moore** (22 Jan 1834 Rockbridge Co. – 17 Sep 1911 Rockbridge Co.) daughter of Samuel Moore & Anne Hayslet[146]

---

[145] David is buried at Thornrose Cemetery, Stauton, Augusta Co. VA.

1) **Nancy** Ann **Drain** (20 Jul 1868 Rockbridge Co. – ...)
2) **James** Anthony **Drain** (15 Mar 1873 Rockbridge Co. – ...)
= ...; **Emma** ... (ca.1883 Rockbridge Co. – ...)
   a) **Bertha Drain** (ca.1898 Rockbridge Co. – ...)
   b) **Leslie Drain** (ca.1902 Rockbridge Co. – ...)
   c) **Juanita Drain** (ca.1905 Rockbridge Co. – ...)
   d) **James Drain** (ca.1908 Rockbridge Co. – ...)
   e) a son (1910 Rockbridge Co. – ...)
E) Mary Ann "**Polly**" **Drain** (1842 – ...)
= 7 Nov 1863 Rockbridge Co.; **Lewis Hostetter** (1838 Collierstown, VA – 8 Dec 1880 Collierstown) son of David Hostetter & Jane Hughes
F) **Andrew** Jackson **Drain** (ca.1847 – 1901 Rockbridge Co.)
= 16 Sep 1869 Rockbridge Co.; **Sarah** Ann **Potter** (30 Nov 1849 Rockbridge Co. – 31 Dec 1926 Rockbridge Co.) daughter of Jacob Potter & Elizabeth Bell
   1) **Gardner Drain** (1 Nov 1870 Colliers Creek, VA – Nov 1892 Rockbridge Co.) unm.
   2) **Frances Drain** (22 Sep 1871 Rockbridge Co. – 8 Nov 1935 Rockbridge Co.)
   = 29 Sep 1899 Rockbridge Co.; **Walter Riley** (1878 – ...) son of Andrew Riley & Annie Flint
   3) **Mary** Eliza **Drain** (25 Jul 1872 Rockbridge Co. – ...)
   = 7 May 1896 Rockbridge Co.; **Howard** Emmett **Loving** (1873 Augusta Co., VA – ...) son of John Loving & Ella ...
   4) **Andrew** Robert **Drain** (10 Sep 1875 Rockbridge Co. – ...)
   = 10 Sep 1897 Rockbridge Co.; **Bessie Hartless** (1880 Rockbridge Co. – ...) daughter of Jesse Hartless & Mattie
      a) **Violet Drain** (ca.1898 Rockbridge Co. – ...)
      b) **Jesse Drain** (ca.1902 Rockbridge Co. – ...)
      c) **Ethel Drain** (ca.1907 Rockbridge Co. – ...)
      d) **Virginia Drain** (ca.1909 Rockbridge Co. – ...)
   5) A. **Robert Drain** (23 Dec 1877 Rockbridge Co. – ...)
   6) **Oliver Drain** (1878 Rockbridge Co. – ...)
   7) **Charles** Gilbert **Drain** (2 Oct 1879 Rockbridge Co. – aft.1931 Collierstown)
   =1 ca.1897; ... (...)
   =2 26 Aug 1906 Rockbridge Co.; Martha "**Mattie**" **Carter** (5 Feb 1868 – 18 Mar 1922 Collierstown) daughter of Nicholas Carter & Mary Ford; =1st ... Thomas

---

[146] Anne (Hayslet) Moore was a niece of Jean (Hayslet) Drane.

=3 31 Oct 1931 Lexington, VA; **Nora** Belle **Vest** (ca.1876 Rockbridge Co. – ...) daughter of Calvin Vest & Eliza McDaniel; =1st ... Mitchell
issue of 1st:
a) **Herbert Drain** (ca.1897 Rockbridge Co. – ...)
issue of 2nd (none by 3rd):
b) **Della Drain** (ca.1909 Rockbridge Co. – ...)
8) **Josephine Drain** (28 Aug 1881 Rockbridge Co. – ...)
= 29 Aug 1909 Rockbridge Co.; **Oliver** Rogers **Blaine** (1886 – ...)
9) **William Drain** (15 Sep 1883 Rockbridge Co. – ...)
= ...; **Emma Brown** (ca.1886 – ...)
10) **Dock Drain** (31 Oct 1884 Rockbridge Co. – ...)
11) **Eva** Florence **Drain** (31 Mar 1887 Rockbridge Co. – 1972 Rockbridge Co.) (twin)
= 16 Oct 1907 Rockbridge Co.; **James** William **Potter** (4 Jan 1888 Rockbridge Co. – 1969 Rockbridge Co.) son of John Potter
& Emma Moore
12) **Herbert Drain** (31 Mar 1887 Rockbridge Co. – +young) (twin)
13) Napoleon **"Pelican" Drain** (1 Jul 1889 Rockbridge Co. – 11 Apr 1965) unm.
14) **Lucky Drain** (1892 – 29 Aug 1893 Rockbridge Co.)
G) **Charles B Drain** (22 Jun 1848 Rockbridge Co. – 28 Mar 1920 Buena Vista, VA)
= 5 Oct 1871 Rockbridge Co.; **Julia Riley** (15 Feb 1854 Rockbridge Co. – 18 May 1916 Rockbridge Co.) daughter of Andrew Riley & Annie Flint
1) **William** Donald **Drain** (24 Jun 1872 Rockbridge Co. – ...)
= 31 Mar 1897 Rockbridge Co.; **Emma Branham** (Mar 1881 Amherst Co. – 1916 Rockbridge Co.) daughter of Seth Branham & Patsy Hicks
a) **Bertha Drain** (5 Jun 1898 – 23 Mar 1955)
= 7 Jun 1921 Buena Vista; **Lloyd** Hudson **Level** (14 Oct 1895 Luray, VA – ...) son of Beauregard Level & Belle Skelton; fought in WWI
b) **Nannie Drain** (27 Nov 1901 Rockbridge Co. – 25 Feb 1989)
= **Jake Carter** (...)
c) **James** Donald **Drain** (12 Aug 1905 Buena Vista – 7 Jan 2008 Frederick, MD)

= ...; **Anne Groshon** (12 Dec 1912 Gaithersburg, MD – 7 Nov 1999 Hagerstown, MD) daughter of Clarence Groshon & Rosa Craver
has issue

d) Russell **"Pete"** Curtis **Drain** (12 Feb 1910 Lexington, VA – Nov 1977 Stanley, VA)
= 4 Jun 1931 Page Co., VA; **Ruth** Margaret **Donovan** (1913 - ...) daughter of Ernest Donovan & Emma Nauman

e) Viola **Drain** (Jun 1916 – ...)
= ...; **...Giles** (...)

2) James **Stuart Drain** (19 Apr 1874 Rockbridge Co. – bef.1900)
= 5 Mar 1895 Rockbridge Co.; **Annie Smith** (...) daughter of John Smith

a) **Robert Drain** (3 Apr 1897 Rockbridge Co. – May 1976 Salem, VA)

3) **Hannah Drain** (Jul 1876 – ...)
= 29 Jan 1899 Rockbridge Co.; **Daniel Tyree** (1856 Amherst Co. – ...)

4) **Calvin M Drain** (14 Apr 1879 Rockbridge Co. – ...)
= 19 Jul 1901 Rockbridge Co.; **Virginia Hicks** (1881 Rockbridge Co. – ...) daughter of James Hicks and Susan ...
has issue

5) **Rosa Belle Drain** (15 Apr 1884 Rockbridge Co. – ...)
= 11 Oct 1908 Rockbridge Co.; **Elisha** Megyson **Smith** (1886 – ...)

6) Albert **Tucker Drain** (Apr 1889 – ...) (twin)
= **June ...** (...)

7) Harry **Lee Drain** (Apr 1889 – ...) (twin)
=1 ca.1909 Rockbridge Co.; **Alice Virginia ...** (ca.1892 VA – bef.1920)
=2 ca.1928 NJ; **Anna ...** (ca.1912 NJ – ...)
has issue

8) **Bertie** Elizabeth **Drain** (26 Jul 1892 Triford, VA – ...)
= 16 Jun 1911 Buena Vista, VA; **James** William **Kelly** (1889 Rockbridge Co. – ...) son of David Kelly & Virginia ...

9) **Mary Drain** (4 Aug 1896 Rockbridge Co. – Oct 1976 Willshire, OH)
= **Jesse Painter** (...)

H) **Margaret Drain** (ca.1849 – ...)
= 1 Feb 1872 Rockbridge Co.; **James Boley** (ca.1844 Bedford Co., VA – ...) son of John Boley & Amelia ...

V) **Nancy Drain** (10 Feb 1810 Rockbridge Co. – 3 May 1882 Mercer Co., OH)
= 20 May 1934 Rockbridge Co.; **James** Tate **Ford** (15 Mar 1913 Rockbridge Co. – 13 Jul 1884 Mercer Co.) son of Ellison Ford & Elizabeth Tate

VI) **David Drain Jr.** (ca.1815 VA – ca.1850 at sea off Panama)
= 22 Apr 1842 Warren Co.; **Lucinda Meachum** (ca.1816 – ...) =2nd Alfonso Smith

  A) **Cincinatus Drain** (ca.1844 IL – ...)
    = 15 Oct 1863 Warren Co.; **Harriet** Ellen **Baldwin** (ca.1848 – ...)
    1) Sarah **Orpha Drain** (30 Sep 1870 – ...)
      = Sep 1888 Driftwood, KS; **Frank** Earle **Randall** (22 Jan 1860 Providence, RI – 1929) son of Stephen Randall & Deborah Joslin

  B) **Andrew** Hayslet **Drain** (ca.1845 Warren Co. – 1925)
    = 30 Dec 1869 Ellison, IL; **Virginia** Whitley **Wornam** (9 Aug 1849 – ...) daughter of Charles Wornam & Jane Gilmor
    1) **Gen. James** Andrew **Drain** (30 Sep 1870 Warren Co. – 23 May 1943 Washington, DC)
      = 24 Jun 1891; **Ethel** Mary **Marsland** (5 Mar 1868 – aft. 1943) daughter of Thomas Marsland & Maria Lord
      a) **Doris** Marsden **Drain** (1892 – 1976)
        = **Edward** Northrup **Hay** (...)
      b) **Kathryn Drain** (1894 – 1973)
        = ... **Lawson** (1890 – ...)
      c) **Gertrude** Virginia **Drain** (1898 – ...)
        = **Frederick van den Arend** (1894 – ...)
      d) **Marion** Whitley **Drain** (9 Nov 1901 – 6 Mar 2000 Clinton, SC)
        = **Clarence Hemphill** (1897 – ...)
      e) **James** Andrew **Drain, Jr.** (21 Oct 1903 – 27 Oct 1993 West Palm Beach, FL)
        = **Barbara** Jane **Atwater** (b.30 Jun 1912)
    2) **Edwin Drain** (ca.1874 – ...)
    3) **Ralph Drain** (20 Sep 1878 Kirkwood, IL – ...)
      = **Jeanetta ...** (ca.1881 – ...)
      has issue
    4) **Dale Drain** (4 Oct 1885 – Aug 1973 Washington, DC)

  C) **William E Drain** (Jul 1849 IL – aft.1910)
    = 17 Feb 1870 Warren Co.; **Almira Ray** (Dec 1846 – bef.1910)
    1) **John Drain** (Nov 1870 IL – ...)

= ca.1899; **Mary** ... (Apr 1884 IL – ...)
has issue
2) **David Drain** (ca.1872 – ...) moved to Los Angeles, CA
= ca.1902; **Carrie Bird** (ca.1884 IA – ...)
no issue
3) **Marvin** Deboski **Drain** (25 Oct 1873 Roseville, IL – 25 Jan 1933
Henderson Co. IL[147])
= 3 Jan 1899 Henderson Co.; **Jessie Henderson** (6 Aug 1881 IL – 26 Mar 1953 Henderson Co.)
has issue
4) **James Leonard Drain** (ca.1874 IL – ...)
= **Christina** ... (ca.1870 IL – ...)
no issue
5) **Lola Drain** (ca.1876 – ...) single in 1910 living in Plymouth Co. IA with father and brother Leonard
6) **Pearl Drain** (1 Aug 1877 Kirkwood – 3 Dec 1946 La Harpe, IL)
= 24 Dec 1896 Henderson Co.; **Ella Gilliland** (6 Oct 1875 IL – 2 Jun 1956 Henderson Co.[148]) daughter of William Gilliland & Nancy ...
   a) **William Drain** (Jul 1898 IL – ...)
   b) **Marie Drain** (May 1899 IL – ...) died young
   c) **Elzie Drain** (ca.1907 IL – ...) (a son)
   d) **Walter Drain** (ca.Dec 1909 IL – ...)
     = ca.1929; **Ruth Louden** (ca.1912 – ...)
   e) **Theda Drain** (ca.1916 IL – ...)
7) **... Drain** (– ...)
8) Eva **Blanche Drain** (Mar 1882 IL – ...) single in 1910
9) **Frederick Drain** (May 1884 IL – ...)
= ca.1915; **Mabel** ... (ca.1894 IL – ...)
has issue
10) **Mathie Drain** (Jul 1885 IL – ...) (a dau)
11) **Virdie Drain** (Jul 1887 IL – ...) (a dau) single in 1910
12) **George W Drain** (Jul 1888 IL – ...)
= ca.1906; **Alice** ... (1888 IL – 1963)
has issue
VII) **Mary Drain** (...)
= 22 Oct 1840 Wood Co. (W)VA; **James Rockenbough** (...)

---

[147] Buried in Stronghurst Cemetery, Henderson Co. IL.
[148] Buried in Stronghurst Cemetery. Henderson Co., IL.

Chapter 11
The Harrison County, West Virginia, Drains

The founder of this branch was one Isaac Drain. Nailing down any definitive information about him has been quite difficult. I have included him as a son of Anthony Drane solely based on Anthony's tendency to name his children from his first marriage from the Old Testament. I have not come across any other viable locations within the family for Issac. Therefore, I am leaving him here, with the caveat that I have no hard evidence that he belongs here.

Issac's parentage is not the only difficult piece for him. The information I am presenting in this chapter is what appears to be the case, but there are several issues which muddy the water with this family. Many of the marriages were between old men and young women, and using the Census is a little confusing because disparate family members lived together. A person's relationship to the head of the household was not recorded on the census until 1880, so the older generations are something of a jumble. However, the saving grace has been that once West Virginia formed its own state, the marriage and death records there became detailed enough to help fill in many of the gaps.

Issac went to Harrison County, which sits in the midst of the Appalachian Mountains, in the early 1800s. Harrison County is in the north central area of what, in 1863, became West Virginia. Like many members of his family, he seemed driven by a desire to see "what is out there." There is also a more practical reason why a son of Anthony Drane would pursue such a venture. Anthony had a lot of children, and his fortunes had greatly dwindled from their pre-Revolution heyday. His marriage to Ann Smith brought a substantial dowry, which helped keep the Drane plantation in Prince George's County afloat. But given the lack of potential inheritance, it would stand to reason that the sons were encouraged to go make their own lives. This reversal in fortune might also explain why so many of the descendants of Anthony spelled their name Drain. The Drane spelling seems tied to the ability of the parents to afford tutors for their children who would have taught them to spell their name the traditional way. Without that, the spelling was typically dictated by what local officials heard when it was spoken aloud. Dince it sounded like a water drain, they usually spelled it like a water drain.

Isaac's wife remains unknown. It is likely he married before going to Harrison County. The records from Prince George's County, Maryland, were largely destroyed in the War of 1812, so a marriage that took place there would easily be lost to history. They had at least three children, Azariah, James, and Elizabeth. These can be deduced from the marriage records of their children.

The first record of Azariah is his 1818 certificate of marriage to Polly Collins. The Collins family had been the first settlers in the area. The effort to piece together the exact number of children Azariah and Polly had has been difficult, but it seems to be ten. Of those ten, most died young, never married, or did not have surviving children. Life for a mountaineer family in pre-Civil War days was very rough. The predominant industry in the area was coal-mining, which added a burden to the health of the residents. Once the State of West Virginia was formed, forestry and farming added some variation to the available job market.

The only sons of Azariah and Polly to marry and leave descendants were Harrison and John. After Polly's death, Azariah married a much younger lady named Mary. They had at least four more children before Azariah died in the late 1860s. The descendants from the second marriage are through sons William Golden and Charles Jackson, both of whom married after 1900. After Azariah's death, Mary married Caleb Ashcraft, who was from the most prominent and prolific family in Harrison County.

The eldest son, Harrison Drain, married a cousin, Rose Ann, or maybe Rosanne, Collins, probably in the mid-1850s. They had four known children, only one of whom was a son, William Harrison, who was usually called Harrison or Harry. Harry married Mary Matson in the 1870s, and she died in 1897. Their eight children included four sons, Richard Cecil, James Lawrence, Hugh Grant, and Harrison Roy, who all married after 1900 and left descendants. Today, the Drains of Harrison County live mostly in the areas of Clarksburg, the county seat, and Shinnston, to the north.

Harrison's and Rose's eldest daughter, Emily, made an interesting marriage. She married her second cousin, Isaac Drain, a grandson of Haddock Drane, Azariah's elder brother. Their numerous descendants are discussed in Chapter 5.

John Drain, the second surviving son of Azariah's first marriage, married Malinda Cunningham in 1848. Although they had nine children, only two would continue the Drain name, sons Robert and Granville. Robert married Alice Martin and had two children, Thurman and Audra. Both of them married after 1900.

Granville Drain married Minerva Ashcraft, a relative of Caleb. They had four children, two sons and two daughters. The elder son, John, was the only one to receive a common name. His sisters were Retha and Dessie, and his brother was called Coke. Presumably, he was named for the coal derivative and not the newly founded soft drink, Coca-Cola. Both sisters married Drain cousins. Retha married her second cousin, James Lawrence, grandson of Azariah's eldest son, Harrison. Dessie married William Goff Drain, a son of Isaac and Emily. William and Dessie were double cousins since both Isaac and Emily were born Drains. There is an old saying that a lady is marrying too close akin when her name doesn't change upon marriage, but what about when she, her husband, and her mother-in-law all have the same birth name?

Isaac Drain's younger son, James, seems to have died pretty early on. He did marry a lady named Rebecca and had at least one child, James Jr. It is the 1855 marriage record of James Jr. to Rachel Thompson Tucker that gives us what little we know of his parents.

Rachel was significantly younger than James Jr. and may have been a second wife, but I have not found a reference to a first wife or older children. Rachel's children were Sylvester, Sarah, and Jackson. Jackson seems to have died young, leaving Sil, as he was called, to be the only male of this line to leave Drain descendants. He married Mary Lefevers and has descendants remaining through his son, George Washington Drain, who lived from 1887 to 1967.

Isaac Drain (ca.1774 Prince George's Co. – btw.1810/1820 Harrison Co. [W]VA)
= probably in Prince George's Co.; ...
I) **Azariah Drain** (ca.1795 – btw.1867/1870)
  =1 1818 Harrison Co.; **Polly Collins** (... – bef.1854)
  =2 17 Feb 1854 Harrison Co.; **Mary** ... (ca.1835 Harrison Co. – ...)
  she =2nd Caleb Ashcraft
  issue of 1st:
  A) **Harrison A. Drain** (... – bef.1880)
    = ...; **Rose Ann Collins** (ca.1820 – ...)
    1) **Emily** Jane **Drain** (1856 – 17 Apr 1931 Shinnston, WV)
      = 1868; **Isaac Drain** (1838 – 1915 Shinnston)
      see: Chapter 5
    2) William **Harrison Drain** (May 1857 Harrsion Co – 3 Oct 1943 Sinnston)
      = ...; **Mary** Jane **Matson** (26 May 1857 – 23 May 1897 Shinnston)
      a) Richard **Cecil Drain** (Apr 1879 Harrison Co. – ...)
        = ca.1899; **Belle** ... (Mar 1876 Harrison Co. – ...)
        has issue
      b) **Mary** Eveline **Drain** (25 Sep 1880 Harrison Co. – 6 Feb 1941 Lumberpost, WV)
        = 25 Nov 1905; **Asa Gallagher** (...)
      c) **Ivy Drain** (* & + Feb 1881 Harrison Co.)
      d) James **Lawrence Drain** (20 Jun 1883 Harrison Co. – 11 Jun 1968 Shinnston)
        = ...; **Retha Drain** (Dec 1885 Harrison Co. – 7 Apr 1945 Shinnston) daughter of Granville Drain & Minerva Ashcraft
        see below
        has issue
      e) **Hugh** Grant **Drain** (28 Jul 1885 Harrison Co. – 27 Jul 1954 Clarksburg, WV)
        = ...; **Nora Minor** (...)
        has issue
      f) **Harrison** Roy **Drain** (20 Dec 1887 Harrison Co. – 29 Oct 1960 Shinnston)
      g) **Bessie Drain** (May 1889 Harrison Co. – ...)
      h) **Alice Drain** (Nov 1892 Harrison Co. – ...)
      i) **Stella Drain** (Mar 1894 Harrison Co. – ...)
    3) **Minerva Drain** (ca.1865 – ...)
      = 5 Feb 1882 Harrison Co.; **James Hagerty** (ca.1860 – ...) son

of William Hagerty & Sarah ...
  4) **Effie Drain** (ca.1868 – ...)
  5) **Pleasant Drain** (ca.1873 – ...)
    = ...; **Charles Hood** (ca.1872 – ...)
B) **Emeline Drain** (ca.1821 Harrison Co. – 9 Jun 1901)
C) **John Drain** (1827 – 15 Dec 1877 Harrsion Co.)
  = 4 Jan 1848 Harrsion Co.; **Malinda** Ann **Cunningham** (1831 Harrsion Co. – Jun 1864 Harrison Co.) daughter of George Cunningham & Sarah Nay
  1) **Sarah Drain** (22 Jun 1849 Harrison Co. – 21 Jul 1932 Marion Co. WV)
    = ...; **Fenton** Hilby **Moore** (1844 – 30 Jul 1913 Marion Co.) son of Elias Moore & Mary ...
  2) **Mary Drain** (ca.1849 Harrison Co. – ...)
  3) **George** William **Drain** (Jun 1850 Harrison Co. – 7 Jul 1853 Harrsion Co.)
  4) **Leonard Drain** (* & + 1853 Harrison Co.)
  5) **Robert Drain** (29 Mar 1862 Harrison Co. – 9 Feb 1890 Harrison Co.)
    = 1 Jan 1888 Harrison Co.; Estella **Alice Martin** (20 Oct 1860 – 14 Jun 1942 Clarksburg, WV) daughter of Elmer Martin & Mary Garrett
    a) **Thurman** Blaine **Drain** (10 Oct 1888 Harrison Co. – 2 May 1928 Harrison Co.)
      = ...; **Lillian** Frances **Moore** (...)
      has issue
    b) **Audra Drain** (4 Apr 1890 Harrison Co. – Jan 1967)
      = ...; **Jerry** Curtis **Harker** (17 Apr 1887 – ...)
  6) **Aaron Drain** (1859 Harrison Co. – 25 May 1875 Harrison Co.)
  7) **Andrew Drain** (1860 Co. – 17 May 1898 Harrison Co.)
  8) John **Granville Drain** (Aug 1861 Harrison Co. – ...)
  = ca.1884; **Minerva** Jane **Ashcraft** (28 Dec 1868 Harrison Co. – 8 Mar 1933 Harrison Co.) daughter of Armistead Ashcraft & Elizabeth Brooks
    a) **Retha Drain** (Dec 1885 Harrison Co. – 7 Apr 1945 Shinnston)
      = ...; **Lawrence Drain** (1883 – 1968)
      see above
    b) **Dessie** Dorothy **Drain** (Jan 1887 – 13 Dec 1957 Clarksburg)
      = ...; **William** Goff **Drain** (1877 – 1961)

see Chapter 5
 c) **John** Thurman **Drain** (Mar 1891 Harrison Co. – 27 Feb 1950 Harrison Co.)
 d) **Coke Drain** (Jan 1894 Harrsion Co. – ...)
 9) **Gideon Drain** (1864 – 17 Nov 1893 Marion Co.)
D) **Azariah Drain** (1829 Harrison Co. – 22 Jan 1879)
= 16 May 1848 Harrison Co.; **Keziah Weekley** (ca.1828 – ...)
 1) **Tabitha Drain** (21 Oct 1853 Harrison Co. –
E) **Richard Drain** (ca.1830 Harrison Co. – 3 Dec 1864 VA)
F) **Mary Ann Drain** (ca.1834 Harrison Co. – ...)
G) **Eleanor Drain** (2 Sep 1835 Harrison Co. – 21 May 1916 Harrison Co.)
H) **Eliza Drain** (ca.1837 Harrsion Co. – ...) probably +young
I) **William Drain** (ca.1839 Harrsion Co. – bef.1867)
J) **Pressley Drain** (May 1841 Harrison Co. – 4 Mar 1922 Harrison Co.)
= 18 Mar 1866 Doddridge Co., WV; **Louisa** Jane **Carroll** (...)
no issue
K) **Ruth Drain** (1841 Harrison Co. – 5 Oct 1870 Harrison Co.)
= ...; **Nathan Ashcraft** (...)
issue of 2nd:
L) a son (24-25 Dec 1855 Harrison Co.)
M) William **Golden Drain** (Dec 1857 Harrison Co. – 3 Nov 1931 Paden City, WV)
=1 ca.1898; **Lucy** ... (June 1877 Harrison Co. – ...)
=2 ...; **Jessie** ... (...)
has issue
N) **Ashberry Drain** (ca.1859 – bef.1870)
O) **Sarah Drain** (ca.1865 Harrson Co. – ...)
P) **Charles** Jackson **Drain** (ca.1867 Harrison Co. – ...)
= 3 Apr 1898 Marion Co.; **Nancy Piles** (ca.1875 Harrison Co. – 1943 Wetzel Co. WV)
has issue
II) **Elizabeth Drain** (1798 – 11 Jun 1873 Athens Co. OH)
= 7 Oct 1819 Harrison County, (W)VA; **James Brandenburg** (...)
III) **James Drain** (... – ca.1825)
= ...; **Rebecca** ... (...)
 A) **James Drain** (ca.1823 – btw.1867/1875)

= 18 Oct 1855 Harrison Co.; **Rachel Thompson** (ca.1835 Harrison Co. – ...) daughter of Richard Thompson & Rebecca Ashcraft; =1st George Tucker
1) **Sylvester Drain** (31 Mar 1856 Harrison Co. – 4 Feb 1928 Harrison Co.)
 =1 ...; **Mary LeFevers** (Mar 1855 Harrison Co. – 26 Feb 1910 Harrison Co.)
 =2 ...; **Mary** Squires **Mason** (...)
 issue of 1st:
 a) **Susan** Himanda **Drain** (17 Aug 1879 Harrison Co. – 11 May 1924)
  =1 ...; **Alva** Grant **Martin** (4 May 1868 – Oct 1900)
  =2 ...; **Joseph** Floyd **Crites** (15 Mar 1884 – 6 Aug 1925)
 b) **James Drain** (Dec 1881 Harrison Co. – ...)
 c) **Charles Drain** (18 Apr 1885 Harrison Co. – 12 Nov 1943 Shinnston)
 d) **George** Washington **Drain** (24 Jul 1887 Harrison Co. – 17 Oct 1967 Shinnston)
  = ...; **Lydia** Myrtle **McIntyre** (...)
  has issue
 e) **Virginia Drain** (Jul 1894 Harrison Co. – 4 Jun 1910 Harrison Co.)
  = ...; **... Bunnell** (...)
2) **Sarah Drain** (ca.1865 Harrsion Co. – ...)
3) **Jackson Drain** (ca.1867 Harrsion Co. – ...)

Chapter 12
The Western Pennsylvania Drains

Kinzie Drane was another son of Anthony Drane and Ann Smith who left Maryland to make a life in newly settled lands. Most researchers try to spell the name Kinsey, which is a little more standard, but the records signed by the three members of the family to carry the name all use the Kinzie spelling.

Kinzie went to western Pennsylvania, settling first in Westmoreland County, southeast of Pittsburgh. There he married Elizabeth Burtner and later moved the family to Allegheny County, which is mostly made up of Pittsburgh and its suburbs. Kinzie and Elizabeth did not marry until 1827, but had already been living as man and wife for at least three years. Their first son, Kinzie Gibbon Drane, had been born in 1824. After their wedding, Kinzie and Elizabeth had ten more children, but only two more sons, Philip and William. Sadly,

William was killed as a young man in the Civil War, fighting for the Union.

Kinzie Gibbon lived from 1824 to 1909. He married Sarah McCollum in the mid-1840s, and they would have thirteen children, but several of them died young. The family made their home in Birdville, just outside of Pittsburgh, along the Monongahela River. For several years, Kinzie served as Birdville's postmaster. At the time of his death, Kinzie had three surviving sons, Charles, Albert, and Ulysses. His eldest son, William, also lived to adulthood, married, and left an only daughter before his premature death in the 1880s.

Charles Drane was the only one of the surviving sons to remain in Pennsylvania. He and his wife, Margaret, also faced the loss of several babies. Margaret bore a total of eleven children, but only four made it past childhood. Of those four, two sons, Kinzie Gibbon and James, have Drane descendants living today. Their children were born after 1900.

Neither Albert nor Ulysses are believed to have left any children behind. Both became wanderers, never settling in one location for very long. Albert went to the southern plains and made a living working in the up and coming oil drilling business. He spent most of his time moving around Arkansas and Oklahoma. Ulysses turns up at different times all over the country. It is not clear what he did for a living, but he seems to have settled into one place by 1930, where the census records him living as a boarder in Dayton, Ohio. Ulysses did marry at least once, in 1900, in Manhattan. His wife was Marion Lee, but they divorced, apparently without having any children together. He died in a nursing home in Dayton in 1960, at the age of 93.

Philip Drane, the younger son of Kinzie and Elizabeth, moved to Butler County, the neighbor to the north of Allegheny County. Here, he and his wife, Susan Hughey, raised their nine children. Unlike the other members of his family, Philip was blessed to have all healthy children, and they all lived to adulthood. However, only two of the five sons fathered children. The elder, Charles, married Ann Logan in 1900. The younger, Russell, married a lady named Helen in the 1940s. The descendants of both brothers primarily continue to live in the Pittsburgh area.

Kinsey Drane (ca.1791 PA – bef.1870)
= 24 Jul 1827 Harrison Twp; **Elizabeth Burtner** (10 Jan 1805 Allegheny Co., PA – 2 May 1884 Tarentem, PA) dau of Philip Burtner & Margaret Negley

I) **Kinsey** Gibbon **Drane**[149] (May 1824 Harrison – 11 Nov 1909 Birdville, PA) Pvt in the Union Army; one time postmaster of Birdville
= ca.1847; **Sarah McCollum**[150] (Apr 1827 – 24 Mar 1911)

  A) **William Drane** (Nov 1848 – bef.1900)
    = ...; **Agnes ...** (ca.1857 – bef.1900)
    1) **Edith Drane** (ca.1879 Allegheny Co. – ...)

  B) **Sarah Drane** (... – aft.1911)
    = **... Hawks** (...)

  C) Rachel **Ann Drane** (Apr 1853 – 24 Sep 1926)
    =1 ...; **... Miltner** (...)
    =2 ...; **David McCononaha** (...)

  D) **Caroline Drane** (ca.1860 – aft.1911)
    = ...; **James Ebensberger** (...)

  E) **Charles Drane** (Dec 1862 – aft.1911)
    = ca.1883; **Margaret ...**[151] (May 1862 – ...)
    1) **Charles Drane** (Feb 1884 – ...)
    2) **Beatrice Drane** (Feb 1887 – ...)
      = ...; **Isador Wibel** (...)
    3) **Kinsey** Gibbon **Drane** (Apr 1889 – 1951)
      = ...; **Sarah Gibson** (1888 – 1937) daughter of Joseph Gibson
      has issue
    4) **James Drane** (Sep 1891 – ...)
      = ...; **Della ...** (...)
      has issue

  F) **Ulysses** Sylvanus Grant **Drane** (1866 – 24 Jan 1960 Dayton, OH)
    = 10 Dec 1900 Manhattan, NY (dv.bef.1930); **Marion** Gertrude **Lee** (...) daughter of Richard Lee & Elizabeth Lynn
    issue ?

  G) **Albert Drane**[152] (...)

---

[149] 1880: Pittsburgh, 14th Ward, Pcts 3 &4, Allegany Co. PA
[150] According to the 1900 Census, Sarah had 13 children, 6 of whom were alive at that time. There is also a grandson, Charles (b.Sep 1874), living with them.
[151] According the 1900 Census, Margaret had 11 children, 4 of whom were then still living.

H) **James K Drane** (ca.1872 – bef.1900)
II) **Nancy Drane** (27 Mar 1828 Harrison – 16 Sep 1883)
= 24 Jul 1848 Harrison; **John Kean** (1824 – 1854)
III) **Margaret Drane** (7 Dec 1829 Harrison – 6 Jan 1912)
= 3 May 1849 Butler Co., PA; **Henry Smith** (ca.1825 – bef.1880)
IV) **Mary** Ann **Drane** (27 Mar 1832 – ...)
= 24 Apr 1855 Armstrong Co.; **Robert Lardin** (5 Jul 1810 Butler Co. – ...) son of Thomas Lardin & Christina Harsh; =1st Hannah Pugh
V) **Elizabeth** Elton **Drane** (Feb 1834 – 7 Jan 1889)
= 15 Mar 1852 Allengheny Co., PA; **Josiah** White **Lefever** (10 Jul 1825 Allegheny Co., – 25 Oct 1902 Allegheny Co.)
VI) **Christina Drane** (28 May 1838 – ...)
= 1858; **Joseph Best** (ca.1834 Allegheny Co. – ...)
VII) **Philip** Anthony **Drane**[153] (6 Sep 1839 Allegheny Co. – 8 Mar 1921[154] Butler Co.)
= 3 Jun 1869; **Susan Hughey** (8 Aug 1851 – 7 Feb 1943 Butler Co.)
  A) **William A Drane** (26 Jul 1870 – 3 Jun 1917)
  B) **Effie Drane** (11 May 1873 – ...)
  = 6 Sep 1892 Butler Co.; **Thomas Humes** (ca.1869 – ...)
  C) **Charles Drane** (24 Dec 1874 – Jun 1953)
  = 25 Apr 1900 Butler Co.; **Ann Logan** (Nov 1878 – Aug 1977) daughter of John Logan & Emma ...
  has issue
  D) **Emily Drane** (1877 – ...)
  = ...; **Charles Sauter** (...)
  E) **Anna Drane** (14 Sep 1882 – 1971 Butler Co.)
  = 25 Jun 1902 Butler Co.; **Albert Freehling** (1880 – 1969) son of George Freehling & Annie ...
  F) **Harry Drane** (Aug 1885 – ...)
  G) **Nettie Drane** (23 Nov 1889 – Nov 1981 Saxonburg, PA)
  = ...; **John Ekas** (b.6 Nov 1888)
  H) **Russell Drane** (31 May 1893 – Aug 1972 Sarver, PA)
  = ...; **Helen ...** (1907 – 1975)
  has issue
  I) **Jesse H Drane** (25 Oct 1895 – 14 May 1991)

---

[152] Listed in both parents' obituaries as living in Arkansas.
[153] 1880: Buffalo Twp, Butler Co., PA, name is written as Drum.
[154] A Sargeant in the Civil War for the Union. Wounded in the Battle of Wilderness, VA.

VIII) **William Drane** (ca.1840 Harrison – 1860s) killed in action in Civil War
IX) **Matilda Drane** (ca.1842 – ...) dunm.
X **Barbara** Ellen **Drane** (ca.1845 – 16 Oct 1848)
XI) **Sarah Drane** (7 Oct 1852 Harrison –)
    = 31 Mar 1872; **Andrew Ebensberger** (ca.1848 – btw.1910/1920)

Chapter 13
The Louisville, Kentucky, Dranes
Including migrations to Florida and Texas

The Dranes of Louisville are actually two families, one is the descendants of Anthony Drane, the youngest son of Anthony Drane and Ann Smith of Prince George's County, and the other is the descendants of Anthony Jr.'s uncle, Stephen Tillet Drane, who is the youngest son of James Drane and Elizabeth Piles.

The first of these lines is actually rather limited in numbers. However, the founder of the line, Anthony Drane Jr., was a very prominent member of Louisville society, and his descendants also rose to places of distinction. Anthony was a career military man who began by attending West Point. After his graduation in 1824, he ultimately rose to the rank of captain. In the late 1820s, he married Elizabeth Ferguson. He spent most of his military career stationed in and around Virginia and Washington, D.C. Most of his five children were born in Virginia. After retiring from the Army, he settled in Louisville, near his uncle, Stephen Tillet Drane, whose family we will discuss shortly.

Only two of Anthony's children married; both were sons. The elder, Joseph Kent Drane, married Mattie Poindexter in the mid-1850s. They had six children who survived to adulthood, but none of the three sons would have children of their own. The eldest of the sons, Poindexter Drane, followed his grandfather into a military career, also matching his rank of captain.

Anthony's younger son, Ossian Anthony Drane, married, had children, but also has no male lines living today to represent the family. Ossian and his wife, Josephine Dickey, had three children, Edgar, Herbert, and a daughter who died infancy. Edgar's only child by his wife, Mary Pope, was a daughter, Marion, who remained a spinster. Herbert married Mary Wright in 1885, and they had three children, Ossian, Mabel, and Helen. Both Mabel and Helen married, and any living descendants would be through them. Ossian joined the Army and fought in World War I with the rank of lieutenant. He survived the war, only be struck down by pneumonia in 1922. He never married.

Shortly after his marriage, Herbert Drane moved his family to Florida, where they were the founders of the town of Lakeland, which is now a suburb of Orlando. He entered local politics, serving as a State Representative from 1903 to 1905 and then returned to the legislature, moving over to the State Senate, from 1913 to 1917. He served as the Senate President the last two years of his time there. In the election of 1916, Herbert Jackson was elected to Congress as a Democrat, retiring from public service at the end of his eighth term in January, 1933. With his death in 1947, the male line of descent from Capt. Anthony Drane became extinct.

Having spent the past five and a half chapters discussing the descendants of Anthony Drane of Prince George's County, we now turn our attention to his younger brothers, all of whom left Maryland and founded branches of the family in different areas of the country. The youngest brother, Stephen Tillet Drane, is the founder of the second batch of Dranes, who were based in and around Louisville and Frankfort, in Kentucky.

Stephen was born in Prince George's County in 1768 and married there in 1793 to Priscilla Sprigg Crabb. The Crabbs and the Spriggs were both prominent families in the region at that time. Stephen and Priscilla had a total of seven surviving children, the first four being born in Maryland prior to the move to Kentucky. In 1801, the family settled in Shelby County, Kentucky, in what would become the town of Shelbyville, which is located about half way between Louisville and Frankfort.

Stephen's eldest son, Edward Crabb Drane, became a doctor and served the people of neighboring Henry County. He married Judith Dupuy, and they had five children. Although all three of their sons married, and two of them fathered children, the male line of descent from Edward became extinct in the 1920s with the death his grandson, Paul Shipman Drane. Although never married, Paul was an accomplished man. He graduated from Harvard University and travelled quite extensively, working for the government in various capacities. He called New York City home in his later years, so that he could be near his sisters, one of whom, Louise, was married to Carr Van Anda, one-time managing editor of the *New York Times*.

The second son of Stephen and Priscilla, Theodore Smith Drane, lived from 1796 to 1869. His wife was Edith Yates, whom he married in 1816. Unusual for the day, they maintained a small family of only four children, two sons and two daughters. The elder son, Stephen, married but remained childless. The younger, Benjamin Franklin Drane, was known as Frank. He and his wife, Bettie MacDonald, had nine children, including five sons.

Frank's eldest son, James, married a lady named Ida. Their only son, Leslie, was still single in the 1930 census, at the age of 42. The second son, Theodore, married twice, but several of his children died in infancy. His surviving son, also named Theodore, married and continued the family into the 20th century. The third son, Frank Jr., never married, and the two younger sons each married after 1900.

The youngest child of Stephen and Priscilla, Stephen Tillet Jr., is the only other son to have living descendants. He married Bertha Ford in 1828, and they had a total of ten children. Stephen Jr. briefly dabbled in politics. He was elected to the Kentucky legislature in 1856, but was defeated when he ran for re-election in 1858. When the Civil War broke out, he received a commission as a captain. After the war, he lived a quieter life in Shelbyville until his death in 1893. His widow outlived him by four years, dying a year before her 90th birthday.

Stephen Jr. and Bertha had seven sons, the eldest of whom was Edward Drane, a physician in Louisville. Edward's only surviving son died childless in 1923. The second son, Richard, never married. The third son was Albert Gallatin Drane, a name he shared with several distant cousins in other chapters. Albert and his wife, Salinda Hinton, produced five children, but only one of the sons, Henry, would have children of his own. Henry's marriage and children all occurred after 1900.

The next son of Stephen and Bertha, Merritt, moved to Navarro County, Texas, shortly after his 1860 marriage to Malvina Neal. Merritt and Malvina settled in the town of Corsicana, about 55 miles south of Dallas. Six of their eight children were daughters. But both the eldest and youngest child were sons. The elder brother, Frank, left a surviving son, Hugh, who married three times and fathered several children after 1900. The younger brother, Merritt, married twice, both times after 1900, so his descendants were all born in 20th and 21st centuries.

The last two sons of Stephen and Bertha were Leonard and William. Leonard served in the Civil War as a sergeant. He was wounded in both hands at the Battle of Perryville. His wounds were not fatal though, and he lived on to 1913. He married two times, but only had children with the first wife, Anna Shawhan. His male line continued into the 20th century through his youngest child, Joseph.

William Drane married Lizzie Skidmore in 1895. They had five children, including sons Bryan, Stephen, and James. Although James married, he left no children. Bryan's and Stephen's descendants continue to live in the Louisville area.

Line 1

Capt. Anthony Drane (19 Dec 1799 Prince George Co.[155] – 5 Apr 1850 Louisville, KY[156]) graduated West Point 1824
= ca.1828; **Elizabeth** Rebecca **Ferguson** (1807 – 1858 Bladensburg, MD) daughter of Richard Ferguson & Elizabeth Booth
I) **Richard** Ferguson **Drane** (13 Dec 1829 – 21 Jan 1930)
II) **Ann** Elisa **Drane** (Jan 1831 – 19 Oct 1833)
III) **Joseph** Kent **Drane** (31 Aug 1833 KY – Apr 1896 Louisville)
 = ...; **Mattie** Winn **Poindexter** (1838 – Jun 1895 Louisville)
 A) **Capt. Poindexter Drane** (May 1859 KY – Jun 1910 Louisville)
  = ca.1898; **Lela Reierson** (Jul 1865 VA – ...) daughter of Oscar Reierson & Mary ...
  no issue
 B) **Joseph** Kent **Drane Jr.** (Jul 1861 VA – Feb 1910 Louisville)
 C) **Mary Drane** (1865 Charlottesville, VA – 12 Mar 1900 Charlottesville)
 D) **Maximilian Drane** (1867 VA – Jun 1895 Louisville)
 E) **Mattie Drane** (Mar 1874 VA – Jan 1922 Louisville)
  = 5 Dec 1905 Louisville; **William** Wade **Wilson** (21 Jan 1879 – ...)
 F) **Rosaline Drane** (1878 KY – 1906 Louisville)
  = ...; **Ewell Button** (...)
IV) **Ossian** Anthony **Drane** (13 Sep 1836 – Oct 1908 Louisville)
 = ...; **Josephine** Frances **Dickey** (ca.1839 – ...) daughter of John Dickey & Bethia Duncan
 A) **Edgar** Duncan **Drane** (1859 – 9 May 1917 Jefferson Co.)
  = ...; **Mary** Rawson **Pope** (1867 – Apr 1930) daughter of Frank Pope & Kate Crutcher
  1) **Marian** Pope **Drane** (Dec 1893 – 4 Nov 1960 Louisville)
 B) a daugher (+inf)
 C) **Rep. Herbert** Jackson **Drane** (20 Jun 1863 Franklin, KY – 12 Aug 1947 Lakeland, FL) FL State Rep. 1903-1905; FL State Senator 1913-1917 (Pres.1913-1915); US Rep. 1917-1933 (D-FL)
  = 31 Dec 1885; **Mary S Wright** (7 Apr 1866 KY – 19 Feb 1946 Lakeland)
  1) **Lt. Ossian** Wright **Drane** (25 Apr 1888 Lakeland – 20 Dec 1922 Lakeland) Served in World War I; never married

---

[155] Prince George Co. Parish Register. Anthony Drane erected a stone on the original burial place of his parents calling himself their youngest son.
[156] Grave of Capt. Drane at Cave Hill Cemetery, Louisville.

2) **Mabel** Adrienne **Drane** (1891 Lakeland – ...)
   = ...; **William S Moore** (...)
3) **Helen** Josephine **Drane** (1895 Lakeland – ...)
   = ...; **James W Passmore** (...)
V) **Ann** Eliza **Drane** (20 May 1837 – ...)

Line 2

Stephen Tillet **Drane Sr.** (4 Sep 1768 Prince Georges Co. – 4 Dec 1844 Shelby Co.,KY)
= 24 Dec 1793 Prince Georges Co.; **Priscilla** Sprigg **Crabb** (11 Jun 1765 Prince Georges Co. – 14 Nov 1831 Shelby Co.) daughter of Robert Crabb & Ursula Sprigg

a. **Dr. Edward** Crabb **Drane** (27 Sep 1794 Prince Georges Co. – 20 Dec 1853 Louisville)
= 18 Apr 1822 Henry Co.,KY; **Judith** Coleman **Dupuy** (12 Mar 1802 – 18 Apr 1894 Louisville) daughter of Joseph Dupuy & Nancy Peay

I) **Joseph** Stephen **Drane** (13 Jan 1823 KY – 22 Mar 1869 KY) Surgeon, served in the Union Army in Civil War
= ca.1849; **Martha** Amelia **Gill** (... – 19 Sep 1850) daughter of Erasmus Gill & Nancy Smith
no issue

II) **Agnes Drane** (18 Apr 1825 KY – 12 Nov 1894)
= ca.1847; **Richard** Anderson **Logan** (ca.1814 – ca.1883) John Logan & Ann Anderson

III) **George** Canning **Drane** (17 Jun 1827 New Castle, KY – 1 Jan 1898 Frankfort, KY) Circuit Court Judge
= 30 Jan 1861 Niagara, NY; **Mary Shipman** (29 Mar 1835 – 3 Dec 1922)

A) **Paul** Shipman **Drane** (13 Jan 1863 Louisville – aft.1920)

B) **Judith** Coleman **Drane** (8 Oct 1868 Frankfort – aft.1920)
= 6 Jun 1895 Frankfort; **Virgil Hewitt** (20 Jul 1840 – 4 Jul 1898)

C) **Edward** Crabb **Drane** (12 Feb 1871 Frankfort – 22 Oct 1900 Elkins, WV) unm.

D) **Louise** Shipman **Drane** (26 Nov 1873 Frankfort – ...)
= 11 Apr 1898 Frankfort; **Carr** Vattal **van Anda** (2 Dec 1865 – 28 Jan 1945 Manhattan, NY) =1st Harriet Tupper; managing editor of *New York Times*

IV) **Martha Drane** (4 Nov 1828 KY – 4 Mar 1883 KY)
= Apr 1851; **Wade F Lane** (ca.1825 – ...)

V) **Edward** Morton **Drane** (8 Nov 1830 Henry Co. – 13 Dec 1914 Frankfort) Postmaster of Frankfort
= ca.1855; **Alice Keats** (ca.1838 – 15 Jun 1881)

A) **Adele Drane** (15 Mar 1856 Louisville – 18 Jun 1922

Frankfort) dunm.
B) **Clarence Drane** (15 Sep 1857 Louisville – Jul 1899 in Mexico) unm.
C) **George** Keats **Drane** (13 Jan 1861 New Castle – 6 Aug 1900 Frankfort) dunm.
D) **Edward Drane** (3 Mar 1865 Louisville – ...) + in infancy
E) **Agnes** Keats **Drane** (15 Jun 1866 Louisville – 15 Feb 1954 Louisville) unm.

b. **Theodore** Smith **Drane** (27 Oct 1796 Prince Georges Co. – 8 Feb 1869 Smithfield, KY)
= 2 Dec 1816 Shelby Co.,KY; **Edith Yates** (11 Apr 1799 – 25 Apr 1877) daughter of Benjamin Yates & Vineta Ford

I) **Dulcena Drane** (ca.1819 – ...)
= 21 Jul 1879 TX; **George Neal** (...)

II) **Stephen T Drane** (6 Jun 1820 – 1 Nov 1894 Henry Co.)
= 26 Nov 1851; Ruth **Ellen Berry** (3 Mar 1830 Henry Co. – 6 Jun 1906 Henry Co.) daughter of Edwin Berry & Eleanor Strode
no issue

III) Benjamin **Franklin Drane** (1 Oct 1822 Smithfield – 25 Mar 1902 Smithfield)
= ...; Mary Elizabeth "**Bettie**" **MacDonald** (Dec 1833 – 1913)

A) **James N Drane** (Feb 1858 Henry Co. – 1933)
= ...; **Ida** Belle **Kalfus** (Jun 1860 – 13 Oct 1950) daughter of Wlliam Kalfus & Nancy Black

1) **Nancy Drane** (15 Aug 1885 Henry Co. – 9 Dec 1968)
= ...; **James Tandy** (17 Aug 1884 KY – 6 May 1972)
2) **Alene Drane** (Feb 1887 Henry Co. – 1922 Henry Co.) unm.
3) **J Leslie Drane** (Oct 1888 Henry Co. – ...)
4) **Ethel Drane** (Mar 1890 Henry Co. – ...)

B) **Theodore S Drane** (1 Jun 1860 Henry Co. – Jun 1925)
=1 ...; **Ora Moore** (... – 1891)
=2 10 Nov 1891 Lousville; **Fannie** Barbour **Bate** (6 Jun 1865 Louisville – Nov 1944 Louisville) daughter of Richard Bate & Susan Robertson

issue of 1st:
1) **Mattie B Drane** (* & + 19 Apr 1888 Smithfield)
2) **Louis K Drane** (1891 – 1894)

issue of 2nd:
3) **Theodore** Robertson **Drane** (3 Aug 1892 Louisville – 7

Mar 1963 Louisville)
= 1918 Jeffersonville, KY; **Doris Bradley** (22 Sep 1900 – 6 Jul 1969 Louisville)
has issue
4) **Lottie** Alexander **Drane** (20 Jun 1895 Louisville – ...)
5) **Richard** Bate **Drane** (14 Jun 1897 Louisville – 9 Dec 1898 Louisville)
6) **Benjamin** Franklin **Drane** (Apr 1899 Henry Co. – ...)
 = ...; **Lola Gunterman** (... – 1930) daughter of Jesse Gunterman & Clara Line
C) **Mary Drane** (16 Mar 1862 – 14 Feb 1960)
 = ...; **H Miller Lail** (28 Jan 1858 – 3 Feb 1934)
D) Benjamin **Frank Drane Jr.** (1864 – 1938)
 = ...; **Beatrice White** (...)
E) **Charles** Edward **Drane** (June 1866 – 1929)
 = ...; **Agnes** Cecilia **Crumlish** (1877 – ca.1951)
has issue
F) **Minta Drane** (1868 – aft.1935)
 = ..; **... Barker** (...)
G) **William** Stephen **Drane** (Feb 1874 – 31 Dec 1935 New Castle)
 = ...; Marion **Vina Watkins** (1876 – 18 Sep 1952 Louisville) daughter of John Watkins & Rachel Totten
has issue
H) **Fannie Drane** (May 1878 – aft.1935) unm.
I) **Alice Drane** (10 Dec 1879 – 11 Mar 1959)
 = ...; **Richard Watkins** (22 Dec 1870 – 15 Jul 1961)
IV) **Emma** Bright **Drane** (1825 – 1886)
 = 1841; **Thomas** Harford **Jackson** (1818 – 1862) son of James Jackson & Winifred Harford
c. **William Drane** (14 Nov 1798 Prince Georges Co. – ...)
d. **Elizabeth** Emma **Drane** (3 Oct 1799 Prince Georges Co. – 1 Feb 1873 Shelby Co.)
 = 13 Feb 1816 Shelby Co; **Jeptha Bright** (19 Mar 1793 Montgomery Co. KY – 19 Feb 1870 Shelby Co.) son of Tobias Bright & Jane Ford
e. **Eleanor** Crabb **Drane** (31 May 1802 Shelby Co. – 14 Jan 1881 Navarro Co.,TX)
 = 12 May 1818 Shelby Co; **William Bright** (1 Jan 1795 Montgomery Co. – 20 Jul 1859 Navarro Co.) son of Tobais Bright & Jane Ford

f. **James** Hiram **Drane** (31 Mar 1805 Shelby Co. – 23 Oct 1892 Shelby Co.)
= 2 Nov 1825; **Nancy Wells** (11 Mar 1801 Shelby Co. – 21 Jan 1883) daughter of Hayden Wells & Nancy Ford
  I) **William C Drane** (31 Aug 1827 – 11 Aug 1834)
g. **Virginia Drane** (ca.1807 Shelby Co. – 1808 Shelby Co.)
h. **Stephen** Tillet **Drane Jr.** (25 Jan 1808 Shelby Co. – 16 Jul 1893 Shelby Co.) KY State Rep 1857-1859; Capt in Union Army
= 21 May 1828 Shelby Co; **Bertha Ford** (30 Oct 1808 Shelby Co. – 29 Aug 1897 Shelby Co.) daughter of Spencer Ford & Susan Bright
  I) **Dr. Edward Drane** (3 Feb 1829 Shelby Co.,KY – 1905)
    = 1 Dec 1858 Jessamine Co., KY; **Margaret F Neal** (5 Aug 1839 – 30 Jan 1910) daughter of Lewis Neal & Louisa Lowry
    A) **Bertha Drane** (...)
    B) **Nannie Drane** (...)
    C) **Merritt Drane** (1864 – Nov 1942 Louisville)
    D) Lewis **Tillet Drane** (Feb 1866 – 1923)
      =1 ...; **Minnie Peatner** (... – bef.1894)
      =2 ca.1894; **Mary Miller** (Jun 1872 – 1953)
      no issue
  II) **Richard Drane** (31 Mar 1831 – ca.1886)
  III) **Albert** Gallatin **Drane** (18 Nov 1834 KY – 19 Apr 1900 Henry Co.)
    = 19 Feb 1862; **Salinda A Hinton** (ca.1836 KY – ...)
    A) **John W Drane** (16 Nov 1862 Shelby Co. – 9 Apr 1925 Shelbyville, KY) dunm.
    B) **Merritt Drane** (7 Apr 1864 Shelby Co. – 10 Nov 1942 Lyndon, KY)
      = **Clara Lindiman** (1880 – 29 Dec 1960 Louisville)
      1) **Salinda** Hinton **Drane** (...)
    C) **Henry** Hinton **Drane** (9 Nov 1865 Shelby Co. – 9 Mar 1953 Shelbyville)
      =1 ca.1896; **Jennie K Calloway** (19 Jun 1874 – 1940) daughter of James Calloway & Minnie Tooley
      =2 ...; **Maude Johnston** (... – 1 May 1961 Madisonville, KY) daughter of Isaac Johnston & Annie Nash; =1st ... Pearce
      has issue
    D) **Richard Drane** (25 May 1867 – 21 Oct 1872)
    E) **Tillet Drane** (Oct 1868 – 29 Oct 1954 New Castle)
      = ca.1899; **Emma L Jackson** (May 1872 – 1947) daughter of

James Jackson & Eliza Bryant
no issue

IV) **Merritt Drane Sr.** (14 Apr 1837 Shelby Co. – 28 Apr 1895 Navarro Co.)
= 6 Dec 1860 Jessamine Co.; **Malvina** Todd **Neal** (9 Jan 1842 KY – 25 May 1896 Navarro Co.) daughter of Lewis Neal & Louisa Lowry

A) **Frank** Neal **Drane** (14 Jan 1862 Corsicana, TX – 1 Dec 1938 Corsicana) killed by power saw, possibly a suicide
= 13 Jan 1885 Wilmington, OH; **Florence** Adelia **Bingman** (13 Jan 1864 OH – 11 Jul 1932 Corsicana)

1) **Hugh** Albert **Drane** (10 Nov 1885 Corsicana – 7 Oct 1967)
=1 10 Nov 1910 Corsicana; **Lula** Love **Wood** (...)
=2 28 Feb 1918 Paris, TX; **Hazel House** (...)
=3 23 Aug 1933 Dallas, TX; **Anna** Belle **Brown** (...)
has issue

2) **Dorothy** Anderson **Drane** (1 Sep 1891 TX – 30 Sep 1937 Robertson Co.,TX) killed in a car crash

B) **Florence Drane** (17 – 19 Nov 1864 Corsicana)

C) **Ora** Bertha **Drane** (10 Jan 1866 Corsicana – 16 May 1882 Corsicana)

D) **Ruth** Hoskins **Drane** (21 Oct 1867 Corsicana – 4 Oct 1915 Dallas)
= 15 Nov 1887 Corsicana; **Charles** Robertson **Bullock** (...)

E) **Lena Drane** (6 Mar 1874 Corsicana – 27 Jun 1919 Corsicana)
= 15 Mar 1893 Corsicana; **Rufus** Nicholas **Elliott** (1870 New Orleans – 7 Jul 1943 Corsicana)

F) **May Drane** (9 Jan 1876 Corsicana – 28 Jun 1880 Corsicana) (twin)

G) **Maud Drane** (9 Jan 1876 Corsicana – 10 May 1908 Corsicana) (twin)
= 1 Jun 1898; **James** Knox **Parr** (...)

H) **Merritt** Arthur **Drane Jr** (15 Oct 1885 Corsicana – Dec 1958 Dallas)
=1 16 Jan 1907 Corsicana; **Frances Hammond** (...) =1st ... Bryant
=2 23 Jan 1913 Corsicana; **Eva Burgess** (...)
has issue

V) **Maggie Drane** (1839 – ...)

VI) **Stephen Drane** (14 Jan 1840 – ...)
  = ...; **Ona Moore** (16 Feb 1841 – 26 May 1865 Henry Co.)
VII) **Leonard Drane** (9 May 1843 Shelby Co. – 5 Nov 1913 Shelby Co.) wounded at battle of Perryville, a Sergeant for the Union
  =1 3 Oct 1876 Shelby Co; **Anna Shawhan** (30 Oct 1848 – 27 Feb 1885) daughter of Henry Shawhan & Sarah Cantrell
  =2 22 Sep 1887; Mary **Elizabeth Duckwall** (Nov 1846 – 1926) issue of 1st (none by 2nd):
  A) a baby (* & + 9 Sep 1877) (twin)
  B) **Maggie** Lynn **Drane** (9 Sep 1877 – ...) (twin)
    =1 ...; **William** Franklin **Miller** (...)
    =2 2 Jun 1916 Cynthiana, KY; **C. T. Eals** (...)
  C) **Henry** Shawhan **Drane** (Aug 1881 – ...)
  D) **Joseph Drane** (Dec 1882 – ...)
    = ...; **Fannie ...** (ca.1885 – ...)
    has issue
VIII) **Mary** Baker **Drane** (1 Nov 1847 – 1 Feb 1922)
  = 4 Jun 1874; **Dr. Samuel R Bass** (Oct 1836 – bef.1910)
IX) **Florence Drane** (1 Jan 1850 – 19 Nov 1867) dunm.
X) **William P Drane** (12 Aug 1854 – 19 Oct 1927 Louisville)
  = 21 May 1895; **Lizzie Skidmore** (1864 – 1950)
  A) **Bryan** Skidmore **Drane** (26 Jul 1896 Shelby Co. – ...)
    = ...; **Roseanna Sachs** (ca.1895 – ...)
    has issue
  B) **Mary Drane** (ca.1897 – ...)
    = ...; **Victor Albanese** (...)
  C) **Stephen** Tillet **Drane** (1898 Shelby Co. – 1971)
    = ...; **Christine Prewitt** (1900 – 1970)
    has issue
  D) **James** Edward **Drane** (18 Nov 1899 – 18 Jul 1987 Henry Co.)
    = ...; **Sylvia Blades** (17 Jan 1902 – 28 Apr 1979 Henry Co.) no issue
  E) **Pearl Drane** (29 Sep 1904 – 23 Oct 1996)
    = ...; **Claude Berry** (12 Jun 1900 – 18 Feb 1966)

Chapter 14
The Georgia Dranes
Including migrations to Alabama and Mississippi

The final portion of the American Drane family is actually two portions, the descendants of a set of brothers who both left Maryland to go to Georgia. Walter and William were among the sons of James Drane and Elizabeth Piles. Born in 1756 and 1765, respectively, the brothers set out for Georgia shortly after Walter's 1782 marriage to Althea Magruder. As it would turn out, William would also marry a Magruder, ten years later, Althea's sister, Cassandra. Althea's and Cassandra's parents were also Marylanders who moved to Georgia about the same time as Walter and William.

As the Drane boys traveled south, likely with the Magruders, they followed the Savannah River, which runs between the states of Georgia and South Carolina. They initially settled in Columbia County, which is situated right on that river. Columbia County remained the home base for Walter's family, while William moved closer to his in-laws in the next county over, McDuffie County. All of the children of these two brothers were born in this part of Georgia.

Walter's and Althea's line seems to be extinct in the male line now, but it did continue a few generations before that happened. Of their seven children, only one was a son, Walter Jr. Like his father, Walter Jr. had the adventurous spirit and moved as a young man to southern Alabama, eventually settling in Lowndes County, which is now a suburban area of Montgomery. Once there, he married Mary Austill. Walter soon found himself involved in the civic affairs of his community and was among the men who organized Lowndes County after its 1830 creation. Later, Walter represented Lowndes County twice in the Alabama House of Representatives.

Walter Jr. and Mary also had seven children, and like his parents, only one of them was a son, William Walter, who was known by his middle name, making him the third Walter Drane in a row. This Walter married Susan Foster shortly after serving in the Civil War.

During the Reconstruction era, Alabama's recordkeeping took a sharp nosedive in terms of completeness and accuracy. I have not been able to locate death dates or places for Walter, Susan, nor five of their seven children. Of these children, three were sons, Foster, William Walter Jr., and Maury. The only reference to the youngest is in the 1880 census, where his name is difficult to read. It may have been written as Manny. So presumably, his name was actually Maurice or Emmanuel. In any event, there is no record of the fates of Foster or Maury/Manny. They are not living with their parents in the 1900 census, but by then they would have been old enough to be on their own. They also do not appear in any subsequent census up through 1930. The only assumption that can be drawn from the available information is that they died as young men, probably unmarried.

The middle son, William Walter Jr., did marry, in 1893. However, he and his wife, Cindy Thomas, appear to have remained childless. Unless there are unknown descendants of him or his brothers, this line of the Drane family became extinct upon his death in 1943.

The descendants of the younger brother to leave Maryland, William Piles Drane, and his wife, Cassandra Magruder, fared much better. They were the parents of eight children, five of whom were boys, Stephen, William Jr., Benjamin, Hiram, and James. All five sons married and have descendants living to this day. They also became quite accomplished gentlemen in their own right and in different ways.

The eldest, Stephen, worked his way from a simple uneducated farmer to a clerk, and later a magistrate, of the local courts. He also served periodically, as needed, in the Georgia militia, first being commissioned a lieutenant in 1818, moving through the ranks quickly, ultimately achieving major general status under the Confederate flag. He was active in local politics, being from time to time elected to be a judge in later life. During peacetime, when he was serving on the bench, he made his living as a surveyor.

Gen. Drane married twice. His only descendants from his first wife, Rebecca Wilson, were through two of their daughters, Mrs. Cassandra Leonard and Mrs. Georgia Sanders. His second wife, Susan Hamrick, was the mother of his only sons to marry, Hamilton Stephen and William Abner. Both sons married and left numerous sons to continue the family name into the 20th century.

Gen. Drane's next younger brother, William Piles Drane Jr., followed his father into politics. After marrying Martha Winfrey in 1827, he moved his family across the state to Talbot County, near the city of Columbus. He served in the Georgia legislature in the 1830s and '40s. William and Martha had five children, although the youngest died in infancy. The remaining four were two sons and two daughters. The elder son, William Winfrey, married Eugenia Brown. They lived their lives as pillars of the community, helping their neighbors survive the hardships of the Civil War and the following Reconstruction. When William Winfrey died in 1910, the funeral had to be held outdoors, because there was no church in Columbus large enough to accommodate the crowd that wished to pay their respects. He and Eugenia had five children, but the male line continues only through their middle son, Eugene Drane, who married Irene Buchanan after 1900.

The third son of William Piles Sr. and Cassandra Magruder was Benjamin Drane. He started his life as a farmer on his father's farm, but after moving to Mississippi in 1838, was repeatedly elected as a judge in Choctaw County. While still in Georgia, he married Sarah Germany, and they had thirteen children. Of these, seven were sons, James, Benjamin Jr., William, Robert, George, John, and Edgar. Only James, John, and Edgar have male lines still surviving. One of the daughters is also of note. Miss Georgia Drane married a fellow named Henry Drane. It took some puzzle solving to figure out who her husband was, but with a little determination I have found he is the son of James Faustus Drane from the Montgomery County, Maryland line in Chapter 6. However, their only two children both died as babies.

Benjamin's son James and his wife, Elizabeth, had three children, two of whom were boys, another set of William and Walter. Although both sons married and fathered sons, the only line that continued to the present day was through William's son Charles, who was born in 1880.

James's younger brother, John, married Alice Booth in 1867. She was a relative of John Wilkes Booth, and the names Wilkes and Booth occur rather often as middle names for their descendants. Settling in Montgomery

County, Mississippi, they are known to have descendants from their second son, Howard. However, there is also an elder son, John Booth Drane, who married Susan Sullivan, but it is not known if they had children.

Edgar Summerfield Drane, the third son of Benjamin and Sarah to leave male issue, remained in Choctaw County all of his life. He married Sarah Love in 1866, and they had four sons, James, William, John, and Albert, who all married after 1900 and have descendants living today, mostly still in Choctaw County and the surrounding area.

Hiram Drane was the fourth son of William Piles Sr. Like many others in his family, he dabbled in politics, serving in the Georgia State Senate during the Civil War. After his first wife, and cousin, Eleanor Magruder, died in 1870, Hiram moved to DeSoto County in northern Mississippi. There, he married Electra Haughton. By this time, his children were grown, so they mostly remained in Georgia. Only his youngest surviving son, Hiram Walter, went with him to Mississippi. Hiram Walter also married twice, fathering fourteen children between the two wives. He has numerous male line Drane descents today in the Memphis area, which is just across the state line from DeSoto County.

Of Hiram Sr.'s elder sons, only William Magruder Drane had any surviving children. He married Margaret Bryan in 1854, settling in Talbot County, Georgia. They had four children, including sons William Arthur and Henry. Henry moved to Texas, but died there unmarried in 1905. William Arthur remained in western Georgia, where he married Lou Butt and fathered six children. The only son to father his own children was another William, this one called William Edgar. He married after 1900, and his descendants remain in the area of Talbot County.

Hiram's youngest brother, James, moved to Choctaw County, Mississippi, with his brother, Benjamin. There he married Matilda Shaw, from a prominent local family, in 1829. They had five children, including two sons, Virgil and James. The elder James Drane had a long and distinguished career in Mississippi politics. He served in both houses of the Mississippi legislature beginning in 1837, including a four-year stint as President of the Senate from 1860 to 1864. It was in this capacity that he signed the Ordinance of Secession, moving Mississippi from the United States to the Confederate States in January, 1861. The end of the Civil War ended his political career, as the Union-controlled elections during Reconstruction did not favor previous office holders. It likely also broke his spirit, since he died a few years later in 1869.

James's elder son, Virgil, lived a quieter life away from his father's politics. He married Mary Dean, but their only surviving children were all daughters. His brother, James William, made up the difference with his household of nine children, six of whom were boys. James married Frances Hemphill in 1854. Ten years later, he returned from the War a lieutenant colonel and severely wounded. However, he would live on until 1896, even marrying a second time after Frances's death.

Their eldest son, James, would finally bring the Drane name back to the Mississippi statehouse in the early 1880s, when he served one term as a Representative. He married his cousin, Belle Hemphill, but their only surviving child was a daughter, Fannie. The remainder of the Mississippi Dranes descend from James's younger brothers, Frank, Jefferson, and Hugh, all of whom married after 1900.

Line 1

Walter Drane (14 Jul 1756 Prince Georges Co. – 20 Nov 1807 Midgeville, GA)
= ca.1782; **Althea Magruder** (ca.1757 Frederick Co., MD – 19 Oct 1833 Columbia Co., GA) daughter of Ninian Magruder & Rebecca Young; =2nd Jonathan Reeves
a. **Rebecca Drane** (ca.1783 GA – 10 Oct 1802 Columbia Co.)
b. **Cassandra Drane** (ca.1786 GA – 29 Jul 1862 Warren Co., GA)
 = 7 Nov 1811 GA; **James Wright** (ca.1780 Warren Co. – 17 Apr 1838 Warren Co.)
c. **Ann Drane** (ca.1790 GA – ...)
 = 21 Jan 1808 Columbia Co.; **David Willson** (ca.1788 GA – ca.1828 Warren Co.)
d. **Elizabeth Drane** (ca.1792 GA – ...)
 = 3 Jul 1811; **John** Ed **Wooding** (...)
e. **Walter Drane** (ca.1796 – 24 Mar 1872 Collirene, AL) served in the AL House of Representiaves 1835-6 and 1843-4
 = ca.1831 Lowndes Co., AL; **Mary Austill** (ca.1807 – aft.1880 Lowndes Co.)
 I) **Mary** Virginia **Drane** (ca.1831 AL – ...)
 = 20 Oct 1847 Lowndes Co.; **John Vasser** (ca.1829 – ...)
 II) **Sarah** Austill **Drane** (ca.1833 Columbia Co. – ...)
 = 12 Sep 1850 Lowndes Co.; **John M Hrabowski** (ca.1825 – bef.1870) son of Thomas Hrabowski & Harriett ...
 III) **Elizabeth Drane** (ca.1836 AL – ... Lowndes Co.)
 IV) William **Walter Drane** (ca.1838 Lowndes Co. – aft.1885 Lowndes Co.) Private is CSA Army
 = 6 Nov 1867 Lowndes Co.; **Susan** Amanda **Foster** (5 Apr 1840 Dallas, AL – ...) daughter of William Foster & Sarah Roberts
 A) **Foster Drane** (ca.1869 Lowndes Co. – bef.1880)
 B) William **Walter Drane Jr.** (Sep 1870 Hayneville, AL – 4 Jun 1943 Hayneville)
 = 28 Dec 1893 Lowndes Co.; **Cinda Thomas** (...) issue ?[157]
 C) **Maury J Drane** (ca.1872 Haynesville – ...)
 D) **Mary** Virginia **Drane** (ca.1875 Haynesville – ...)
 = 5 Sep 1899 Lowndes Co.; **J. Y. Alexander** (ca.1870

---

[157] Unless there are descendants of this marriage, this branch of the Drane family is extinct in the male line.

Lowndes Co. – ...)
- E) **Margaret Drane** (13 Feb 1878 Haynesville – 20 Jul 1909 Enterprise, AL) (twin)
  = 23 Oct 1895 Lowndes Co.; **Dr. Joel** Carter **Sellers** (14 Mar 1870 Pike Co. AL – 23 May 1926 Enterprise) son of Joseph Sellers & Lucinda Carter
- F) **Rosa F Drane** (13 Feb 1878 Haynesville – 10 Aug 1901 Andalusia, AL) (twin)
  = ...; **Clive** Eskel **Reid** (1 Jan 1875 – 3 Jan 1913) son of George Reid & Laura Harris
- V) **Emma Drane** (ca.1839 Lowndes Co. – ... Lowndes Co.)
  = 3 Dec 1858 Lowndes Co.; **William Crook** (ca.1836 Lowndes Co. – ...)
- VI) **Caroline Drane** (ca.1841 Lowndes Co. – aft.1910 Lowndes Co.) unm.
- VII) **Clarinda Drane** (ca.1844 Lowndes Co. – ...Lowndes Co.)
  = 10 Sep 1860 Londes Co.; **Charles Patterson** (ca.1840 Lowndes Co. – ... Lowndes Co.)

f. Mary **(Polly) Drane** (28 Oct 1799 Columbia Co. – 31 Dec 1859 Dougherty Co., GA)
= 17 Apr 1817 Columbia Co.; **William Wilder IV** (27 Sep 1788 Warren Co. – 25 Jun 1860 Dougherty Co.) son of Sampson Wilder & Sarah Barfield

g. **Effie Drane** (ca.1801 Columbia Co. – ...)
= 22 Mar 1821 Columbia Co.; **David Perryman** (...)

Line 2

William Piles **Drane** (14 Jul 1765 Prince Georges Co. – 6 Feb 1847 Columbia Co., GA[158])
= 31 Oct 1792 Columbia Co.; **Cassandra Magruder** (13 Sep 1768 McDuffie Co., GA – 26 Feb 1860 Columbia Co.) daughter of Ninian Magruder & Rebecca Young

a. **Elizabeth Drane** (7 Jun 1793 – ... Tolbert, GA)
  = 17 Mar 1825; **Jonathan** Edward **Wooding** (... – 1844)

b. Mary **Eleanor Drane** (18 Nov 1795 Columbia Co. – 1866 Coweta Co., GA)
  = 1812 Columbia Co.; **Anselm** Buge **Leigh** (1794 – 1853 Coweta Co.)

c. **Maj. Gen. Stephen** Hamilton **Drane Sr** (20 Feb 1798 McDuffie Co. – 19 Nov 1880 McDuffie Co.) Gen. in CSA
  =1 7 Jan 1819 Columbia Co; **Rebecca Wilson** (9 Jan 1793 GA – 19 Jan 1859 Columbia Co.) daughter of John Wilson & Mary Roberson
  =2 10 Nov 1859 ; **Susan** Frances **Hamrick** (23 Nov 1839 Wilkes Co., GA – 27 Jun 1901 McDuffie Co.)
  issue of 1st:
  I) **Mary Drane** (1820 GA – 1887 GA) never married
  II) **John Drane** (5 Nov 1821 GA – ca.1859 GA) never married
  III) **Cassandra** Magruder **Drane** (4 Feb 1826 GA – 1892)
    = 11 Apr 1844 Columbia Co.; **Uriah Leonard** (1821 – 1863)
  IV) **Sarah Drane** (1830 – ...) never married
  V) **Georgia** Rebecca **Drane** (2 Aug 1831 Columbia Co. – 12 Mar 1902 Harlem, GA)
    = 1857; **Andrew Sanders, MD** (7 Feb 1832 SC – 17 Aug 1895 Harlem)
  VI) **Frances Drane** (1834 GA – ...) never married
  issue of 2nd:
  VII) **Catherine** Luke **Drane** (7 Nov 1861 Columbia Co. – ...)
    = 10 Feb 1881; **William** Augustin **Watson** (12 Feb 1859 Columbia Co. – 24 Apr 1937 Thomson, GA)
  VIII) **Hamilton** Stephen **Drane Jr.** (29 Nov 1863 Thomson – 4 Feb 1933 Augusta, GA)
    =1 17 Nov 1885 (dv.); **Emma Bacon** (20 Jun 1860 McDuffie Co. – 15 Jul 1918 Macon, GA) =2nd ... Marshall
    =2 ...; **Martha Smith** (...)

---

[158] Buried in Drane family cemetery in Dearing, GA.

issue of 1st:
A) **India** May **Drane** (17 Oct 1886 Harlem – 20 Apr 1889 Harlem)
B) **Gordon** Holliday **Drane** (31 Mar 1890 Augusta – 21 Jun 1957 Atlanta) Pvt in WWI
  = ...; **Anna** Mae **Cobb** (... – 28 Feb 1919 Macon)
  has issue
C) **Casey** Bentley **Drane** (a daughter) (15 Sep 1891 – 28 Feb 1919)
D) **Howard** Wayne **Drane** (4 Oct 1897 – 27 Apr 1965)
  = ...; ... **Wiggins** (...)
  has issue
E) **James** Emmitt **Drane** (...)
  = ...; **Alma** Louise **Owens** (...)
  has issue
issue of 2nd:
F) **Hamilton** Stephen **Drane** (Sep 1920 Augusta – Sep 1956 Tampa, FL)
  = ...; **Edries** Jean **Farr** (18 May 1920 Thomson – 8 Dec 1978 Tampa)
  has issue
G) **Martha** Jean **Drane** (1929 – 1972)
  = ...; ... **Aiken** (...)
IX) **William** Abner **Drane** (15 Oct 1869 Columbia Co. – 31 Oct 1904 Thomson)
= 10 Mar 1891; **Cornelia** Frances **Radford** (28 Dec 1874 McDuffie Co. – 8 Jan 1962 Greensboro, GA)
A) **John** Stephen **Drane** (Jul 1892 Columbia Co. – Jan 1893 Columbia Co.)
B) **Angus** Bailey **Drane** (22 Nov 1893 Harlem – May 1982 Columbia Co.)
  =1 10 Mar 1912 Union Point, GA; Willie **Corine Allen** (19 Jan 1891 Thomson – 2 Jul 1932 Union Point)
  =2 ...; **Claire** Frances **Autry** (...)
  has issue
C) **Mary** Frances **Drane** (2 Sep 1895 Columbia Co. – 29 May 1935)
  = 11 Aug 1913 Union Point; **Herbert Rhodes** (18 Dec 1888 Powellton, GA – ...)
D) **Allie** Mae **Drane** (28 Jul 1897 Columbia Co-)
  =1 19 Jul 1914 Union Point; **Lawrence Brake** (19 Sep 1892

Green Co., GA – 17 Jul 1929 Union Point)
=2 ...
=3 ...
E) **Alphonso** Roger **Drane** (21 Sep 1899 Columbia Co. – ...)
=1 ...; **Agnes** Agatha **Guill** (23 Sep 1898 – 27 Sep 1943 Union Point)
=2 ca.1939; **Evelyn Burnett** (29 Oct 1912 – 14 Jun 2003 Union Point)
has issue
F) **William** Abner **Drane Jr.** (22 Feb 1902 Thomson – Jul 1905 Thomson)
G) **Nellie Drane** (Dec 1903 Harlem – 1904 Harlem) (twin)
H) **Ellie Drane** (b & d. Dec 1903 Harlem) (twin)
X) **Susan** Eugenia **Drane** (21 Nov 1871 Columbia Co. – 28 Nov 1958 Washington DC)
= 17 Jan 1890 Columbia Co; **William** Bunyon **Reynolds** (6 Mar 1856 Columbia Co. – 25 Apr 1925 McDuffie Co.)
d. **Dr. William** Piles **Drane Jr** (30 Jan 1800 McDuffie Co. – 15 Jul 1870 Prattsburg, GA) served in the GA legislature.
= 6 Dec 1827 Columbia Co; **Martha** Hughes **Winfrey** (16 Dec 1806 Columbia Co. – 2 Dec 1873 Talbot Co., GA) daughter of Jesse Winfrey & Frances Spencer
I) **Minerva** Spencer **Drane** (7 Dec 1828 Columbia Co. – 12 Feb 1873 Talbot Co.)
= 10 Sep 1846 Columbia Co.; **William** Parker **Matthews** (20 Aug 1820 Baldwin Co., GA – 16 May 1879 Prattsburg) son of Josiah Matthews & Jane Brown
II) **William** Winfrey **Drane** (24 Sep 1830 Columbia Co. – 7 Feb 1910 Friendship GA)
= 16 Jun 1859 Marion Co., GA; Mary **Eugenia** Nesbitt **Brown** (17 Jul 1833 Crawford Co., GA – 8 Aug 1922 Marion Co.) daughter of Col.William Brown & Amanda Gray
A) William **Albert Drane** (27 Oct 1860 Marion Co., GA – 2 Jan 1932 Albemarle Co., VA)
= aft.1880; **Hettie McKennie** (14 Sep 1856 VA – ...) daughter of Kinchen McKennie & Nancy ...
no issue
B) **Minnie Drane** (1865 – aft.1932)
= 19 Jan 1887; **R. A. Olphant** (...)
C) **Eugene Drane** (16 Jul 1871 – 16 Nov 1921)
= ...; **Irene Buchanan** (28 Jan 1874 – 13 Sep 1946) daughter of

Francis Buchanan & Susie Brooks
has issue
   D) **Walter Drane** (7 Dec 1874 – 3 Aug 1932 Columbus, GA)
   = ...; **Margaret** LaFontaine **Smith** (... – 1964)
   1) **Eugenia** Nesbitt **Drane** (19 Feb 1892 – Dec 1985)
      = ...; **Henry R Forst** (9 Jan 1891 – Mar 1986)
   E) **Bertha Drane**[159] (Apr 1878 – 1965)
   = 7 Oct 1897 Marion Co., GA; **Joseph J Dunham** (1859 – 1927) son of James Dunham & Martha Wood
III) **Maj. Walter** Hugh **Drane** (8 Jan 1832 Plattsburg, GA – 28 Mar 1905 Batesville, MS) moved to MS 1866; served as a surgeon for the CSA in the Civil War
= 21 Oct 1858; **Mary** Frances **Spencer** (30 Dec 1838 Farmville, VA – 19 Dec 1907) daughter of Matthew Spencer & Louisa Neal
   A) **William** Winfrey **Drane** (2 – 11 Jul 1870 Batesville)
   B) **Walter** Hugh **Drane Jr.** (1 Jul 1871 Batesville – 22 Oct 1957 Savoy, TX)
   = 19 Nov 1902 Coffeeville, MS; **Mary** Louise **Brannon** (7 Jul 1877 Coffeeville – Sep 1959 Savoy) daughter of Wiley Brannon & Sarah Garner
   has issue
   C) Louisa **Neal Drane** (8 Aug 1875 Batesville – 12 Oct 1940 Batesville)
   = ...; **Lemuel** Braxton **Lester** (7 Nov 1869 – 16 Sep 1947 Batesville)
IV) **Mary** Julia **Drane** (25 Dec 1834 Talbot Co. – 8 Mar 1896 Marion Co.)
= 4 Dec 1851 Talbot Co.; **Capt. Thomas** Jackson **Matthews** (22 Nov 1822 Baldwin Co., GA – 17 Feb 1874 Marion Co., GA) son of Josiah Matthew & Jane Brown
V) **Andrew** Jackson **Drane** (* & +4 May 1837 Prattsburg)
e. **Benjamin Drane** (29 Dec 1803 Columbia Co. – 14 Jun 1889 Winona, MS) a judge
= 2 Nov 1826 Columbia Co; **Sarah Germany** (9 Jan 1809 Columbia Co. – 17 Oct 1859 Choctaw Co.)
   I) **James G. Drane** (1829 GA – 1888 MS)
   = ...; **Elizabeth H ...** (Nov 1829 GA – aft.1880)
   A) **William** Thomas **Drane** (1 Mar 1857 Copiah Co. – 20 Dec 1938 Lincoln Co., MS)
   = 26 Dec 1877 Copiah Co.; **Sarah E Furr** (13 Jun 1859 – ...)

---
[159] Went to Mexico in her later years.

daughter of Joseph Furr & Rebecca ...
1) **Charles A Drane** (2 Aug 1880 Lincoln Co. – 26 Apr 1946 Lincoln Co.)
= ...; **Catherine Cagle** (24 Jan 1880 – 21 Dec 1968 Lincoln Co.)
has issue
2) **Benjamin Drane** (Dec 1881 Lincoln Co. – ...)
3) **Anne Drane** (Jan 1885 Lincoln Co. – ...)
4) **M M Drane** (a daughter) (11 Dec 1887 Lincoln Co. – 5 Dec 1891 Lincoln Co.)
5) **Josephine Drane** (Nov 1888 Lincoln Co. – ...)
6) **James Drane** (Aug 1890 Lincoln Co. – ...)
7) Eric **Lee Drane** (13 Feb 1891 Lincoln Co. – 18 Sep 1967 Lincoln Co.)
8) **Luther Drane** (Aug 1894 – ...)
9) **Ethel Drane** (26 Jul 1897 Copiah Co. – 30 Oct 1969 Lincoln Co.)
= ...; **Otis** Adrian **Smith** (18 Nov 1892 East Lincoln, MS – 25 Feb 1956 Brookhaven, MS)
10) **Mary** Emma **Drane** (9 Apr 1902 Copiah Co. – 21 Jan 1856 MS)
= ...; **Rea** Everett **Anding** (10 Sep 1894 MS – 21 Feb 1985 MS)
B) **Walter Drane** (Nov 1861 Copiah Co. – 1939 Copiah Co.)
= 7 Nov 1889 Copiah Co.; **Martha** Drake **Boyanton** (Dec 1866 MS – ...) daughter of Harmon Boyanton & Miriam Williams
1) a daughter[160] (+inf)
2) a daughter (+inf)
3) **Stella** Allene **Drane** (19 Oct 1895 Copiah Co. – 12 May 1896 Copiah Co.)
4) **Charles** Edward **Drane** (7 Apr 1897 Copiah Co. – 1 Oct 1918 Great Lakes, IL[161]) unm.
C) Mary Elizabeth "**Mollie**" **Drane** (7 Sep 1866 Copiah Co. – ...)
= aft.1900; **Oliver C Barnes** (22 Mar 1862 – 10 Mar 1917 Copiah Co.)
II) **Elvina** Eugenia **Drane** (ca.1829 Columbia Co. – ...)
= ca.1849; **William Shoemaker** (ca.1813 – ...)

---

[160] The three infant daughters of Walter are buried together, two without name or dates, in Wesson Cemetery in Copiah Co.
[161] Died of pneumonia while serving in the US Naval Reserve. He was a Petty Officer 3rd Class.

III) **Dr. Benjamin B Drane** (5 Dec 1830 Columbia Co. – ...)
=1 ...; **Harriet Guy** (ca.1834 – 1865 Atlanta) daughter of Maj. Curtis Guy & Eliza Scurlock
=2 ca.1872 MS; **Margaret A E Gage** (ca.1848 – ...) daughter of Rev. James Gage & ... Sanders; =1st Benjamin Land
issue of 1st (none by 2nd):
A) **Guy Drane** (ca.1863 MS – aft.1880)

IV) **William Drane** (24 Dec 1833 – 24 Dec 1856 Choctaw Co., MS)

V) **Robert** Alexander **Drane** (7 Dec 1834 GA – ca.1885 TX)
= 1871; **Eliza Hargrove** (ca.1842 GA – ...)
A) **Sarah** Elizabeth **Drane** (ca.1873 Columbus, TX – ...)
= ...; **Jacob F. Wolters** (2 Sep 1871 New Ulm, TX – ...) son of Theodor Wolters & Margaret Wink

VI) **Mary** Eunice **Drane** (23 Dec 1836 GA – 1890)
=...; ... **Stewart** (...)

VII) **George** Washington **Drane** (5 Jul 1839 MS – ...) went to South America
= ...; **E H Wood** (...)

VIII) **John** Henry **Drane** (28 Aug 1841 MS – 11 Ap 1906 Montgomery Co., MS)
= 15 Aug 1867; **Alice Booth** (28 Aug 1845 – 14 Aug 1915 Montgomery Co.)
A) **John** Booth **Drane** (9 Jun 1870 – 1 Oct 1912 Montgomery Co.)
= ...; **Susan** Anna **Sullivan** (...)
issue ?
B) **Mary** Alice **Drane** (1873 Winona – 1976 Washington DC)
= 17 Oct 1907 Montgomery Co; **J S Taylor** (...)
C) **Howard** Judson **Drane** (2 Mar 1877 Winona – 22 Nov 1951 Montgomery Co.)
= 11 Dec 1914 Liberty, MS; **Annie** Ray **Brown** (15 Mar 1891 Liberty – 12 Apr 1977 West Monroe, LA)
has issue
D) **Lee D Drane** (May 1880 Winona – 1930 Winona) fought in Spanish American War
married, but no issue
E) **Sarah** Belinda **Drane** (Feb 1884 Winona – ...)
= 28 Aug 1908 Montgomery Co; **Clifton** Mardigras **Bondurant** (...)
F) **Johnye** McLean **Drane** (1887 Winona – Sep 1961)

= 8 Sep 1907; **Martin V Harpole** (1985 – 1931)
IX) **Edgar** Summerfield **Drane** (1 Oct 1843 MS – 23 Mar 1900 Choctaw Co., MS)
= 6 Dec 1866; **Sarah** Adine **Love** (5 Sep 1847 Choctaw Co. – 16 Nov 1910 Choctaw Co.) daughter of James Love & Sarah Bowen
  A) **James** Benjamin **Drane** (13 Oct 1870 Weir, MS – 6 Oct 1945)
    = ...; **Lillie** Dell **Hunt** (18 Sep 1880 Sturgis, MS – 4 Apr 1956)
    has issue
  B) **William** Edgar **Drane** (15 Sep 1873 Choctaw Co., MS – 24 Sep 1961 Starkville)
    = 30 Nov 1898 Choctaw Co., MS; **Effie Robinson** (6 Jul 1877 Choctaw Co. – 31 Jul 1955 Starkville) daughter of Alexander Robinson & Frances Love
    has issue
  C) **John** Edwin **Drane** (4 Jul 1877 – 7 Jan 1962 Weir, MS)
    = 19 Jul 1916; **Fannie** Jane **Henderson** (16 Dec 1887 – 24 Sep 1978 Weir)
    has issue
  D) **Albert** Johnson **Drane Sr** (24 Jul 1880 Weir – 30 Nov 1967 Hazelhurst, MS)
    = 17 Aug 1917; **Anne Furr** (1 Mar 1894 – 7 Feb 1982)
    has issue
X) **Sarah** Virginia **Drane** (May 1845 MS – 17 Jul 1904 MS)
= ...; **Alfred Orr** (... – bef.1900)
XI) **Georgia** Ann **Drane** (21 Mar 1848 MS – 10 Jul 1901)
= ca.1868; **Henry C Drane** (11 Oct 1845 KY – 29 Aug 1872 Choctaw Co.)
see Chapter 6
XII) **Elizabeth Cassandra Drane** (4 Mar 1850 MS – 28 Oct 1895 Choctow Co.)
= ...; **William H Tabor** (3 Feb 1846 Winston Co., MS – ... Bankston, MS) son of John Tabor & Martha Anderson
XIII) **Louvo** Alice **Drane** (20 Jan 1852 MS – 11 Feb 1854 MS)
f. **Hiram Drane** (20 Feb 1806 McDuffie, Co. – 14 Sep 1889 DeSoto Co., MS) elected to the Georgia State Senate in 1852
=1 20 Dec 1827 Columbia Co.; (his cousin) **Eleanor Magruder** (20 Jul 1809 McDuffie Co. – 19 Nov 1870) daughter of John Magruder & Sarah Pryor
=2 7 Jan 1875 DeSoto Co.; **Electra** Ann **Haughton** (8 Feb 1823 – 13 Jan 1878) =1st ... Jackson

issue of 1st:
I) **Mary Drane** (11 Dec 1828 – 11 Jun 1829)
II) **William** Magruder **Drane** (20 Apr 1830 Talbot Co. – 21 Feb 1871 Marion Co.)
= 20 Dec 1854 Talbot Co; **Margaret** Angeline **Bryan** (26 Jul 1834 – 26 Aug 1915 Marion Co.) daughter of Isaac Bryan & Mary Warren
  A) **Minnie Drane** (26 Jun 1857 Marion Co. – ...)
  = 11 Dec 1877; **Osborn Bullock** (7 Jun 1852 Marion Co. – ...) son of Cordy Bullock & Jane Combs
  B) **Dr. William** Arthur **Drane** (27 Oct 1860 Marion Co. – 6 Jan 1932 Marion Co.)
  =1 27 Oct 1880 Buena Vista, GA; Mary Elizabeth "**Lou**" **Butt** (26 May 1863 Marion Co. – 9 Jul 1906 Marion Co.) daughter of Edgar Butt & Martha Mathis
  =2 ...; **Mary** Susan **Bennett** (23 Jun 1873 – 8 Nov 1942 Columbus)
  issue of 1st (none by 2nd):
  1) **Mary** Lou **Drane** (...)
    = ...; **E R Jordan** (...)
  2) **Minnie Drane** (...)
    = 1 Jan 1905 Buena Vista; **Cecil Burt** (...) son of William Burt
  3) **William** Edgar **Drane** (20 Sep 1882 Marion Co. – 2 May 1934 Muscogee Co., GA)
    = 21 Jun 1904 Meriwether Co., GA; **Luella Davis** (20 Nov 1882 Meriwether Co. – 16 Aug 1942 Muscogee Co.) daughter of Joseph Davis & Emma Betts; =2nd ... King
    has issue
  4) **Marguerite Drane** (1 Nov 1890 – 10 Jan 1957)
    = ...; **Frank** Williford **Lowe** (28 Sep 1885 – 5 Aug 1951)
  5) **Dr. (Lt.) Arthur** Hall **Drane** (1893 – 1 Apr 1919 Columbus) served in WWI in he US Navy
    = ...; **Ella** Bess **McMichael** (...) daughter of E. H. McMichael
    no issue
  6) **John** Elizabeth **Drane** (a daughter) (14 Dec 1896 – 7 Mar 1955)
    = 20 Aug 1915; **Lovard** Goodin **McMichael** (26 Aug 1893 – 7 Mar 1972) son of E. H. McMichael
  C) **Henry Drane** (27 Sep 1862 GA – 21 Jan 1905 TX[162]) never

---

[162] Buried in Methodist Cemetery in Marion Co., GA, date of death is from tombstone.

married
- D) **Margaret Drane** (1871 GA – 1961)
  = ...; **Edgar Hornaday** (5 Feb 1859 – 6 Dec 1939 Schley Co. GA)
- III) **Sarah** Frances **Drane** (17 Aug 1832 – 20 Aug 1834)
- IV) **Patrick** Henry **Drane** (12 Jan 1835 GA – 23 Sep 1887 Cockrun, MS) Fought in Civil War as a Pvt. for the CSA; unm.
- V) **Martha B Drane** (21 Aug 1838 GA – ...)
  = Feb 1856 GA; **James Matthews** (...)
- VI) **Eleanor** Elizabeth **Drane** (21 Nov 1840 GA – bef.1887)
  = ...; **Henry Manes** (...)
- VII) **Louisa Drane** (23 Jan – 30 Oct 1843)
- VIII) **Julia** Augusta **Drane** (10 Oct 1844 Talbot Co. – 24 Jan 1912 Montgomery, AL)
  = 31 Oct 1865 Talbot Co; **Charles Knowlton** (1 Jul 1841 Marion Co. – 1916 Montgomery)
- IX) **Andrew** Jackson **Drane** (4 Jun 1847 Taylor Co., GA – ...)
  =1 18 Feb 1868 DeSoto Co.; **Emma Cummings** (...) died in childbirth
  =2 ...**Burt** (...)
  =3 **Futrelle Othello** (...) =1st ... Farrar
  issue of 1st:
  - A) a child (+inf)
  issue of 3rd (none by 2nd):
  - B) **Louisa** Futrelle **Drane** (...)
    =1 ...; ... **Rainey** (...)
    =2 ...; ... **Owens** (...)
- X) **Hiram** Walter **Drane** (12 Nov 1849 New Tabattan, GA – 5 Jul 1931 Memphis, TN)
  =1 14 Feb 1878; **Callie** Pierce **Spencer** (15 Sep 1854 – Mar 1886) daughter of Matthew Spencer & Louisa Neal
  =2 5 Oct 1887; **Sarah** Ann **Hayward** (15 Dec 1859 Yala Bushie, MS – 13 Jul 1937 Memphis)
  issue of 1st:
  - A) **Ruth** Aurela **Drane** (29 Nov 1878 – 3 Aug 1973)
    = 22 Dec 1904; **Thaddeus** Alonzo **Wood** (...) Judge
  - B) **Vera** Lyle **Drane** (28 Aug 1880 – ...)
  - C) Hiram **Dudley Drane** (13 Nov 1882 – 4 Aug 1914)
    = 11 Oct 1908; **Eleanor Van Hooks** (...)
    has issue
  - D) **Julia** Neal **Drane** (13 – 23 Aug 1883 Desoto Co., MS)

E) **William** Linton **Drane** (6 Aug 1884 De Sota Co. – 25 Sep 1885 DeSota Co.)
F) **Chester** Alexander **Drane** (25 Mar 1886 DeSota Co. – 16 Jun 1887 DeSota Co.)
issue of 2nd:
G) **Ethel Drane** (3 Jun 1889 – ...)
= 14 Dec 1916; **Edgar Giles** (...)
H) **Walter** Earl **Drane** (2 Nov 1890 – Jan 1985 LA)
= 21 Oct 1923; **Ruby** Belle **Waller** (25 Feb 1906 – 28 Feb 1992 LA)
has issue
I) **Miriam** Magruder **Drane** (7 Jan 1893 DeSota Co. – ...)
= ...; ... **Hopkins** (...)
J) **Haywood** Benton **Drane** (26 Apr 1894 Love Station, MS – 22 Aug 1966 Natchez, MS) Elected State Rep. 1923, Army Capt in WWII
= 21 Jan 1925; **Louisa** Catherine **Sloan** (8 Apr 1906 Natchez – 11 Aug 1987 Natchez) daughter of Theodore Sloan & Jessie Cory
has issue
K) **Hugh** Wanzer **Drane** (10 Feb 1896 – ...)
= ...; **Florence** Hurdaugh **Glenn** (...)
no issue
M) **Thomas** Gerald **Drane** (22 Jun 1898 DeSoto Co. – Nov 1967)
= 17 Aug 1920; **Rose Lindsay** (...)
has issue
N) **Salome Drane** (22 – 23 Apr 1900 DeSota Co.)
O) **Herbert Drane** (2 Jul 1901 – 10 Apr 1990)
= 31 Oct 1925; **Sallie** Edna **Early** (25 Jan 1905 – Dec 1973)
no issue
XI) **Thomas** Jefferson **Drane** (29 Jan 1852 – 6 Feb 1856)
g. **Col. James** William **Drane Sr.** (24 Feb 1808 Columbia Co. – 8 Mar 1869 Choctaw Co.) served in the MS House 1837-1843 and the MS Senate 1849-1866, serving as President of the Senate 1860-1864, thus signing the Ordinance of Succession
=1 16 Dec 1829 Columbia Co.; **Matilda** Blanche **Shaw** (7 Mar 1813 Columbia Co. – 27 Jul 1859 Choctaw Co.) daughter of James Shaw & Mary...
=2 27 May 1862; **Amelia Edwards** (...)
issue of 1st:
I) **Mary** Cassandra **Drane** (10 Oct 1830 Columbia Co. – 28 Mar

1892 Huntsville, MS)
= 18 Nov 1846; **Maj. William** Carroll **Staples** (12 Feb 1822 – 7 Jun 1884 Huntsville) son of John Staples & Sally Stovall

II) **Virgil** Lee **Drane** (23 Dec 1832 – 28 Aug 1903) fought in Civil War for CSA
= ...; **Mary G Dean** (23 Oct 1842 – 7 Dec 1895)
  A) Beulah **Lena Drane** (ca. 1869 Choctaw Co. – ...)
    = 28 Aug 1889 Choctaw Co.; **W.D. Sheedy** (...)
  B) **Lulu Drane** (16 Mar 1870 Choctaw Co. – 26 Mar 1904)
    = 31 Jan 1893 Choctaw Co.; **Joseph** Pinckney **Quinn** (ca. 1868 – 1940)
  C) **Mary** Belle **Drane** (ca.1873 Choctaw Co. – ...)
    = ...; **Seth** Thomas **Adams** (...)
  D) **Carrie** Lee **Drane** (2 Dec 1874 Choctaw Co. – 23 May 1940)
    = ...; **P F Simpson** (27 Nov 1872 – 23 Oct 1955)
  E) **Alexander Drane** (ca. 1877 Choctaw Co. – ...)

III) **Lt. Col. James** William **Drane Jr.** (14 Apr 1833 Columbia Co. – 8 Aug 1896 MS) fought for the CSA, severely wounded
=1 7 May 1854; **H Frances Hemphill** (1836 – 20 Sep 1884) daughter of Gen. James Hemphill
=2 21 Jul 1885 Oktibbeha Co., MS; **Sarah** Guion **Bardwell** (31 Dec 1842 – 1923) daughter of Rev. Horatio Bardwell & Joanna Rogers; =1st Col. Newton Whitfield
issue of 1st (none by 2nd):
  A) **James Drane** (25 Apr 1855 – 20 Sep 1889 Chester, MS) served 2 years in MS House of Reps.
    = 23 Nov 1881 Choctaw Co; (his cousin) **Belle Hemphill** (21 Oct 1860 Choctaw Co. – 1 Oct 1956) =2nd Richard Stubblefield
    1) **James** Andrew **Drane** (May 1883 Choctaw Co. – ...)
    2) **Fannie** Belle **Drane** (3 Aug 1886 Choctaw Co. – 1 Jan 1963)
      = aft.1910; **Alfred** Homer **Barwick** (29 Jul 1880 Braxton, MS – 5 Jul 1928 Braxton) son of James Barwick & Elizabeth Lacy
    3) **Annie** Kate **Drane** (Jun 1888 Choctaw Co. – ...)
  B) **Butler Drane** (4 Oct 1858 Choctaw Co. – 1860 Choctaw Co.)
  C) **Dr. William Drane** (29 Dec 1860 Choctaw Co. – 17 Apr 1896 Choctaw Co.)
  D) **Frank Drane** (26 Oct 1863 Choctaw Co. – 4 Nov 1931)
    = 20 Feb 1898 Choctaw Co.; **Lucy Carter** (6 Dec 1875 – 24 May 1939)
    1) **Katherine Drane** (Sep 1899 Choctaw Co. – ...)

2) **Frank Drane** (ca.1902 Choctaw Co. – ...) (twin)
3) **James Drane** (ca.1902 Choctaw Co. – ...) (twin)
E) **Dr. Jefferson** Davis **Drane** (6 Dec 1865 MS – 13 Oct 1904 Choctaw Co.)
= 6 Dec 1887 Choctaw Co.; **Louisa** Eleanor **Sission** (Apr 1871–1926) daughter of Charles Sission
1) **Charles Drane** (Aug 1889 Choctaw Co. – ...)
2) **Ada Belle Drane** (Sep 1891 Choctaw Co. – ...)
3) **James Drane** (Aug 1893 Choctaw Co. – ...)
4) **Upton Drane** (20 May 1895 Choctaw Co. – 11 Jun 1896 Choctaw Co.)
5) **Mary Drane** (Oct 1896 Choctaw Co. – ...)
6) **Mattie Drane** (Feb 1889 Choctaw Co. – ...)
F) **Anna** Maria Blanche **Drane** (24 Jul 1870 MS – 26 Apr 1898)
= 2 Sep 1897 Choctaw Co.; **Charles Sisson** (...)
G) **Mary Drane** (9 Jan 1872 MS – Feb 1955) never married
H) **Hugh** M **Drane** (10 Sep 1874 MS – Oct 1854)
= 28 Jun 1903 Attala Co. MS; **Ella Colbert** (1884 – 1940)
has issue
I) **Lillian Drane** (1 Mar 1877 MS – 27 Jul 1896) never married
IV) **Matilda** Celeste **Drane** (13 May 1838 – Jan 1865)
= 5 Feb 1860; (her cousin) **Hobart** Doane **Shaw** (...)
V) **Benjamin Drane** (ca.1846 MS – ...)
h. **Mary Drane** (20 Jul 1810 GA – ...)

Chapter 15
The Last Odds and Ends

This book has been my effort to trace out all of the known lines of descent of the Drane family who settled in Maryland during the colonial period. This however, does not include all Drane families in the United States. There were several later immigrations of Dranes and Drains who are likely somehow connected to the Dranes that originated in Hertfordshire, but that connection is not known.

The Drane name shows up in English records as far back as the 1200s, and there were pockets of them living throughout England in the 1500s. There is no record, to the best of my knowledge, of how these pockets were related to one another or how they are connected to the various later Drane immigrants. But here is a quick rundown of those later immigrant families and what little I have found of them.

One Drane who does show up in the American colonies prior to the Revolution is a William Drane who married Ann Powers in 1760 in New York City. This Drane could possibly be connected to the Maryland Dranes, but there are no other known details of his life to be able to use to try to connect him anywhere. By 1850, the first U.S. Census with any amount of detail, there are several Dranes with a birthplace listed as New York. They are presumably descended from William and Ann. These lines settled largely in western Ohio and southern Indiana, and from there went to points further west.

In the 1810s, several Drains emigrated from Ireland through the port of Philadelphia. This line remained mostly in Philadelphia throughout the 1800s, with a few members going to western Pennsylvania. We have already discussed the 1849 immigration of a branch to Baltimore in Chapter 3. This was also an Irish branch, but one that still used the Drane spelling.

Finally, there is a Scottish branch descended from three brothers who came from Argyllshire, which is on the west coast of Scotland, in 1837. They settled in southeastern Ohio, largely in Washington County, and seem to have remained in the vicinity for the most part. This branch uses the Drain spelling.

Whether the name is spelled Drane, Drain, or Draine, and comes from England, Ireland, or Scotland, it is a safe bet they are still one huge family. This includes the numerous branches that remain in England to the present day.

Sources Consulted

Below are some of the published works used for this book. In addtion to these, the electronic and microfilm records of the Jesus Christ of Latter Day Saints Church were used extensively as was the U.S. Census records on file at the National Archives in Lakewood, Colorado.

Cemetery Records. <http://www.findagrave.com> 2010–2012.

Coldham, Peter Wilson. The Kings Passengers to Maryland and Virginia. Westminster: Heritage Books, 2006.

Drane, Larry David. <http://www.idrane.com> 2008–2012.

Herr, Carol Draine. Telephone interview. February 5, 2012.

Jevne, Louise Priscilla Armstrong. Drane Families of Maryland and Some Descendants. Lansford, ND: self-published, 1973.

Jourdan, Elise Greenup. The Land Records of Prince George's County Maryland 1733-1739. Westminster: Heritage Books, 2008.

Kanely, Enda Agatha. Directory of Minsters and the Maryland Churches They Served 1634–1990. Westminster: Willow Bend Books, 1991.

Nelson, Jr., Ralph D., et.al. Delaware – 1782 Tax Assessment and Census Lists. Wilmington: Delaware Genealogical Society, 1994.

Wilcox, Shirley Langdon, editor. Prince George's County Maryland Land Records 1696-1702. Westminster: Heritage Books, 2007.

Index of Names

ABELL, Edith 155
  Wilbur 155
ADAMS, Amy 115
  James 115
  Mary 101
  Seth 233
ALBANESE, Victor 213
ALBERTE, Mary 120
ALDERMAN, Ernest 154
  George 154
ALESHIRE, Mary 153
ALEXANDER, Amzi 99
  Charles 99
ALLEN, Annie 92
  Charles 102
  Corine 224
  Richard 102
ALLISON, Ora 23
  Sherman 23
ANDERSON, Elizabeth 174,177
  Lelia 102
  Martha 229
  Thomas 177
ANDING Rea 227
ANDREWS, John 102
ARMSTRONG, Ann 173,174,177
  Jacob 37
  Robert 177
ASHCRAFT, Armistead 192
  Caleb 189,190
  Minerva 74,190-192
  Nathan 193
  Rebecca 193
ASHFORD, Craven 71,76
  Sapphronia 71,76
ATWATER, Barbara 185
AUDRAIN, James 164
AUSTILL, Mary 215,221
AUSTIN, Frances 32
AUTRY, Claire 224
BACON, Emma 223
BACOT, Mary 149,158
BAILEY, Ada 22
BAIN, Gona 27
BAIRD, Martha 110,119
BALDWIN, Harriet 173,185
  Mamie 27
BALL, Ann 24
BATTARD, Jerusha 95
BANKHEAD, Rowena 120
  Thomas 120
BANKS, Alfred 19
BARBER, Elizabeth 150
BARDWELL, Horatio 233
  Sarah 233
BARFIELD, Sarah 222
BARKLOW, Thomas 118

BARNETT, Rachel 26
BARNES, Chiles 93
  Laura 115
  Oliver 227
BARNWELL, Lola 19
BARRY, Catherine 46
BARWICK, Alfred 233
  James 233
BASS, Robert 37
  Samuel 213
BATE, Fannie 209
  Richard 2069
BATES, Elizabeth 95
  Joe 95
BAYLESS, Eddie 34
  Eva 34
BEALL, Rebecca 72
BEARDEN, Alabama 20
  Charles 101
  Edgar 101
  Oscar 20
BEATTY, Mary 24
BECKER, Ferdinand 93
  Josephine 93
BECKETT, John 67,72
BELL, Elizabeth 182
  John 123
BELT, Eleonora 154
  Miles 25
  Newton 26
  Polly 26
BENCH, Ferdinand 119
BENNETT, Mary 230
BERRY, Claude 213
  Edwin 209
  Ellen 209
  Hamilton 21
BETTS, Emma 230
BINGMAN, Florence 212
BIRD, Carrie 186
BISHOP, Benjamin 144,154
  Elijah 154
BLACK, Nancy 209
BLADES, Sylvia 213
BLAINE, Oliver 183
BLAKELEY, Andrew 163,167
  Mary 36
BLAYLOCK, Amanda 153
BOBBITT, Eliza 94
  James 94
BOCK, Frank 117
BOCOCK, Daisy 153
  Thomas 153
BOISEAU, Louise 84,94
BOLEY, James 184
  John 184
BOLLES, James 179

240

BONDURANT, Clifton 228
BONSALL, Louisa 88,102
   Mary 88,102
BOOKOUT, Naurma 27
BOOTH, Alice 218,228
   Elizabeth 206
   John Wilkes 218
BOREN, Chaney 76
   James 77
BOWEN, Sarah 229
BOWKER, Sylvia 57
BOWMAN, Renie 152
BOYANTON, Harmon 227
   Martha 227
BOYCE, Mahala 124
BRADLEY, Doris 210
BRAKE, Lawrence 224
BRANDENBURG, Elizabeth 121
   James 193
BRANDT/BRENT, Nancy 1,2
BRANHAM, Emma 183
   Mary 89
   Seth 183
BRANNON, Mary 226
   Wiley 226
BRIGHT, Jeptha 210
   Susan 211
   Tobias 210
   William 210
BRIMM, Joseph 162,167
BROCK, Seldon 59
BRODY, Bernadetta 106,112,129
   Richard 106,129
   Thomas 129
BROOKS, Elizabeth 192
   Susie 226
BROWN, Anna 212
   Annie 228
   Eliza 158
   Emma 183
   Eugenia 218,225
   Jane 225,226
   Leah 155
   Leona 179
   Nancy 74
   Ora 28
   Vernon 153
   William 225
BRUNDAGE, Elizabeth 167
BRUNER, Cline 128
BRUNNER, Frank 151
BRYAN, Isaac 230
   Margaret 219,230
BRYANT, Emma 212
BUCHANAN, Francis 226
   Irene 218,225
BUCKLER, Price 123

BUCKNER, Elliott 92
BULLOCK, Charles 212
   Cordy 230
   Osborn 230
BUNNELL, Elizabeth 110,119
BURCH, Sarah 112,125
BURGESS, Ann 73
   Eva 212
BURLEY, Elaine 152
BURNETT, Evelyn 225
   Nancy 165
   Thomas 165
BURNHAM, Esther 153
   Ivy 153
BURRADELL, Sarah 94
BURT, Cecil 230
BURTON , Comfort 61
BUSBY, Lydia 14,18
BUTTON, Ewell 206
BUTT, Edgar 230
   Lou 219,230
BUTTS, John 89
BYARD, James 60
BYRD, Leonora 120
CAGLE, Catherine 227
CALDWELL, Margaret 70,75
CALLOWAY, James 211
   Jennie 211
   Jonathan 59
CALVERT, Cecilius (2nd Lord Baltimore) 1 40,66,146
   Elisha 125
   George (1st Lord Baltimore) 3
   Jerry 125
CAMPBELL, Anne 29
CAMPER, Hazel 152
   Waldo 152
CANTRELL, Sarah 213
CARMAN, Alfred 127
   Margaret 127
CARR, Fannie 34
   Susan 16,26
CARROLL, Louisa 193
   Nancy 74
CARTER, Elizabeth 129
   Jake 183
   Lucinda 222
   Lucy 233
   Lula 181
   Mattie 182
   Nicholas 181,182
CARVER, John 166
   Manuel 166
CARY, Maude 174,177
   William 177
CASTNER, Marion 91
CHAMBERS, Mary 145,157

William 157
CHARLES I, King 2
CHARLTON, George 35
  Harvey 35
  Herman 35
CHILDERS, Silas 25
CHOAT, Mary 6
CHUMLEY, Joseph 117
CHURCHILL, Eula 166
CLAGNETT, Martha 98
CLARK, Agnes 60
  Deborah 8,18
  Elmira 31
  James 30,62
  John 61,64
  Minnie 64
  Sally 165,166
  Whittington 60
  William (Chief Wyniaco) 62
CLARKE, Rebecca 129
CLAYTON, John 99
  Louisiana 86,99
COACHMAN, Estelle 120
COBB, Anna 224
COCHRAN, Junius 166
COKER, Angela 62
COLBERT, Ella 234
  George 9,37
COLEMAN, Rebecca 19
COLLARD, Mary 126
COLLINS, Polly 188,189,191
  Rose 74
  Rose Ann 189,191
COMBS, Altha 29
  Audie 31
  Elsie 30
  Jane 230
CONDER, Amanda 115
CONKLIN, Hubbard 115
  Robert 116
CONSER, Dorothy 58
COOKE, Elizabeth 68,73
COOLEY, Lizzie 91
COOLIDGE, Calvin, Pres. 146
COOMBS, Henry 100
  Victoria 100
CORNELL, Minnie 175,179
  Robert
CORSON, Alanson 143,150
CORY, Jessie 232
COUCH, Henry 31
COURSEY, George 64
COWDELL, Catherine 156
COX, Nancy 90
CRABB, Priscilla 203,204,208
  Robert 208
CRABTREE, Amanda 34

Tilman 36
Trula 35
CRADDOCK, William 12,37
CRAIN, Lee 99
CRAVER, Rosa 184
CREECH, Bessie 32
CREIGHTON, Louisa 58
  Mary 52,57
  Vernon 52,57
CRITES, Joseph 194
CROOK, William 222
CROSS, Marie 92
CRUMLISH, Agnes 210
CRUTCHER, Kate 206
CULLY, Cecilia 121
CUME, Polly 106,108,109,114
  William 114
CUMMINGS, Emma 231
CUNNINGHAM, George 192
  Malinda 190,192
DADE, Anna Maria 70,75
  Balwin 75
DAISEY, Nancy 63
  Nellie 63
DALTON, Martin 165
  Nancy 165
DARNELL, John 33
DAUGHERTY, Elizabeth 117,124
DAVENPORT, Mary 123
DAVIS, Emma 33
  Floyd 20
  Hezekiah 104
  Ida 34
  Joseph 230
  Lexie 20
  Luella 230
  Missouri 165
  Valerie 86,99
DAWSON, Thomas 89
DEAN, Mary 220,233
DeBARDELEBEN, Henry 93
DeGEAR, Abraham 56
  Peter 56
DEJARNETTE, Francis 124
  Isaac 124
DELL, Emma 63
DENHAM, George 122
  Samuel 122
DENNIS, Bud 115
  John 114
  Mary 107,114
  Sye 115
DEPP, Henry 99
  Mary 99
deWOLF, Susannah 151
DICKERSON, Mayse 153
DICKEY, Gabriella 97

John 206
Josephine 202,206
DICKSON, John 22
DINKLE, Mary 123
  Thomas 123
DIX, Lena 97
  Susan 75
DODD, Lucinda 99
  Susan 26
DONOVAN, Ernest 184
  Ruth 184
DOTY, Mary 165
DOW, Lorenzo 52,53
DOWN, Susanna 40,41,44
DRAIN, Aaron 192
  Abraham 54,59
  Adam Vernon 31
  Adda Temperance 30
  Adeline 61
  Albert 21,51,59
  Albert Sterling 28
  Albert Tucker 184
  Alfred 31
  Alice 21,191
  Allen James 175,176,181
  Allison 167
  Alta 22
  Amanda 62,74,180,181
  Anna Maude 35
  Anne 64
  Andrew 62,192
  Andrew Hayslet 172,173,185
  Andrew Jackson 52,176,182
  Andrew Johnson 32
  Andrew Robert 176,182
  Andy Green 22
  Annie 63
  Appie 23
  Archie 74
  Armenia 61
  Arthur Lee 15,22
  Ashberry 193
  Audra 192
  Azariah 188,189,191,193
  Benjamin Stanford 53,59
  Bert 28
  Bert Frances 164 167
  Bertha 24,27,182,183
  Bertie Elizabeth 184
  Bertie Mae 34
  Bessie 191
  Bonnie 28
  Calvin 184
  Capatola Vanlura 181
  Carl Wade 180
  Carma 75
  Celestia 168
  Charles 20,57,176,180,183,194
  Charles Floyd 75
  Charles Gilbert 176,182
  Charles Jackson 189,193
  Charley 23, 24,74
  Chester 23
  Cincinatus 172,173,185
  Clara 64
  Clarence 63
  Coke 190,193
  Columbia Luellen 29
  Cora 25,62
  Cornelia 21
  Dale 1736,185
  Daniel 51,54,59,61,62,64,75
  Daniel Boone 31
  David 23,69,73,161,169-173,175-177,
    181,185,186
  David Floyd 181
  David Lee 19
  Deidamia 163,167
  Dela Audrey 31
  DeLange 63
  Delilah 14,36
  Della 183
  Denver Lee 24
  Dessie Dorothy 74,190,192
  Dewey 35
  Dock 183
  Dollie 26
  Dora 22
  Doris Marsden 185
  Dortha 28
  Earl 75
  Edith Myrtle 22
  Edward 13,32,74
  Edwin 53,58,173,185
  Effie 32,192
  Eleanor 193
  Electra 64,75
  Elisha 20
  Eliza 75,193
  Eliza Jane 18
  Eliza Louisa 74
  Elizabeth 19,23,33,54,58,59,61,64,188,
    193
  Elizabeth Amanda 59
  Ella 14,37
  Ellen 20,61
  Elmira 61
  Elsworth 75
  Elzie 186
  Emeline 192
  Emily 64
  Emily Jane 70,74,189-191
  Emma 27,64
  Emmeline 54,64

Ernest 21
Ernest Franklin 34
Ernest Jackson 25
Ethwel 182
Ethel Lena 178
Eva Blanche 186
Eva Florence 183
Fannie Pauline 36
Flora 30,60
Florence 62
Flossie 74
Frances 26,29,182
Francis 74
Frank 62
Frederick 186
Gardner 54, 61,182
General 74
George 14,28,37,53,58,59,177,186
George Edward 27
George Franklin 34
George Keever 180
George Washington 15,16,20,22-26,32, 52,75,190,194
George William 192
Gertrude 64
Gertrude Elizabeth 177
Gertrude Virginia 185
Gideon 193
Gilbert 20
Gladys 60
Gracie 24
Granville 74,190,191
Habrick 62
Halsey 59
Hannah 61,184
Harold 64
Harold Wesley 180
Harriet 60,61
Harrison 74,189,191
Harrison Roy 189,191
Harry Joseph 60
Harry Lee 184
Helen 64
Helena 63
Henry Ward 34
Herbert 183
Herschel 63
Hezekiah 69,73
Homer 30
Howard 61
Hoyt 24
Hugh 28
Hugh Grant 189,191
Ida 21,23,32,74
Idella 20
Iris Pearl 34
Isaac 55,64,69,70,73,74,161,187,188-191
Ivie 28
Ivy 191
Jack 20
Jackson 190,194
Jacob 54,63,74
Jane 59
James 12-16,18,24,26,36,54,55,64,75, 173,176,182,188,190,193,194
James Alexander 29
James Andrew 185
James Anthony 175,176,181,182
James Donald 183
James Harvey 34
James Henry 180
James Hiram 24
James Humphrey Bates 19
James Lawrence 189-192
James Leonard 186
James Mathis 180
James Sterman 25
James Stuart 176,184
James Washington 23
James William 21
Jayson 28
Jemima 75
Jennie 16,60
Jesse 182
Jessie 28,180
Jessie Bressie 34
Joel 21
John 12,13,15,16,21,26.27,29,32,59-61, 74,167,172,176,177,181,185,189, 190,192
John David 25
John Elmer 20
John Enos 26
John Franklin 28
John Granville 192
John Green 15,19
John Ivan 35
John Jesse 19
John Masters 24
John Thurman 193
John Ulysses 29
John Wesley 24,27
John Wilson 14,33
Johnnie 29
Joseph 21
Joseph Albert 60
Joseph Frederick 181
Josephine 21,183
Joshua 50,64
Josie 22
Juanita 182
Julietta 181
June 22

Kansada 21
Katherine 53,59
Kathryn 185
Katy Elizabeth 24
Kindness 12,18
King Solomon 14,36
Larue 31
Laura 27,62,75
Leila 58
Lela Gay 57
Leonard 192
Leroy 21
Leslie 182
Leu 28
Lillie 25
Lola 186
Lorenzo 19,173,177
Lorenzo Dow 15,19,21,52,53,58
Lottie Louisa 25
Louisa 26,52,58
Louisa Betha 30
Louise Ivy 59
Loy 28
Lucky 183
Lucy 60
Luney Edward 34
Luther 62
Magnolia 22
Manuel 74
Margaret 12,16,18,21,32,51,58,61,63, 75,184
Margaret Ann 59
Margaret Pluma 19
Marie 186
Marion Whitley 185
Marshall 28
Martha 30,32,62,64,75
Martha Elizabeth 36
Martha Sarah 29
Marvin Deboski 186
Mary 13,19,20,27,32,34,57,61,63,64, 75,184,186,192
Mary Ann 24,58,182,193
Mary Eliza 182
Mary Elizabeth 27
Mary Euvenia 64
Mary Eveline 191
Mary Jane 23,32
Mary Josephine 22
Mary Matilda 60
Mathie 186
Matilda 58
Melvin Lewis 178
Merritt Wade 29
Minerva 191
Miranda 62
Miranda Jane 58

Mollie 26
Mose 20
Mose Allen 23
Motie Mary 35
Myrtle 24,32
Nancy 14,21,26,168,184
Nancy Ann 182
Nancy Dessie Celinda Jane 37
Nancy Jane 25
Nancy Keziah 19
Nancy Virginia 34
Nannie 183
Naomi Mae 36
Napoleon 176,183
Nelson 63
Nervia 31
Nora 26
Oliver 182
Oscar Grove 178
Otis 31
Otis Leotis 32
Ott Hubert 35
Paul 24
Pearl 20,186
Pearley 15,21
Perlina 22
Perry 167
Pleasant 192
Pocahontas 168
Pressley 193
Ralph 173,185
Raymond Roy 178
Reason Anthony 168
Rebecca 12,13,23,28,33,37
Retha 190-192
Rhoda Alice 30
Richard 193
Richard Cecil 189,191
Richard Clarence 23
Richard David 23
Riley Arthur 178
Risie Katherine 35
Roan 22
Robert 23,27,54,63,64,74,176,182,184, 190,192
Robert Lee 26,29
Robert Murphy 22
Rosa Belle 184
Rose 22
Roy 27
Ruanna 29,30
Ruby 28
Rueben 50,51,64
Russell 50,64
Russell Curtis 184
Ruth 193
Sadie 60

Salina 26
Sallie Ann 61
Samuel 181
Samuel Edward 35
Samuel Jackson 30
Sarah 13,14,16,26,28,33,36,51,59,61,
 64,190,192-194
Sarah Ann 33
Sarah Emmeline 26
Sarah Ida 30
Sarah Orlena 36
Sarah Orpha 173,185
Senora 74
Shepherd 51,52,56-58
Sherman 15,20
Sims 57
Solomon 13,14,33,51,53,54,59-61
Stanford 52,58
Stella 191
Stephen Shepherd 52,57
Susan 180
Susan Himanda 194
Susan Louise 26
Susanna 51,59
Sylvester 190,194
Tabitha 193
Temperance Gertrude 31
Thankful 172,177
Theda 186
Theresa 58
Thomas 13,14,32,36,60,61,162,163,167
Thomas Franklin 33
Thomas Leonard 31
Thomas Toy 28
Thomas Woodrow 27
Thurman Blaine 192
Vera 28
Vernon 28,51,59
Vernon Creighton 52,57,58
Vernon Lyell 53,58,59
Vernon William 178
Viola 75,184
Violet 182
Virdie 186
Virginia 182,194
Virginia Lee 25
Wallace Lee 22
Walter 186
Wesley 28
Wesley Newton 16,17,25,29,31
Willard 62
William 15,19,20,21,51,53,58,59,61,
 163,164,167,172,175,177,181,183,
 185,186,193
William Alexander 25
William Andrew 27,180
William Burtis 26

William Donald 181
William Edward 62
William Fisk 52,58
William Goff 74,190,192
William Gordon 189,193
William Harrison 189,191
William Harvey 34
William Oliver 63
William Reason 14,36
William Robert 33
William Thomas 164,167
Willis Andrew 29
Wilton 13,32
Winnie Juanita 35
Woolsey 64
DRAINE, Adha Jane 154
 Adolphia Neomia 154
 Albert Benjamin 153
 George Henry 152
 Herbert William 153
 James Harrison 153
 Joseph McKinney 153
 Robert Leroy 152
 Susan Priscilla 153
 Walter Leslie 153
DRANE, Ada Belle 234
 Ada May 98
 Adele 208
 Adeline Florence 151
 Agnes 46,208
 Agnes Keats 209
 Albert 47, 86,100,121
 Albert Gallatin 110,120,204,211
 Albert Johnson 219,229
 Alene 209
 Alexander 233
 Alfred 87,88,97,103,104,163,166
 Alfred Osbourne 103
 Alice 45,92,210
 Alice Macrae 91
 Allie Mae 224
 Alma 96
 Alphonso Roger 225
 Alvin 108,109,112,115,117,127
 Amelia Washington 91
 America Emaline 89
 Andrew Jackson 41,44,81,85,98,226,
 231
 Angus Bailey 224
 Ann(e) 9,37,47,67,72,76,77,96,166,
 221,227
 Ann Elisa 206
 Ann Eliza 207
 Anna Maria Blanche 234
 Anna Maria Louisa 70,75
 Anne Dade 70,76
 Annie 104

Annie Kate 233
Annie Lou 94
Anthony 3-8,65-69,71,72,76,79,80,
 85-87,98,111,121,146,161,169-171,
 201,203,206
Arabella Rogers 121
Arthur 125
Arthur Hall 230
Augusta 90
Avis 44
Baldwin Dade 71,76
Benjamin 76,94,124,217-220,226-
 228,234
Benjamin Franklin 203,204,209,210
Bernard 47
Bernetta 125
Bert Frances 167
Bertha 211,226
Bessie 96
Bettie 102
Bettie Thomas 93
Bettie Wheeler 92
Beulah Lena 233
Birdie 90,121
Bob 128
Brent Skinner 149,159
Bryan Skidmore 205,213
Burdie 120
Burnetta 116
Butler 233
Carl 57
Carl Bryant 116
Caroline 89,174,179,222
Caroline Harding 94
Carrie Etta 179
Carrie Lee 233
Caey Bentley 224
Cassandra 72,221
Cassandra Magruder 217,223
Catherine 44,98
Catherine Luke 223
Celina Belle 112,127,128
Charles 42,45,46,57,84,94,98,103,104,
 108,127,166,218,227,234
Charles Edward 210,227
Charles Haddox 83,91
Charles Marvin 120
Charles Monroe 110,121
Charles Naylor 116
Charlotte 77
Chester Alexander 232
Christopher Columbus 119
Clara 96,101
Clarence 112,127,130,209
Clarinda 222
Clelland 121,127
Cleveland 112,128

Clifford Ellis 126
Clint 127
Clinton 112,127,130
Coleman 128
Cora 124
Cova 127
Daisy 151
Daniel 43,47,94
Daniel Merida 112.127
David 43,46,80,87,88,102,104
Davis Clark 111,122
Della 126,127
Dewey Edward 163,166
Dicy 124
Dorothy 152
Dorothy Anderson 212
Drusie 97
Dulcena 209
Earl 152,179
Edgar Duncan 202,206
Edgar Summerfield 218,219,229
Edith 104,120,121
Edna 128
Edward 83,92,204,209,211
Edward Crabb 203,208
Edward Kemper 145,155,156
Edward Morton 208
Edward Washington 71,76
Edwin 86,99
Edwin Booth 97
Edwin Snyder 103
Effie 128,130,222
Eleanor 8,18,77,105,106,129
Eleanor Crabb 210
Eleanor Elizabeth 231
Elijah 112,129
Elijah Lee 125
Elina 126
Eliza 67,68,72,76,157,165
Eliza Ann 119
Eliza Brown 158
Eliza Harwood 159
Eliza Jane 157
Eliza West 156
Elizabeth 6,8,9,18,37,42,45,89,104,106
 129,166,221,223
Elizabeth Ann 98,159,165
Elizabeth Cassandra 229
Elizabeth Collins 95
Elizabeth Emma 210
Elizabeth Madeline 156
Ella 90
Ella Vera 179
Ellen 46,126,145157
Ellen West 154
Ellie 225
Elmer 47

247

Elmore 107,115
Elmore Frederick 108,116
Elnora Catherine 119
Elsie 57,152
Elvina Eugenia 227
Emily 88,103,119
Emma 43,44,163,166,222
Emma Bright 210
Emma Lou 177
Emma Martha 165
Emmett 84,96
Endamile 109,119
Eric Lee 227
Ernest 98
Esifane 111,121
Essie 129
Estelle 123
Etta Lillian 107,115
Ethel 209,227,232
Eugene 86,100,218,225
Eugenia Nesbitt 226
Everett 151
Fannie 210
Fannie Belle 220,233
Fielden David 111,124
Fillmore 76
Florence 212,213
Florence Effie 152
Florence Parrish 101
Foster 216,221
Frances 223
Frances Helen 152
Francis 57,103
Francis Marion 145,156
Frank 56,220,233,234
Frank Condie 87,88,103
Frank Neal 204,212
Frank Parker 149,159
Frederick 100
Frederick Blount 149,159
Fredonia 93
Gallie Walton 110,120
George 109,110,113,130,179
George Canning 208
George Christopher 119
George Keats 209
George Monroe 97
George Thomas 111,118,122,144,149,158
George Washington 69,75,81,84,85,97,121,143,150,154,218,228
George Washington Lafayette 42,45
George William 86,100,101,129
Georgia Ann 84,94,218,229
Georgia Rebecca 217,223
Gertrude 47
Gilbert 126

Gladys Dora 117
Glenn Robert 167,166
Gordon Holliday 224
Gustavus Leuman 87,88,104
Gustavus Savage 69,70,75
Guy 228
Haddock 69,73,189
Hallie 128
Hamilton Stephen 217,223,224
Harriet 101,119,143,150
Harriet Elizabeth 56
Harriet Ellen 89
Harris 143,152
Harry 86,100
Harry Raymond 175,178
Haywood Benton 232
Hazel 121,166
Helen Josephine 202,207
Helen Wesley 95,96
Henrietta 120
Henry 84,103,113,129,130,158,218,219,229,230
Henry Clay 94
Henry Gustavus 103
Henry Hinton 204,211
Henry Marion 90
Henry Martyn 148,149,158
Henry McClellan 104
Henry Shawhan 213
Henry Tupper 84,93
Herbert 103,232
Herbert Jackson, Rep. 202,206
Hiram 76,143,150,217,219,229
Hiram Alanson 151
Hiram Dudley 231
Hiram Walter 219,231
Hobert 125
Holden 179
Hollis 125
Homer 126
Honor 124
Howard Judson 219,228
Howard Wayne 224
Hugh 82,89,93,220,234
Hugh Albert 204,212
Hugh McClure 83,92
Hugh Nelson 145,156
Hugh Wanzer 232
Hughanna 90
Ida 126
Ida May 120,121
Ina 115
India May 224
Isabel 158
James 2,5,6,8-11,18,37,39-44,46,47,49,51,52,56,67,68,73,94,105,106,108,109,112,117,119,124,127,129,130,

141-144,150,163,166,174,204,205,
    209,215,217-220,226,227,233,234
James Andrew 233
James Anthony 1-4,70,74,76,145,146
James Benjamin 229
James Edgar 124
James Edward 213
James Emmitt 224
James Erasmus 144,155
James Faustus 84,93,218
James Franklin 179
James Haskin 84,94
James Hiram 211
James Lee 129
James Louis 121
James McClure 83,92
James Newton 123
James Robert 115
James Thomas 141,142,145-147,150
James Walter 96
James William 76,220,232,233
Jane 41,76,87,104
Jefferson Davis 220,234
Jennie 96,177
Jennie Elizabeth 92
Joe 112,129
Joe Bates 84,96
Joel Clelland 128
Joel Thomas 111,112,125
Joelynn 94
John 6,9-11,18,41,43-46,49-51,53,56,
    57,86,94,99,119,126,127,143,150,
    157,210,218,219,223
John Angier 144,145,155
John Elizabeth 230
John Booth 219,228
John Edwin 229
John Henry 228
John Leonard 52,56
John Magruder 84,94
John Robert 112,125
John Roland 174,179
John Stephen 224
John Weslesy 97
John William 97,110,121
Johnye McLean 228
Jonathan 143,150
Joseph 46,47,97,98,108-111,116,119,
    121,124,165,205,213
Joseph Clark 123
Joseph Kent 202,206
Joseph Lamar 145,156
Joseph Russell 120
Joseph Stephen 208
Joseph Walter 111,123
Joseph William 122
Joseph Ira 57

Josephine 99,227
Juanita 115
Judith Coleman 208
Judson 109,119
Judson Scott 86,99,101
Julia 118
Julia Auguta 231
Julia Florence 178
Julia Neal 231
Justinian 6
Kate 42,158
Katharine 159,233
Kinzie 69,71,76
Kirby 127
Lalla 121
Lallah Page 100
Larry David 144
Laura 93,96
Lawrence 47
Lee 57,228
Lee Andrew 112,126
Lena 212
Lennie 90
Leona 57
Leonard 213
Leslie 204,209
Lettice 122
Lewis 174
Lewis Thomas 93
Lewis Tillet 211
Lillian 234
Lillian Belle 153
Lillie Julie 166
Lorena 121
Lottie Alexander 210
Louis 109,110,117,209
Louis Edwin 120
Louisa 91,92,231
Louisa Futrelle 231
Louisa Jane 103
Louisa Neal 226
Louise 95
Louise Shipman 203,208
Louvo Alice 229
Lucille 166
Lucious 96
Lucy 167
Lucy Belle 101
Lula 100,130,166
Lulu 233
Luther 227
Mabel 100
Mabel Adrienne 202,207
Mabel Elise 103
Madelyn Alice 117
Maggie 212
Maggie Lynn 213

249

Malvina 96
Mamie 122
Mamie Belle 100
Margaret 41,44,47,102,103,222,231
Margaret Ann 110,119
Margarette Maryette 151
Marguerite 230
Maria 144,154
Mariah 145,158
Marian 92,95,148,149,159
Marian Pope 202,206
Marie 47,104
Marien 145,157
Mark Anthony 86,100
Martha 94,98,106,118,129,162,165,
  167,208,231
Martha Ann 116
Martha Jane 121
Martha Jean 224
Martha Parthenia 129
Martha Pattie 96
Martha Salina 117
Martha William 167
Marvin 110,115
Mary 44-47,67,89,90,92,96,99,104,
  118,123,158,174,206,210,213,222,
  223,230,234
Mary Alice 124,156,228
Mary Ann 72
Mary Baker 213
Masy Belle 233
Mary Cassandra 232
Mary Cora 117
Mary Eleanor 223
Mary Elizabeth 166,179,227
Mary Emma 227
Mary Esthert 179
Mary Estraline 177
Mary Ethel 123
Mary Eunice 228
Mary Frances 224
Mary Harding 97
Mary Jane 119
Mary John 165
Mary Julia 226
Mary Lou 230
Mary Macrae 91
Mary Virginia 221
Matilda 87,88,96,104
Matilda Ann 104
Matilda Celeste 234
Mattie 90,122,206,209,234
Maude 92,124,179,212
Maude Isobel 103
Maureen 96
Maurice 86,99
Maury/Manny 216,221

Maximilian 206
May 57,212
Mecy 123
Meredith 112,126
Meredith Prewitt 111,112,125
Merle Melvin 152
Merritt 204,211,212
Merritt Arthur 204,212
Mildred 94
Millis 112,127,128
Minerva81, 90
Minerva Sarah 126
Minerva Spencer 225
Minnie 225,230
Minta 210
Miriam Magruder 232
Mollie 94
Morton Dewey 151
Moses Lloyd 108,116
Myra 155
Myrtle 91,92,123
Nancy 106,129,166,209
Nannie 211
Nellie 66,67,95,120,225
Nellie Grant 101
Nelson 119
Neppie 126
Nettie 130
Nina 103
Nora 90
Nova 115
Olive 91,117
Olivia 90
Ora Bertha 212
Oran John 57
Oren Glenn 123
Oscar 112,127
Osceola 95,96
Ossian Anthony 202,206
Ossian Wright 202,206
Owen 125
Patrick Henry 231
Parthena 111,121
Paul 93,108,115
Paul Shipman 203,208
Paul Snyder 103
Paul Tifflin 163,166
Pearl 126,213
Peter Hezekiah 162,163,165,170,171
Peter Tifflin 162,165
Philip 84,96
Philip Brooks 145,156
Philip Elmore 109,117
Poindexter 202,206
Polly 162,167
Pressley Harrison 107,114
Priscilla 143,150

Priscilla Ann 157
Priscilla Elizabeth 155
Priscilla Lamar 157
Rachel 10,37,44,67,72,93,147
Rachel Catherine 116
Ralph 103
Rebecca 44,67,72,221
Rebecca Sprigg 96
Rhoda 57
Rhua 128
Richard 9,10,18,39,42,47,106,111,121, 145,157,204,211
Richard Bate 210
Richard Ferguson 206
Richard Henry 144,155
Richard Hooker 148,158
Richard Kane 86,99,101
Richard Keene Scott 85,98
Richard Lamar 144,145154,155
Robert 43,46,103,110,119,159,218
Robert Alexander 228
Robert Brent 146-149,158
Robert Leroy 143,150
Robert Wesley 84,94,95
Robert William 174,177
Roberta Ruffner 156
Rosa 102,179,222
Rosaline 206
Rose 47
Ruanne Catherine 125
Ruth Aurela 231
Ruth Hoskins 212
Sabrina 85,99
Sabrina Scott 99
Saffronia 56
Salina 122
Salina Dorsey 122
Salinda Hinton 211
Sallie 63,162,167
Sallie Mattie 120
Salome 232
Salter Lloyd 149,158
Samuel 119,120
Samuel Dade 71,76
Sarah 56,90,98,106,107,118,127,223
Sarah Adeline 122
Sarah Austill 221
Sarah Belinda 228
Sarah Elizabeth 228
Sarah Emmaline 114,117
Sarah Evelyn 156
Sarah Frances 178,231
Sarah Jane 89
Sarah Nevell 101
Sarah Virginia 229
Seth 119
Silas 117

Solomon 112,128
Stella 121
Stella Allene 227
Stephen 76,77,106,109,118,170,171, 203,205,209,213,
Stephen Hamilton 217,223
Stephen Tillet 201-205,208,211,213
Stonewall Jackson 84,95
Sudie Ethel 126
Susan 57,96,126,179
Susan Eugenia 225
Susan West 155
Theodore 204,209
Theodore Robertson 204,209
Theodore Smith 203,209
Theresa 44
Thomas 5-9,18,37,39,41, 44,56,65,67, 68,72,73,79,87,89,105,106,109,111, 112,114,163,166,179
Thomas Eldridge 82,90
Thomas Emmett 111,124
Thomas Gerald 232
Thomas Givens 106-109,114
Thomas Harding 81,82,89
Thomas Jarvis 82,90
Thomas Jefferson 81,84,87,97,102, 109,118,232
Thomas Lamar 142,150
Thomas Marion 143,144,151
Thomas Offurt 72,80,81,83-85,89,147
Thomas Smith 162,165
Thomas Walter 108,116
Thurman 125
Tillet 211
Una 15
Upton 234
Vera Lyle 231
Verbal 128
Vernon 96,125
Vessie 112,127
Victor 128
Viola 47,120
Virgil Lee 220,233
Virginia 121,211
Virginia Crittenden 121
Walter 76,106-108,114,116,215,216, 218,221,226,227
Walter Earl 232
Walter Elliott 115
Walter Gordon 103
Walter Harding 81,83,90,92
Walter Hugh 226
Washington 70,71,76,80,85,98
Wesley 83,84,91,95
William 41,44,45,57,77,90,95,97, 102-104,107,108,130,144,149,154, 157,159,163,165,166,173,177,205,

210,211,213,215,218,219,228,233, 236
William Abner 217,224,225
William Albert 225
William Anthony 69,73,86,99
William Arthur 219,230
William Edgar 219,229,230
William Emerson 110,120
William Henry 174,177
William Henry Harrison 110,119
William Hezekiah 161,165
William Ira 179
William Isaac 179
William Leuman 87,88,102
William Lewis 179
William Linton 232
William Magruder 219,230
William McClure 83,91,92
William Piles 217-219,223,225
William Robert 125
William Stephen 210
William Thomas 114,115,226
William Walter 216,217,221
William Whitley 110,119
William Winfrey 218,225,226
Willie 44, 97
Willie Clyde 94
Wilma 125
Winnie Ruth 123
Zachary Taylor 86,99
DRAYNE, John Wilson 36
DREDDEN, William 61
DREW, Della 126
　George 126
　Naomi 126
DROAK, Jennie 32
DUCKWALL, Elizabeth 213
DUFF, Hubbard 98
DUGGER, Marsilla 33
DUNAWAY, Eual 30
　Martha 28
DUNCAN, Bethia 206
　Catherine 114
　Elizabeth 128
　Emma 126
　Katharine 115
DUNHAM, James 226
　Joseph 226
DUNIGEN, Estella 24
DUNLAP, Charlotte 31
　Minnie 178
　Nellie 178
DUNN, John 143,150
　Joseph 150
DUNSTEN, Elizabeth 6
DUPUY, Joseph 208
　Judith 203,208

DURHAM, Cornelia 61
　George 60,61
　Martha 118
　Samuel 60
DUVALL, Susannah 67,73
DYER, Fanny 128
　Gladys 128
　Harold 128
DYKES, Sally 35
EARLE, Frank 173,185
EARLS, Nancy 162,165
EARLY, Sallie 232
EDMUNDS, Bettie 100
EDWARD III, King 68
EDWARDS, Amerla 232
　James 167
ELBERT, Elizabeth 54,59
ELIZABETH I, Queen 2
ELLIOTT, Eliza 128
　Fielden 124
　Irene 111,124
　Nancy 123
　Rufus 212
　William 91
　Willie 91
ELLIS, Christopher 99
　Francis 101
　George 99
ELLISON, George 36
ENDICOTT, Augusta 148,158
　Moses 158
ERRAND, Ernest 154
EUBANKS, Francis 29
　Ica 32
　Richard 32
　Sarah 31
　William 29
EVANS, Elizabeth 23
　Lenora 120
　Mary 33
　Thomas 42,45
EVE, Paul 93
　Sarah 93
EVELEIGH, Susan 115
　William 115
EXETER, Nelly 45
FALLS, Madison 33
　Malvina 14,36
FANCHER, Charles 22
　Rebecca 10-12,18
FARMER, Orvis 178
　Selena 62
FARNEY, Jacob 44
FARR, Edries 224
　John 70,75,76
FARRINGTON, Arathusa 167
FAULKNER, Myrtle 31

FEAZEL, William 157
FENTON, Bluford 123
  Caleb 122
  James 122
  Sarah 111,122
  William 122,123
FENTRESS, Mattie 128
FERGUSON, Elizabeth 201,206
  Elvira 31
  Richard 206
FIELD, Matilda 95
FIELDS, Gladys 21
FISH, Martha 154
FISHER, Catherine 102
  Mary 143,151
FLESHER, Jefferson 180
  William 180
FLETCHER, Rhoda 51,56
FLINT, Annie 181-183
FLOURNOY, Rosa 93
FOLLIN, Maggie 110,121
  William 121
FORD, Alverder 129
  Bertha 204,205,211
  Eleanor 37
  Ellison 185
  James 185
  Jane 210
  Mary 181,182
  Nancy 211
  Spencer 211
  Vineta 209
FORST, Henry 226
FOSTER, Lettice 122
  Susan 216,221
  William 221
FOUCHEE, Daniel 119
FOWLER, Mae 20
FOWLKES, Asa 94
  Mattie 94
FRAZEE, Jonathan 150
  Margaret 142,143 150
FRAZELL, Charles 8,18
FRAZER, Maud 153
FREEMAN, Martha 97
FRIEND, Margaret 150
FRISINO, Biaggio 47
  Joseph 47
FURR, Ann 229
  Joseph 227
  Sarah 226
GAGE, James 228
  Margaret 228
GALBRAITH, Marhsall 95
GALLAGHER, Asa 191
  John 89
  Sarah 80, 81,89

GALLATIN, Albert 110
GALLOPS, Frank 117
GARDNER, Alwilda 31
  Ella 155
  Emma 28
  Etta 155
  James 31
  Lewis 29,30
  Safrona 30
  William 26
GARNER, Sarah 226
GARRARD, Edward 155
GARRETT, Mary 192
GENOVESE, Antoinette 47
GERMANY, Sarah 94,218,226
GIBSON, Frances 156
  Sarah 91
GILBERT, Molly 108,117
  Samuel 117
GILBREATH, Temperance 23
GILES, Edgar 232
GILL, Erasmus 208
  Martha 208
GILLIAND, Ella 186
  William 186
GILLOCK, Elizabeth 101
GILMAN, John 41
GILMOR, Jane 185
GILSTRAP, Martha 33
GIVENS, Rachel 106,114
GIVINS, Sarah 9
GLADWELL, Eliza 124
GLASS, Belva 97
GLASSCOCK, Anna 115
  Samuel 115
GLASSELL, Ashton 91
GLENN, Benjamin 32
  Florence 232
GODDARD, Ralph 156
GOLSBOROUGH, Ada 118
GOODING, Mary 45
GOSLIN, Benjamin 124
  Elizabeth 111,122
  Lucinda 111,124
  Rueben 122,124
GRACEY, Lucy 91
  Maria 92
  Matthew 91
GRADY, James 94
GRAHAM, Elizabeth 70,74
  Frank 149,156
GRAY, Amanda 225
  Joshua 44
GREEN, Benjamin 34
  George 166
  John 165,166
  Thomas 165

GREGORY, Sarah 125
GRIFFIN, Anne 96
GRIMES, William 8,18
GROS, Squire 29
GROSHON, Anne 183
  Clarence 183
GUILL, Agnes 225
GUNN, David 156
GUNTERMAN, Jesse 210
  Lola 210
GUY, Curtis 228
  Harriet 228
GWINN, Sarah 18
HADDOX, Amelia 83,91
  Joseph 91
HAGERTY, James 191
  William 192
HALL, Easter 9-11,18
  Irvn 62
  Minnie 62
  Sarah 77,150
HAMBLOCK, Emma 108,116
HAMBROCK, Hanna 118
HAMMOND, Frances 212
HAMRICK, Susan 217,223
HANNON, Charles 179
HARDIE, George 67,72
HARDING, Mary 80,81,89,147
  Walter 89
HARFORD, Winifred 210
HARGROVE, Eliza 228
HARKER, Jerry 192
HARMON, David 63
  Harvey 63
  Nancy 62
  Sarah 64
  Woolsey 64
HARNED, Elizabeth 112,127,128
  John 128
HARPER, Paralee 21
HARPOLE, Martin 229
HARRELL, Moses 114
  Prudence 107,108,114
HARRIS, Benjamin 46
  Bud 126
  John 126,151
  Laura 222
  Mary 143,151
  Rachel 76
HARSSON, Catherine 95
  Henry 95
HART, Thomas 102
HARTLESS, Bessie 182
  Jesse 182
HARTLEY, Pearl 29
HARVEY, Ella 94
HARWOOD, Eliza 159

HAUGHTON, Electra 219,229
HAY, Edward 185
  John 114
HAYNES, Absalam 167
HAYSLET, Andrew 177
  Anne 181
  Jean 87,171-173,175-177
HAYWOOD, Sarah 231
HEARNE, Easter 56
HEATON, Josie 22
HEGWOOD, Eugene 37
HEMBREE, Grace 27
HEMPHILL, Belle 220,233
  Clarence 185
  Frances 220,233
  James 233
HENNIGER, William 128
HENDERSON, Fannie 229
  Jessie 186
HENDRICKS, 26
HENRY, James 120
  Katharine 110,120
HERRINGTON, Sarah 119
HEWITT, Virgil 208
HICKS, James 184
  Patsy 183
  Virginia 184
HILL, Dalton 30
  James 77
  Monroe 25
  Nancy 25
HILLER, Robert 156
HINKLE, Lillie 56
HINTON, Mary 57
  Salinda 204,211
HIPSHER, Catherine 56
HOFFMAN, William 98
HOFSTETTER, Sophia 125
HOLDER, Eva 36
  Manson 36
HOLLAND, Mary 13,14,33
  Robert 33
  Wiley 93
HOLLIDAY, Elizabeth 99
HOLMAN, Allen 27
HOLT, Lee 36
  Stanley 152
HOOD, Benjamin 13,23
  Charles 192
HOOK, Anna 108,117
HOOPER, Alma 93
HOPKINS, Grace 153
HORNADAY, Edgar 231
HORTON, Alice 153
  Isaac 153
HOSTETTER, David 182
  Lewis 182

HOUK, Harry 57
  Maud 57
  Naomi 116
HOUSE, Hazel 212
HOYE, Ann 154
  Eliza 144,154
  Mary Ann 145,157
  William 154,157
HRABOWSKI, John 221
  Thomas 221
HUDSON, Thomas 27
HUFF, Nancy 115
HUFFMAN, Elizabeth 98
HUGHES, Jane 182
HUMPHREY, Grace 156
  Jane 156
  John 156
HUNDLEY, Joe 178
HUNT, Lillie 229
HURLEY, Caroline 52,57
  Isaiah 129
  James 20
  Sidney 129
HURT, Fannie 95
INMAN, Ina 178
  Joseph 178
IRISH, Al 152
  Frank 151
  Lena 143,151
  Myrtle 152
ISBELL, Adeline 20
JACK, Margaret 64
JACKSON, Andrew, Pres. 41
  Emma 211
  James 210,211
  Lettie 180
  Matilda 62
  Stonewall 181
  Thomas 210
JACOBS, John 58
  Lewis 58
JAKES, Emily 6
JAMES I, King 2
JOBE, Eugene 36
JOHNSON, Clara 62
  Clark 61
  Ellen 19
  George 95
  Hannah 63
  Jettie 94
  Lemuel 27
  Mary 61
  Nancy 116
  Robert 92
  Walter 120
JOHNSTON, Isaac 211
  Maude 211

JONES, Fannie 166
  Georgia 152
  Minnie 163,165
  Sarah 33
  Susannah 114
  Sylvia 152
  Wessie 115
  William 32,35,36
JORDAN, Hallie 101
  Louis 101
JOSLIN, Deborah 185
JUHASCIK, Anna 60
  John 60
JUST, Henrietta 110,121
KALFUS, Ida 209
  William 209
KEATS, Alice 208
KEESEE, John 92
  Thomas 92
  Viola 127
  William 127
KEITH, Benjamin 118
  Susannah 109,118
KEITHLEY, Harry 124
  Thomas 124
KELLY, David 184
  Ida 126
  James 184
KENNEDY, Margaret 21
KERNAN, Julia 41,44
KETCHUM, Cliff 122
KETTERING, William 157
KEY, Francis Scott 142
KIMMEY, James 61
KIRK, Arthea 28
KIRKENDALL, Wallace 24
KNIE, Paul 151
KNOWLTON, Charles 231
KODER, Elmira
KOLLOCK, Elizabeth 50,51,53,56
  Shepherd 56
KOHLHOUSE, Margaret 41,44
LACY, Elizabeth 233
  John 23
LAIL, Miller 210
LAMAR, Priscilla 141,142,145-147,150
  Richard 77
  Robert 77,150
  William 141
LAND, Benjamin 228
LANE, Margaret 13,32
  Martha 35
  Wade 208
LANGELY, Ida 115
LATHAM, Elizabeth 20
LAWLESS, Mercy 111,121
  Nancy 118

LAWRENCE, Benjamin 118
  Polly 109,118
LEAVELL, Benjamin 98
LECOUNT, Lydia 61
LEFEVERS, Mary 190,194
LEIGH, Anselm 223
LENEHAN, James 178
  Mildred 178
LEONARD, Nettie 151
  Uriah 223
LESLIE, Hiram 116
  Peter 116
LESTER, Lemuel 226
LETT, Green 90
LEUMAN, Elizabeth 87,88,102
LEVEL, Beauregard 183
  Lloyd 183
LEWIS, Catherine 45
LILES, Emma 21,22
LINAH/LINEA 54,59
LINDIMAN, Clara 211
LINSAY, Rose 232
LINE, Clara 210
LIONEL, Prince (Duke of Clarence) 68
LIRSEY, Hannah 125
LITTLE, Effie 123
  Josiah 123
LIVERS, Arnold 67,72
LLOYD, Salter 158
  Virginia 148,149,158
LOCHER, Sarah 77
LOCKET, Mary 91
LOGAN, John 208
  Richard 208
LOGGINS, Carrie 166
LOLLAR, Jennie 31
LONG, Cora 163,165
  Daniel 122,165
  Henry 45
  Nicholas 121
  Phebe 162,165
LOONEY, Mima 116
  William 116
LORD, Maria 185
LOUDEN, Ruth 186
LOUDERBACK, Frank 103
  Louisa 103
LOVE, Frances 229
  James 229
  Sarah 219,229
LOVING, Howard 182
  John 182
LOWE, Frank 230
LOWRY, Louisa 211,212
LOWTHER, Herbert 178
LUCAS, Clara 128
LUCKET, Mary 92
  Thomas 92
LUSK, Lela 179
LYELL, Mary 53,58
LYMES, John 129
LYON, Leland 35
LYONS, Judson 123
MACDONALD, Bettie 203,209
MACKABEN, Fred 152
MACRAE, Bailey 91
  Mary 91
MAGIER, John 49
MAGRUDER, Althea 215,216,221
  Cassandra 215,217,218,223
  Eleanor 219,229
  John 229
  Nathan 72
  Ninian 221,223
  Samuel 96
  Susannah 67,72
MAHOLLAN, Elizabeth 117
MANES, Henry 231
MANSFIELD, Thomas 99
MALLOY, Dolly 24
MARCH, Absalam 121
  David 121
MARINER, Gilbert 56
MARLOWE, Rebecca 180
MARSLAND, Ethel 185
  Thomas 185
MARTIN, Alice 192
  Alva 194
  Elmer 192
  Frank 157
MARTINEZ, Emma 178
MASON, Mary 194
MASTERS, John 24
  Nancy 24
MASTERSON, Anna 151
MATHIS, Willard 35
MATSON, Mary 189,191
MATTHEWS, Frances 102
  James 231
  Josiah 226
  Nancy 82,90
  Thomas 226
MATTINGLY, Elizabeth 116
  Emily 115
  John 115
MAUPIN, Armistead 86
  Marcellus 86,99
MAYHEW, Ina 180
  Thomas 180
MAYS, John 177
MAZE, Anna 63
McCALLISTER, Aisom 26
McCANDLESS, Eleanor 145.157
McCLURE, Elizabeth 83,91

Hugh 91
McCONNELL, Ina 25
  Walter 25
McDANIEL, Eliza 183
McDONALD, Mattie 126
McELMURRY, Sally 100
McGRATH, Mary 93
McGUFFIN, Halen 114,117
  James 117
  Pearl 125
  Samuel 114
McINTYRE, Lydia 194
McKEE, William 153
McKENNIE, Hettie 225
  Kinchen 225
McKINLEY, Lydia 123
  Patrick 41,44
McLAUGHLIN, Samuel 109,117
McMICHAEL, Ella 230
  Lovard 230
McNAB, Alfred 13,33
McPHERSON, John 22
  Nancy 97
  William 22, 97
MEACHUM, Lucinda 172,173,185
MEADE, Julia 124
MEADOR, George 128
  Vitula 128
MEADOWS, Clarence 31
MEEKS, William 178
MICHEK, Rosalia 60
MILAM, Polly 127
MILES, James 34
MILLER, Alice 91
  Ardella 29
  Ella 45
  Isaac 61
  Jacob 150
  James 29
  Jesse 31
  Juliue 45
  Maggie 31
  Mary 61,211
  Monroe 29
  Rebecca 115
  Sarah 150
  William 213
MILLSAP, Herbert 91
  Uriah 91
MILWEE, Sarah 22
MINOR, Nora 191
MISKEL, Martha 29,30
MITCHELL, Anna 95
  Catherine 15,19
MOCKBEE, Mary 65,72
MONROE, George 25
MOORE, Andrew 179

Elias 192
Emma 183
Fenton 192
George 77
Jane 176,181
Lillian 192
Mary 101
Matthias 56
Ora 209,213
Robert 95
Samuel 181
Sarah 51,52,56
William 207
MORELOCK, Samuel 12,37
MOREMAN, Martha 58
MORGAN, Carrie 111,124
  William 124
MORRIS, Edward 63
  Maggie 63
MORROW, Charles 156
MOSELY, Mary 62
  Andrew 62
MOSS, Ernest 156
MUNFORD, Thomas 92
MURPHY, Joe 30
  Josh 25
  Mary 89
  Mattie 25
NALL, Howell 129
  John 129
NASH, Annie 211
  Doc 33
NAUMAN, Emma 184
NAY, Sarah 192
NEAL, George 209
  Lewis 211,212
  Louisa 226,231
  Malvina 204,212
  Marchie 29
  Margaret 211
NEEL. Virginia 121
NEELY, Nannie 166
NEFF, Frances 129
NEWMAN, John 11,18
NEWTON, Maude 117
NICHOLS, Elizabeth 65,67,72,79
  William 65,67,72
NOLAND, Garland 100
NORRIS, Margaret 45
NORTHCROSS, Pluma 19
NORVELL, John 124
  Mary 124
OAKES, James 162,167
OFFURT, George 80
OGILVIE, Agnes 86,100
  Sam 100
OLINGER, Mary 25

OLIVER, Ada 35
O'NEAL, Flossie 153
ORNBURN, Roscoe 123
ORR, Alfred 229
OSBORN, Levi 88,104
OTHELLO, Futrelle 231
OTTO, Paul 154
OWENS, Alma 224
PAGE, Thoams 26
PAINTER, Jesse 184
PARENT, Jane 106,114
PARKER, Catherine 148,158
  Elisha 58
  Harriet 54,59
  Sarah 53,58
  Theophilius 158
PARKS, Ed 152
PARR, James 212
PARSLEY, Liz 25
PASCOE, Harold 120
PASSMORE, James 207
PATTERSON, Alvin 128
  Charles 222
  Jane 88,104
PAUL, Mary 129
  Susan 107,108,114,115
  Thomas 114,129
PAYNE, Shenobea 20
PEACHER, Lucy 124
PEARCE, Isaac 106,129
PEATNER, Minnie 211
PEAY, Nancy 208
PEDEN, Alonzo 101
  Ebley 101
PENDELTON, Isabelle 152
PERRY, Alice 126
PERRYMAN, David 222
PETERS, Sarah 34
PETERSON, Mary 157
PETTY, James 122
  Perry 122
PHILLIPS, Scott 24
  Susanna 52,56
PICKERING, Fannie 35
  Isaac 35
PIERCE, Minnie 117
PIKE, Russell 118
PILBIRN, John 118
PILES, Elizabeth 68,73,105,215
  Leonard 69,73
  Nancy 193
POINDEXTER, Mattie 202,206
POPE, Frank 206
  Mary 202,206
PORTER, Cora 96
  Nancy 175,181
  William 181

POTTER, George 124
  Jacob 182
  James 183
  John 183
  Sarah 176,182
POTTINGER, Samuel 73
POTTS, Osie 123
POWERS, Ann 236
PRATT, Helen 93
PREWITT, Allen 106,129
  Christine 213
  Jane 127
  Meredith 106,129
  Sarah 106,111,125
PRICE, Charles 90
PRINCE, Ann 6
PRITCHARD, Junia 101
PROBUS, Ivy 127
PROVINCE, Eliza 94
PRYOT, Sarah 229
PULFREY, Mae 57
  Minnie 57
PURCELL, Cyrus 122
  Julie 122
QUALLS, Manerva 164,167
QUINN, Joseph 233
RADFORD, Cornelia 224
RAGLAND, Ella 153
  George 153
RAINSBY, Jessie 103
RAMSEY, Owen 89
RANDALL, Frank 185
  Stephen 185
RAY, Almira 173,185
  Margaret 60
  Thaddeus 157
READ, James 101
  Rice 101
REECE, August 46
  John 19
REES, Samuel 124
  Thomas 124
REEVES, Jonathan 221
  Rhoda 86,100
  William 100
REICH, Pleasant 165
REID, Clive 222
  George 222
REIERSON, Lela 206
  Oscar 206
REYNOLDS, John 12,18
  Mary 36
  Urania 151
  William 225
RHODES, Herbert 224
RICE, Margaret 43,46
RICHARDS, Mary 154

Nancy 23,32
RICHARDSON, James 115
  Katharine 156
  Viola 114
RICHESSON, Cynthia 163,167
  Michael 167
RICHEY, Jim 21,22
  Mary 21
  Phoebe 22
RILEY, Andrew 181-183
  Julia 175,176,183
  Margaret 175,181
  Walter 175,182
RITTER, Jemima 100
ROADEN, Novella 20
ROBBINS, Aaron 32
  Elizabeth 16,23
  Richard 23,32
ROBERSON, Mary 223
ROBERTS, Benjamin 94
  Sarah 221
ROBERTSON, Susan 209
ROBINSON, Alexnader 229
  Effie 27, 229
ROCKENBOUGH, James 186
RODDIN, George 117
RODRIGUEZ, Primitivio 92
ROGERS, Amanda 32
  Forerst 20
  Joanna 233
  John 29
ROLLING, Richard 121
ROUNDS, Abigail 172,177
ROUZEE, Matt 21
ROWE, Minnie 27
RUBLE, William 177
RUFFNER, Sarah 156
RUMANS, Roy 123
RUNNELL, John 13,32
RUSSELL, Minnie 24
SACHS, Roseanna 213
ST.JOHN, Samuel 90
SAMONS , Mary 26
SANDERS, Andrew 223
SANDS, Samauel 116
SAPPINGTON, John 10,37
SCHROER, Otto 156
SCHULTZ, Lee 57
SCOTT, Catherine 85-87,98
  Egbert 60
  Sabritt 98
SCRUGGINS 30
SCURLOCK, Eliza 228
SEAMORE. Beulah 29
SELLERS , Joel 222
  Joseph 222
SEMON, Anna 123

William 123
SEENEY, Elizabeth 60,61
SELF, Maxie 34
  William 34
SELL, Sarah 6,40,44
SELZ, Kunigunde 46
SETTLE, Frances 86,98
  Laura 99
  Nathaniel 100
  Thomas 101
  Warner 101
  William 98
SHACKELFORD, Susan 163,167
SHAFER, Clara 96
SHARP, Joel 19
  Nancy 14,15,18
SHAW, Hobart 234
  James 232
  Mary 144,155
  Matilda 220,232
SHAWHAN, Emma 205,213
  Henry 213
SHELTON, Elsie 62
SHEPHERD, Catherine 97
SHERRILL, Ruanna 12-14,16,18
SHIPMAN, Mary 208
SHIRCLIFF, Mabel 101
SHOWEMAKER, William 227
SIMMONS, Caldonia 116
SIMPSON, Jerome 28
  Laura 27
SIMS, Ann 101
SISSION, Charles 234
  Louisa 234
SKELTON, Belle 183
  Mary 24
SKIDMORE, Lizzie205, 213
SKINNER, Maria 149,158
  Tristrim 58
SLAYTON, Flossie 153
SLICER, Eleanor 154,157
SLOAN, Louisa 232
  Theodore 232
SMILEY, Celia 128
SMITH, Alfonso 173,185
  Ann 69,73,87,146,169-171,184,201
  Belle 123
  Caroline 151
  Elisha 184
  Essa 178
  Haddock 69
  Harry 152
  Howard 91
  Inga 152
  Isabelle 118
  James 73,76
  Jennie 23

John 127,184
Joseph 118
Mamie 95
Margaret 226
Martha 223
Mary 89,145,155
Nancy 161,165,208
Otis 227
Phoebe 112,127
Robert 156
Sol 95
Theodocia 112,127
SMYTHE, Alice 179
SNIDER, Cyrus 152
 Hamilton 153
SNYDER, Rebecca 88,103
SOLLERS, Barbara 41,42,45
SORENSEN, Hannah 152
SOULE, George 56
SPENCER, Callie 231
 Mary 226
 Matthew 226,231
 William 27
SPILLERS, Harrison 30
 James 29
SPRIGG, Ursula 208
SPROUL, Theodore 151
SPURGEON, Eliza 180
 Viola 179
STACY, Arizona 25
STAFFORD, Pearl 100
STANDOFF, Nancy 175,176,181
STANFIELD, Mack 90
STAPLES, John 233
 William 233
STATON, Clara 26
STEENBERGEN, Hattie 100
 William 100
STEIMER, Stephen 125
STEVENS, John 156
 Mary 156
 Sarah 124
STEVENSON, Georgia 97
STEWART, Charles 151
 Dewey 152
 Florence 30
 William 151
STIBBENS, William 24
STICE, Lucinda 122,123
STIPE, Alice 166
STONE, Martha 125
STOVALL, Sally 233
STRADER, Jerushia 179
STREET, Nora 62
 Robert 62
 William 63
STRICKLAND, Fannie 33

Moore 34
STRODE, Eleanor 209
STUBBLEFIELD, Richard 233
SULLIVAN, Susan 219,228
SUMMER, Sarah 101
SUMNER, Jethro 81
 Melinda 81,89
SUTTON, Rosita 178
TABOR, John 229
 William 229
TALBERT, Harry 46
TANDY, James 209
TATE, Elizabeth 185
TAYLOR, Edwin 156
 Mary 114,129
 Pearl 90
 Snowden 9, 34
 William 90
 Zachary, Pres. 9
TEETERS, Catherine 180
TEMPLETON, Martha 23
TETHERLY, Rosanna 177
THACKER, Jim 35
 Loos 35
THOMAS, Cinda 217,221
 David 32
 Elizabeth 93
 Mary 19
THOMASON, Emma 34
 George 34
 Worley 34
THOMPSON, Eliza 123
 John Layaette 28
 Rachel 190,193
 Richard 193
 Ruth 165
THORNBERG, Joel 35
 Leona 35
THURMAN, Margaret 109,119
TICHENOR, George 119
TIFFLIN, Nancy 162,165
TINDER, Anna 123
 James 123
TIPTON, Alice 116
 John 116
TITSWORTH, Grace 25
TOALSON, Catherine 122
TODD, Elizabeth 37
 Lancelot 10,37
 Sarah 10,37
TINGLER, Myrtle 179
TOLLEY, Mary 33
TOOLE, Mary 158
TOOLEY, Minnie 211
TOTTEN, Rachel 210
TOWNE, Anna 158
TRABUE, Benjamin 102

Henry 102
TRAUGHBER, Harriet 82,89
  James 89
  John 89
TRENT, Elizabeth 154
TROTT, Margaret 46
TRUMBLE, Elizabeth 177
TUCKER, George 193
  James 114
  John 22
  Susan 107,108,114
TUPPER, Harriet 208
  Tullius 97
TURNER, George 58
  Nellie 53,58
TYE, Mary 24
TYLER, Elizabeth 68,73,105,141
  Eva 143,151
  Harlow 151
  Robert 73
TYPPER, Grant 57
TYREE, Daniel 184
VALENTINE, Mary 63
van ANDA, Carr 203,208
van den AREND, Frederick 185
van HOOKS, Eleanor 231
van HOOSER, Walter 36
van ZANT, James 117
VASSER, John 221
VEACH, Fleta 166
VERNER, Minnie 120
VEST, Calvin 182
  Nora 182
WADLEY, Della 24
WALKER, Dolly 36
  John 36
WALLER, Ruby 232
WALTHALL, Mary 167
WARDER. Elizer 121
WARREN, Mary 230
WASHINGTON, George, Pres. 42
  Martha 120
WATERS, Ruamy 118
WATHEN, John 101
  Lucy 101
WATKINS, John 210
  Lucinda 26
  Richard 210
  Robert 30
  Vina 210
WATSON, James 122
  Martha 148,158
  Marvin 180
  William 223
WEATHERLY, Mary 58
WEBB, Arthur 90
WEBBER, Douglas 156

WEBSTER, George 178
WEEKLY, Keziah 193
WEIDEMAN, Raymond 117
WELLS, George 114
  Hannah 153
  Hayden 211
  Martha 105,106,109,111,112,114
  Nancy 211
WENAKY, Anna 152
WEST, Catherine 75
  Charles 127
  Erasmus 144,154
  Estella 127
  Mary 124
  Roy 128,152
  Susan 144,154
  William 152
WESTBROOK, Elizabeth 107,114
WHEELER, Elizabeth 92
  Fannie 99
  James 92
WHITE, Appie 23
  Beatrice 210
  John 12,18
  Mary 70,74
WHITFIELD, Newton 233
WHITLEY, Julia 109,110,118
WIGAL, Mary Frances 180
WILCOX, Mary 151
WILDER, Sampson 222
  William 222
WILERSON, Bruce 95
WILLEN, Keziah 42,45
WILLIAMS, Benjamin 153
  Mary 91,96
  James 101
  John 102
  Mary 102
  Milton 101
  Miriam 227
  Ruby 20
  Thomas 20
  Willie 153
WILLIG, George 92
WILLSON, David 221
WILSON, Bonnie 31
  Goodrich 154
  James 60
  John 223
  Lillian 156
  Lillie 94
  Matthew 154
  Rebecca 217,223
  William 27,206
WINFREY, Jesse 225
  Martha 217,225
WINK, Margaret 228

WITT, Eugenia 100
WOLTERS, Jacob 228
  Theodor 228
WOOD, Lula 212
  Maria 166
  Martha 226
  Thaddeus 231
WOODING, Jonathan 223
  John 221
WOODRUFF, Nancy 114
WOODWARD, John 68,73
WORNAM, Charles 185
  Virginia 173,185
WRIGHT, Adeline 63
  Anna 58
  Anne 63
  Frederick 62
  James 221
  Margaret 63
  Mary 202,206
  Philip 63
  Roxana 62
  Sarah 60
  William 33
WYNN, John 21
  Nancy 15,21
YATES, Benjamin 209
  Edith 203,209
YEARBREY, William 162,167
YERKES , Beulah 96
  Elias 96
YOKLEY, Lena 34
YOUNG, Rebecca 221,223
ZAHN, Virginia 59

Made in the USA
San Bernardino, CA
08 January 2013